CENTER FOR ORIGINS RESEARCH

IN CREATION

Christian Perspectives on the Origin of Species

EDITED BY PAUL A. GARNER
Biblical Creation Ministries

Center for Origins Research Issues in Creation
Number 4
January 16, 2009

WIPF & STOCK · Eugene, Oregon

CHRISTIAN PERSPECTIVES ON THE ORIGIN OF SPECIES

Copyright © 2009 Center for Origins Research. All rights reserved. Except for brief quotations in critical publications or reviews, no part of this book may be reproduced in any manner without prior written permission from the publisher. Write: Permissions, Wipf and Stock Publishers, 199 W. 8th Ave., Eugene, OR 97401.

ISBN 13: 978-1-60608-523-3

www.wipfandstock.com

Manufactured in the U.S.A.

Abstract

Christianity and creationism are often linked to species fixity, but this opinion has not been the only position taken by Christians on the question of the origin of species. This compilation collects Christian writings on species from the seventeenth century through the twentieth century, highlighting the diversity of opinions.

Contents

Preface	1
1. Francesco Redi (1626–1697)	3
2. Carolus Linnaeus (1707–1778)	7
3. William Herbert (1778–1847)	23
4. Louis Agassiz (1807–1873)	35
5. Asa Gray (1810–1888)	55
6. Fleeming Jenkin (1833–1885)	89
7. St. George Jackson Mivart (1827–1900)	97
8. Erich Wasmann (1859–1931)	113
9. Harold C. Morton (ca. 1925)	119
10. Byron C. Nelson (1893–1972)	131
11. Dudley Joseph Whitney (1883–1964)	135
12. Douglas Dewar (1875–1957)	143
13. George McCready Price (1870–1963)	147
14. Harold W. Clark (1891–1986)	153
15. Frank L. Marsh (1899–1992)	167

Preface

PAUL A. GARNER

It was not until the seventeenth century that the word "species" began to develop a distinctively biological meaning. Until that time, there was no clear concept of a "species" in the sense that we understand it today. The closest approximations to a biological taxonomy in the mediaeval world were the bestiaries, highly fanciful catalogues of animals and birds, and the ancient herbals, which listed plants according to their perceived medicinal properties.

However, with the age of discovery new continents began to be explored, and the number of known varieties of animals and plants grew rapidly. Catalogues listing a few hundred types soon gave way to those listing thousands. The need arose for a system by which this burgeoning faunal and floral diversity could be described and classified.

This need was met by the binomial system that has become the foundation stone of modern taxonomy. It was developed by the celebrated Swedish naturalist, Carolus Linnaeus (1707-1778), who formalised the method of identifying each species by a unique combination of generic and specific descriptors.

Since the time of Linnaeus, the true nature of species has been the subject of intensive discussion and debate. Are species the fundamental units of nature–immutable and unchanging? Or are they simply units of convenience–dynamic and malleable? Such questions have engaged the interest of scientists and philosophers for the last three hundred years.

The purpose of this monograph is to survey the range of views on these matters expressed by scholars from within the Christian tradition since the seventeenth century. I have sought to discover from their writings what these scholars were thinking about the origin and nature of species. What views did they express? Was there any uniformity? Or did they encompass a variety of different positions? Was there ever what we might call a "consensus" Christian view?

Selections from fifteen Christian scholars have been included, ranging in date from the seventeenth to the twentieth centuries.[1] They are intended to be representative, though not exhaustive or comprehensive.

---

1   Where spelling or other errors occur in the original texts, I have indicated this with *sic*. However, I have not sought to correct those instances where authors have failed to italicize genus and/or species names.

Some are from well known and popular authors, such as Louis Agassiz and Asa Gray. Others are less well known, and their writings are reprinted here for the first time since they were originally published.

Among these scholars a surprisingly wide range of views is expressed. Some undoubtedly propounded the immutability of species, a view that had become particularly popular in the period leading up to the publication of Darwin's *On the Origin of Species* (1859). However, in most cases the beliefs of those advocating fixity seem, interestingly enough, to have been motivated by considerations other than biblical literalism. Certainly it is difficult to regard prominent supporters of fixity such as Louis Agassiz and Fleeming Jenkin as fundamentalists. Other scholars, including some notable contemporaries of Darwin, quickly came to accept unlimited species change. Indeed, one of the leading nineteenth century spokesmen for what today we might call "theistic evolution" was the American Presbyterian Asa Gray.

However, I have also included a number of contributions by a disparate group of Christian scholars, often dismissed or misunderstood today, whose views are not represented by the extremes either of species fixity or unlimited change. Instead, these authors accepted the evidence that species could change, but believed that they did so within limits. They rejected fixity as incompatible with scientific observation, but felt that Darwin had extrapolated the observed changes well beyond what was justified by the data. If there is a bias in my selection, it is towards the inclusion of these more obscure authors, precisely because they are so often neglected today. It is also true that the views of some scholars changed over time, with perhaps Linnaeus being the best example. Often regarded as the proponent *par excellence* of species fixity, Linnaeus actually came to a very different perspective later in life. I am pleased to include in this collection a new translation by Tim Griffith of Linnaeus' *De Peloria*, in which his developing doubts about species fixity are expressed very clearly.

The views represented in this monograph do not necessarily accord with those of the monograph's editor or of the Center for Origins Research. Unlike some of our contributors, I reject species fixity and unlimited evolutionary change on biblical and scientific grounds. Nevertheless, I have included authors of these persuasions to demonstrate the diversity of opinions that have been expressed by Christians on this issue. The truth is that there has never been a uniform Christian "view" on the origin and nature of species. The choice popularly portrayed between creation and evolution, between fixity and unlimited change, does not represent the spectrum of views expressed by Christians over the last three centuries, nor does it reflect the views of modern creation biologists based on the insights provided in the Bible. It is a false dichotomy and the truth about species change probably lies somewhere between these two extremes.

1. Francesco Redi

(1626–1697)

Redi, F. 1668. *Experiments on the Generation of Insects*. The Open Court Publishing Company, Chicago [1909 edition]. Our extract is from pp. 21-27.

Many have believed that this beautiful part of the universe which we commonly call the earth, on leaving the hands of the Eternal, began to clothe itself in a kind of green down, which gradually increasing in perfection and in vigor, by the light of the sun and nourishment from the soil, became plants and trees, which afforded food to the animals that the earth subsequently produced of all kinds, from the elephant to the most minute and invisible animalcule. But the Earth, not content with producing dumb animals, desired the glory of being the Mother of Man. Hence, we are told by Lactantius that the Stoics asserted that human beings sprang forth from the soil of hill and plain like sprouting mushrooms. It was the general belief that they did not originate everywhere, but arose in some special place or country; hence the Egyptians, the Ethiopians, and the Phrygians gave the credit to their own lands, and the Arcadians, Phœnicians, and inhabitants of Attica put forth their claims. The Athenians, as a sign that the fathers of the human race originated in Greece (being born from the soil direct as even now grasshoppers are supposed to be born) wore golden ornaments in the hair fashioned like the grasshopper. But whatever may have been the country of origin, according to the teaching of Archelaus, a pupil of Anaxagoras, light, arid soil would not do nor would a mere sand bank serve the purpose of creation. It was necessary that the ground should be rich, warm, and capable of germination, whereupon a milky substance would be produced forming the first food of man and beast.

Those creatures living in the early days of the world were, according to Empedocles and Epicurus, born all at once, hastily and in disorder from the womb of Earth, still unused to motherhood. Such haphazard generation resulted in great confusion; some animals were born without mouths and without arms, others without eyes and without legs; some creatures with monstrous grafting of hands and feet tumbled about headless; still others were seen with a human head and the body of a beast; others had foreparts of beasts and the nether limbs of man; and certain ones were perhaps made in such guise as the poets describe the

Minotaur of Crete, the Sphinx, the Chimera, the Siren, and winged horse of Perseus, or like the Atlante of Corena described by Ariosto:

> "Nature's own work, no artificial steed,
> His dam a mare, a griffin fierce his sire
> Who 'queathed his plumage and his wings, indeed
> His head and fore feet and the beak entire.
> In other parts he to the mare came nigher;
> Fleet as the wind was Hyppogriff in speed."

But at last the great mother, perceiving that such monstrosities were neither good nor likely to endure, and having become more expert in the art of generation, succeeded in producing men and animals according to their species. Democritus bears witness that men first appeared in the form of small worms, which little by little assumed human shape; or, as Anaximander relates, on escaping from the womb of Earth they were enveloped in a kind of rough, spiny skin, not unlike the burr of a chestnut. After a long period of fertility, during which many monstrous and marvelous generations were brought forth, the Earth Mother became at last exhausted and sterile and lost her power of producing men and the larger animals, still she retained enough vigor to bring forth (besides plants that are presumed to be generated spontaneously) certain small creatures such as flies, wasps, spiders, ants, scorpions, and all the other terrestrial and aerial insects, called by the Greek ἔυτομαζῶα and by the Latins, *insecta animalia*. The schools, both ancient and modern, all agree in this, and constantly teach that the Earth has continued to produce these creatures and will produce them so long as she exists. They do not, however, agree as to the manner in which these insects are generated, nor how life is communicated to them; for they say that not only does the Earth possess this occult power, but that it is possessed by all animals living and dead, also by all things produced from the Earth, and finally by those which are about to decay and return to dust. Hence others have claimed putrefaction itself to be the all-potent cause of generation, and still others, natural heat. Many additional causes have been adduced, conforming to the divers modes of thought of different sects, who speak of active and efficient forces, the world soul, so to say—the spirit of the elements, ideas, the heavens, their light and motion, and higher influences. Nor was there lacking the assertion that the generation of all insects is caused by the generative principle residing in the original and sentient vegetative souls, of which particles remain alive in the dead bodies of animals and plants, in a quiescent state, which is changed into activity by contact with surrounding heat and communicates new life to corrupt matter. There is still another class of wise persons who hold it to be true that generation proceeds from certain minute agglomerations of atoms, which contain the seed of all things, These persons say further that the seed was created by God at the beginning of the world and scattered in all directions for the fertilization of the elements, bestowing upon them, not a transitory, but a permanent fecundity as stable as the elements themselves; in this way, they say, are to be interpreted the words of the Sacred Book, "God created all things together." But that great philosopher of our time, the immortal William Harvey, also held that all living things are born from seed as from an egg, be it the seed of animals of the same species or elsewhere derived; thus he says, "Because this is common to all living creatures, viz: that they derive their origin either from semen or eggs, whether this semen have proceeded from others of the same kind, or have come by chance or something else. For what sometimes happens in art occasionally occurs in nature also; those things, namely, take place by chance or accident which otherwise are brought about by art, of this health (according to Aristotle) is an illustration. And the thing is not different as respects generation (in so far as it is from seed) in certain animals; their semina are either present by accident, or they proceed from an univocal agent of the same kind. For even in fortuitous semina there is an inherent motive principle of generation, which procreates from itself and of itself; and this is the same as that which is found in the semina of congenerative animals—a power, to wit, of forming a living creature."[1] But at first he had said that those invisible seeds, like atoms floating in the air, were scattered hither and thither by the winds; although he never explains whence or from whom they take origin; only it may be gathered from the above quoted words that he believes that those fortuitous seeds, flying in the air and carried by winds, proceed from an agent not univocal, to express myself in the language of the schools, but equivocal. Perhaps, however, he would have stated his opinion with greater clearness and precision if the notes which he had collected on this subject had not been dispersed during the tumult of civil war, to the deplorable loss of the republic of philosophy. Many persons would have difficulty in believing that Harvey could have hit upon the truth, in as much as they obstinately assert that it is impossible to indicate the efficient cause of the procreation of insects. The subtlest philosopher of past centuries, after vainly seeking it in our world, declared that the immediate cause of the generation of insects was none other than the Omnipotent Hand of Him whose knowledge transcends all, that is, the great and good God, from whom all flying animals received their spirit directly, as Ennius thought, if we are to believe Varro, who wrote in the fourth book "De Lingua Latina": "Ova parire solet genu' penneis condecoratum; Non animus, ut ait Ennius. Et post. Inde venit divinitu' pulleis insinuans se ipsa anima." Hereupon others add that it is no wonder Galen should confess so modestly in his book his inability to find this origin, and therefore prays

---

1   Anatomical Exercises on the Generation of Animals (1651). Translated by Robert Willis. Works of William Harvey. London: Sydenham Society, 1847. p. 427.

all philosophers who may happen to fall in with it to let him know of it. But he, holding opinion contrary to the Platonists, was never able to believe that the Power and Wisdom which produces perfect animals, could be the same which stoops to form scorpions, flies, worms, and such like, called imperfect by the scholastics. What may be the truth among so many opinions or what comes nearest to it, I am unable to say, nor is it now in my power or intent to decide, but if it happens that I disclose my own belief on the subject, I do so with much hesitation, and fear, as I imagine that the lines sung by our divine poet sound in my ear:

> "Aye to that truth which has the face of falsehood
> A man should close his lips as far as may be,
> Because without his fault it causes shame."

Although content to be corrected by any one wiser than myself, if I should make erroneous statements, I shall express my belief that the Earth, after having brought forth the first plants and animals at the beginning by order of the Supreme and Omnipotent Creator, has never since produced any kinds of plants or animals, either perfect or imperfect; and everything which we know in past or present times that she has produced, came solely from the true seeds of the plants and animals themselves, which thus, through means of their own, preserve their species. And, although it be a matter of daily observation that infinite numbers of worms are produced in dead bodies and decayed plants, I feel, I say, inclined to believe that these worms are all generated by insemination and that the putrefied matter in which they are found has no other office than that of serving as a place, or suitable nest, where animals deposit their eggs at the breeding season, and in which they also find nourishment; otherwise, I assert that nothing is ever generated therein.

2. Carolus Linnaeus

(1707–1778)

Linnaeus, C. 1749. *Amoenitates academicae, seu dissertationes variae physicae, medicae, botanicae, antehac seorsim editae, nunc collectae et auctae cum tabulis aeneis. Accedit hypothesis nova de febrium intermittentium causa.* Cornelius Haak, Leiden, Netherlands. Our extract is from pp. 55-73. Translated 2008 by Timothy Griffith.

Linnaeus, C. 1744. De Peloria
Peloria,

Praeses: Doctor Carol Linnaeus, Professor of Medicine and Botany at the Imperial Academy Regg. Monspel. Stockholm & Associate of Uppsala, and his secretary,

Defended by

Daniel Rudberg,
Vermeland,
In Uppsala, 1744. December 19. In the Charlemagne auditorium

Preface

Recently a plant was discovered in my country that is of such a marvelous character that one doubts whether nature has ever produced an example like it. I thought, therefore, that I would accomplish something both useful and enjoyable for the educated world and especially for those who are interested in the wonders of the plant kingdom, if I brought into public light everything which I have already observed about this plant without delay, although a number of things could still be added due to the recentness of the discovery. In doing this I could both preserve the eternal memory of this amazing phenomenon which has never been observed before by a botanist, as well as ensure that experts in this field will make studies of their own and attempt with further observation to investigate it more closely and so acquire a fuller understanding of this plant.

Indeed, there can be no doubt that if something so miraculous as this and so worthy of the attention of scholars, a transformation of a plant such as has never been seen before, had been brought before a careful and intelligent observer in another country, the discovery would have been put on public display and gossip in educated circles, publications, and curious discussion everywhere would soon have been competing to spread news of this amazing trick of nature, which in this case strays, as it were, or rather departs altogether from its own otherwise regular laws. Expect all this, as well as great profit because there is so certain a hope that by understanding this plant's nature better, previously unknown truths of the highest importance will come to light (especially to explain vegetation and thus serving to further the science of botany). So then, I thought it best to publish some observations of my work as well as my thoughts on this matter that may contribute something towards this end we desire so much. But we call this plant, which practically names itself, Peloria, from the story of this *auspicious* labor of mine.

1. Description
PELORIA is a species of plant whose:
ROOT filiform, repent, white, perennial, and about the thickness of a pigeon's feather.
STEM simple, erect, a foot in height, occasionally with a branch or two, terete, green, annual, and about the thickness of a pigeon's feather.
LEAVES numerous, sparse, linear, acute, flat, smooth, green, the size of the leaves of *Abies nostratis*, an inch long, erect and spreading upwards and out, sub-sessile, with most of the little leaves having their beginnings from the upper flanges of the *branchlets*.
SPIKE terminal, with flowers nine or twelve (at most eighteen), sub-sessile, almost erect.
CALYX a perianth that is shortly, equally divided into five parts to the base, green, glabrous, persistent.
COROLLA consisting of an infundibular *tube* that is long, cylindrical, tapering more at the bottom but slightly ventricose in the middle, straight, yellow, paler toward the base, covered with brown hairs internally, and with the apex terminating in a limb; with the *limb* spreading, five-parted, obtuse, equal, a more saturated yellow than the tube, itself far shorter than the tube. Directly on top of the tube five equal petals or *nectaries* are adnate in a ring, these subulate, spreading, sessile, hollow on the inside, likewise yellow, and about the same length as the tube.
STAMENS five, with *filaments* proceeding out of the floral receptacle (not adnate to the petal like in most gamopetalous flowers), green, shorter than half the length of the tube, equal; with *anthers* yellow, oval, incumbent.
PISTIL with a green *ovary* located above the floral receptacle; with *style* as long as the stamens, filiform, somewhat green; with *stigma* somewhat thickened.
PERICARP with an oval *capsule* having two locules, slightly larger than

the calyx, dehiscing on two sides.
SEEDS numerous, angular.

2. Character

The GENERIC CHARACTER is easily understood from the description itself.

CALYX a gamosepalous *perianth*, five-partite, equal, very short, persistent.

COROLLA gamopetalous, infundibuliform provided with five nectaries at the base.

The *tube* subcylindrical, not very ventricose, long, straight.

The *limb* spreading, five-partite, obtuse, equal.

The *nectaries* five are subulate, colored, spurred, flat, divergent, issuing in a ring from above the base of the tube.

STAMENS The *filaments* five, hairy equal, shorter than half of the corolla tube, and inserted onto the receptacle.

The *anthers* are subrotund, incumbent.

PISTIL The *ovary* ovate.

The *style* filiform, as long as the stamens.

The *stigma* somewhat thickened, obtuse.

PERICARP The capsule ovate with two locules, bivalvate, with convex receptacles adnate to the partition.

SEEDS many, angular.

Observations: It is clear from the given generic character that our Peloria cannot be assigned to any known genus,[1] first because the nectaries (resembling five equal spurs) growing out of the tube are so unique that it is clear from this alone that its general character is different from all other known genera.

3. Location

The place where this plant grows is especially noteworthy, since it is the only place as of 1744 where the plant has ever[2] been observed; and since it has been overlooked and ignorance is easily able to remove

---

[1] I was shocked recently in 1748 when I saw a dry plant from Siberia sent by the esteemed Gmelin, which he called *Swertia floribus quadrifidis: nectario incurvo ad singulas lacinias*, for the plant seemed as if it were composed out of *Herba Gentianae* Fl. Succ. 203. and Peloria flowers. Certainly they corresponded to all the flowers in number with the given character, only lacking a fifth of the number and with a slightly shorter and more open corolla tube; but otherwise, the calyx, corolla, stamens, pistils were the same. Furthermore, even the nectaries which define the essential character were completely the same.

[2] Afterwards, however, in 1745 and 1746 it was collected in various places, such as Loefstadia Roslagia, Upsalia, etc. with a few flowers on the same stem as the Linaria: and also in 1746 it was seen in Germany, according to the esteemed Albrecht von Haller.

it from the eyes of the curious. This place, however, is an island in the sea, located about seven miles from Uppsala, called Sodra Gaesskiaeret, in the kingdom of Sweden, in the Province of Roslagia, in the Parish Riala and Sacello Nordliusteroe. It grows here frequently, and not only in one place; there have been a number of places found where a particular growth of this plant can be seen, especially in those areas where the sea at some point has washed up sand and gravel onto the land.

4. History

In the year 1742 a Roslagian enthusiast by the name of M. Zioeberg, after spending a few years at the Uppsala University studying Botany and other sciences, left to return to his native soil in order to search for whatever rare plants could be found there. He discovered this first plant and put it into his plant-book, as he had never seen it before. He was himself, however, unaware what its nature and character was, and how valuable his discovery would be.

In the same year, Professor of Theology Doctor Olof Celsius, who is well versed in Botany and was spending most of his time collecting plants growing in Upland, approached Mr. Zioeberg wanting to see his plant collection. He immediate noticed something unusual about it, though at first sight it seemed similar to another known plant and he thought it was a small variety of a known species. But at that time he was prevented from proceeding to explore and learn more about this plant by its condition, as none of it could be seen that was not dried up and glued to paper.

Not long afterward, it happened that Doctor Celsius showed this plant to the Celebrated praeses, who at first glance seemed to recognize it, but then because of its clearly outlandish flowers, finally stated that it was a Linaria and at the same time suspected that some other plant's flowers had been deliberately glued on just to create trouble for botanists. Therefore opening its corolla with a pin, he observed a structure previously unobserved by Botanists, and because of it was inflamed with an incredible desire to see this plant alive. But unless Doctor Celsius had convinced him that it had been taken from Roslagia by the aforementioned enthusiast, he would have believed that the plant was not a native of Europe, but rather an import from the Cape of Good Hope or Japan or Peru or some other remote part of the world.

Then without delay the praeses went to Zioeberg, and when he discovered that the man still remembered the place where the plant had been taken from, he convinced him to go there at once and bring him the same plant taken with its stem and root. After this was done, it was planted in the Academic Garden of Uppsala, but there it withered up because of the shortness of its root.

In 1743, there would have been an opportunity to take the plant whole, except that the running of Alandi cattle pastured on this island caused disaster for this plant as well as for all the other plants growing there.

In 1744, when the summer was nearly over, the same problem arose even earlier in the year due to the livestock of another group of people.

5. Linaria

Linaria is a plant extremely well-known to botanists related to the genus
Antirrhinum, whose synonyms are:

Antirrhinum foliis lanceolatis-linearibus consertis, caule erecto, spicis terminatricibus
sessilibus, floribus imbricatis. Roy leid. 297. Fl. Svec. 501.
Antirrhinum foliis linearibus sparsis. Linn. Clift. 324.
Antirrhinum foliis linearibus ascendentibus congestis, ramis spica florali densa terminatis. Hall. Helv. 614.
Linaria vulgaris, flore majore. Bauh. Pin. 212. Basil. 62. Morif. Hist. 2. P. 499. S. 5. T. 12. F. 10. Tournef. Inst. 170. Paris. 23 Vaill. Paris. 117. Zannich. Venet. T. 174. Boerh. Lugdh. i. p. 231.
Linearia lutea vulgaris. Bauh: hist. 3. p. 456. Raj. hist. 752. syn. 3. p. 281. Blackw. herb. t. 115. Ger. emac. 550.
Linaria vulgaris. Besl. eyst. aest. ord. I. t. 14. f. 3.
Linaria vulgaris nostras. Park. theatr. 458. Rob. ic. 2 t. 128.
Linaria prima. Dod. purg. 182. pempt. 183.
Linaria vulgo dicta. Gesn. hort. 265.
Linaria. Gesn. coll. 86 Caesulp. syst. 350. Riv. mon. 82. Chabr. sciagr. 480.
Osyris linaria. Trag. hist. 357. Dalech. hist. 1332. Lob. obs. 222.
Osyris linaria f. urinaria. Lob. ic. 406.
Osyris major. Tabern. ic. 126.
Osyris. Fuschs. hist. 545. Matth. diosc. 1209. Camer. epit. 930. Ruell. Stirp. 640. Till. ic. 70.
Herba urinalis. Dorst. Herb. 148.
Skeiskraut. Brunsf: hist. 2. p. 43.

I consider it unnecessary to describe this plant, which is so well known to botanists, since almost every authority has described and sketched it before now, and since it grows frequently throughout Europe. It is even known to the country people of Sweden under the name *Flugeblomster*.

6. Origin

In stating that the Peloria originated and was derived from the Linaria, I will at first (and rightfully so) seem to propose something amazing and unbelievable. It wouldn't require any greater miracle for a pear tree to produce narcissuses, or for a thistle to produce a fig, or briars grapes. Nevertheless, so many good reasons persuade us that the Peloria did in fact originate from the Linaria, that nobody in examining and comparing the two could deny it.

1) The Peloria GROWS among Linariae. Wherever the Peloria is found, there are also Linariae growing profusely in the gravel. The Peloria, however, always is found in smaller numbers.

2) The Peloria, at least as far as external appearances go, is so SIMILAR to the Linaria that nobody could distinguish the two before the flower has budded, no matter how carefully he considered its number, shape, position, proportion, and all the attributes of the plant, from its root, to its trunk, to its branches and leaves.

3) There is also a peculiar ODOR which is always observed in the Linaria, and easily distinguishes this from other plants. But any expert will affirm that the same odor is found in the Peloria, as well as taste, and even as a medicine, one has the very same effect as the other.

4) The COLOR of the flowers is identical. The flower of the Peloria is pale towards the base just as much as the Linaria, but toward the top it is yellow. Then there is also the hairy brown palate. In *Linaria* it is no different than a fat tongue, and is positioned between the two lips of its corolla, but in *Peloria* it descends below the neck of the corolla above the stamens, where it covers the entire interior side of the corolla. This brown hair is rarely found in other plants, but it is characteristic of these two.

5) The *calyx, pericarp, and seeds* are obviously similar. Therefore, since the Peloria corresponds to the Linaria in location, root, stem, leaves, calyx, pericarp, seeds, color, and taste, nobody would disagree that the Peloria came from the Linaria.

7. Variety

An example like the Peloria has never been seen among the many varieties we see in both the plant and animal kingdoms.

Multiplied and "double" flowers are so common in the plant kingdom that nothing is more widely known. In similar plants there may be many petals, the stamens may protrude, and frequently even the pistils themselves; but they produce no seeds unless the pistil has remained and has been pollinated by simple flowers. The flower may be filled out with larger petals or only the number of petals increased, as in *Hepatica, Anemone,* and *Diantus;* or there may be an enlarged corolla, as in certain gamopetalous flowers; or a multiplication of ray florets may exclude the disc florets, as in *Helianthus,* or *Tagete;* or the disc florets may exclude the ray florets since the corollas are larger, as in *Tagete, Matricaria,* and *Bellis;* or there may be a greater number of petals, with the nectaries excluded, as in *Aquilegia stellata;* or the number of nectaries may be greater, as also in *Aquilegia,* or the *nectaries* may be larger as in *Helleborus aconiti folio, flore globoso croceo. Amanni ruthen.* 76. There may be a colored and larger calyx, as in *Primula*; or with an increased involucre, as in *Cornus herbacea*; or with five petals joining into one, as in the *Saponaria concava anglica C. B.*

Flowers bearing offshoots may come from the plant either from the center of the flower by a raised peduncle, as in *Geum, Rosa,* and *Ranunculus*; or there may be offshoots from the sides, where the peduncles holding up the florets rise out of the calyx, as in the *Calendula, Bellis,* etc.

In some it is possible to see a number of stems growing together, so that the plant becomes fasciated, as in *Asparagus, Ranunculus,* and *Hesperis.*

In others the leaves vary or there is an enlarged surface, as in plants that are said to be crispate, for example, *Lactuca, Cichoreus, Nasturtius, Malva, Apium, Asplenium, Rumex, Tanacetum, Cardiaca, Reseda,* and *Brassica*; or there is a greater number of leaves (four or five leaves), as in *Lysimachia, Salicaria, Anagallis,* etc.

Nothing is more common than for color to vary, and it is observed as well in leaves: such as a white spotting on the leaves, as in *Cyclamen, Amaranthus, Acetosa, Ranunculus, Trifolium, Empetrum*; or black spotting on the leaves, as in *Persicaria, Arum, Ranunculus, Hieracium, Orchis, Cypripedium, Satyrium*; or red spotting on the leaves, as in *Amaranthus, Ranunculus, Urtica, Menyanthes*; or black dotting, as in the *Plantago, Anagallis*; or variegated lines lengthwise, as in the reeds and grasses. But the odd nature of *Peloria* differs from these variations and all others which are currently known to us.

8. Diversity

When the Peloria and Linaria are placed side by side, it is very easy to tell the difference between them.

1) Linaria's corolla at the base has a spurred *nectary*, which is subulate, acute, bent down perpendicularly, terete, and positioned against the other side of the calyx.

Peloria's corolla, however, in this place has five subulate *nectaries*, which are flat, equal, arranged in a circle, and in the shape of petals, so that it would be easy to believe that they were flat petals rather than concave nectaries except for the fact that they are divided crossways.

2) Linaria's corolla is *perforated* from the side by the flower's ovary, so that when the corolla has fallen away, a hole in the middle of its side can be seen.

But Peloria's corolla is *inserted* into the base or the lowest part, where the corolla comes out into the tube, before it puts out its out five nectaries.

3) Linaria's corolla extends to a subrotund *neck*, pressed together on top from either side, but it is somewhat flat and semi-concave underneath.

Peloria's corolla *neck* is semi-cylindrical and slightly ventricose, equal on every side, and nowhere pressed together.

4) Linaria's corolla *limb* is formed into the same shape as a dragon's head is commonly imagined; hence the flower is called personate (Tournefort). It is clearly arranged in two lips, the upper of which is bifid and reflexed on the sides; but the lower is trifid and obtuse. The convex palate protrudes between the lips, encloses the mouth, and stretches out from the lower lip with a concave throat underneath. *Vid. Gener. plantar. 514. 589.*

Peloria's corolla has *limb* that is quinquifid, plane, obtuse, equal, and does not have the slightest hint of a lip or irregularity. So, this highly irregular flower is transformed by a monstrous birth into something regular, which is, of course, a characteristic never observed previously.

5) Linaria has *stamens* in its flower positioned under the side of the corolla, attached to it, and located in the same plane as the style.

Peloria's *stamens* surround the pistil and are not attached to the corolla at all, although Giulio Pontedera and many other botanists believe the essence of a gamopetalous corolla is that the stamens' filaments grow off the corolla.

6) Linaria has four *stamens*, the outer two of which are longer, the inner two shorter. Their anthers lean in toward each other.

Peloria always has five *stamens* of equal length, with anthers and filaments disconnected from each other.

7) Linaria's *stamens* are the same length as the corolla itself, so that they touch the edge or neck of the corolla with their anthers.

Peloria's *stamens* are not even half the length of the tube, although their anthers produce an equal amount of pollen. Thus, its process of reproduction is not hindered by this deformity at all.

9. Classes

A transformation as great as we have described in this flower requires not only that *Peloria* be assigned to a genus different from the *Linaria* or *Antirrhinus*, but a different class as well.

	LINARIA	PELORIA
RAJUS	Vasculiferous Monopetalae; with flower expressing a mouth	Vasculiferous Monopetalae; with flower regular and entire.
RIVINUS	Irregular Monopetalae; with pericarpium bicapsular.	Regular Monopetalae; with pericarpium bicapsular.
TOURNEFORT	Anomalous Monopetalae; with flower personate.	Infundibuliformes; with pistil going into fruit.
MAGNOLIUS	External calyx and external gamopetalous corolla; with flower irregular.	External calyx and internal gamopetalous corolla; with fruit dry.
LINNAEUS	Didynamia; Angiosperma	Pentandria; Monogynia
ROYENUS	Ringens; Angiosperma	Oliganthera; with stamens five
HALLER	Stamens 4, irregular; with fruit bilocular.	Isostemonous; with fruit below the flower.
LUDIVIGIUS	Irregular Monopetalae; Tetranthera.	Regular Monopetalae; Pentanthera.

10. Genus

This *Peloria*, as much as can be gathered from observations made thus far, seems to propagate itself with its own seed and never return to the Linaria where it originated. For it grows freely in its native soil and in many places; its flowers have always been observed to be perfectly alike, as often as they have ever been seen; and there is no reason to suspect that they will return to the flowers of the Linaria. Once they have received their form, they retain it as consistently and exactly as any other natural flower. Time and further study will establish the truth of this matter more certainly. But, if it remains beyond doubt (as is mostly likely) that it is always propagated by its own seed, it will become very common and its structure will no longer be able to be explained under one and the same character as the Linaria. In that case it should receive it its own specific character, and thus establish a new genus; even if it obviously corresponds to the Linaria in stature, smell, taste, and nature and differs only in its flowers. Otherwise we would assign two different characters within one genus; and this would be inconsistent with the practice of fundamental botany, which establishes that plants that differ in flower should also differ in genus. (See *Fundam. Botanic. No. 166.171.181.*)

11. Name

Every plant genus should receive a name distinct from the others, so it does not matter if a bell-shaped flower is lacking a pistil. Therefore I have called this plant PELORIA, a name, I think, appropriate, as its comes from the Greek word πέλωρ which is derived from πέλω, and means "turn" and "monster", since in this plant the order of common nature seems to be overturned. Likewise, the monstrous child from Apollonius Rhodus is called πέλωρ τέκος. Indeed, nothing could be more monstrous than what occurs in this plant, that degenerate progeny of a plant, which previously produced regular flowers, would produce regular flowers.[3] would produce regular flowers for a plant which previously produced regular flowers. It is not just different from its mother genus but also from the whole class, and by its example (which is without equal in Botany) has made it so nobody can recognize it anymore because of the difference of its flower.

Certainly this is no less of a prodigy than if a cow gave birth to a calf with the head of a wolf. Plutarch says rightly (2.472) "We don't look for a fig or an olive tree from a grapevine: and the fig doesn't grow from a reed." *Anth. 50.*

12. Conclusion

It has been the good fortune of our century to discovery many phenomena not only unknown to previous ages, but altogether amazing. That aphids give birth to granddaughters from the conception of their grandmothers is a thing in which the normal laws of nature seem to be altered. But the observations conducted by Reaumurius confirm it, although there are many things still to be investigated before something so paradoxical can be considered beyond all possibility of doubt.

When Trembley's polyp was cut into tiny pieces, out of each of them was born a new polyp equally complete as it had been before the division, something which goes against all the mechanico-physiological principles hitherto received.

And what should I say of coral? They are rocks at first, then turn to plants, and finally become refuges for zoophytes and members of the animal kingdom, as the most illustrious Bernard de Jussieu observes. These three are, of course, discoveries of the greatest importance disproving all the belief of previous centuries.

Our forefathers wanted to persuade us that *Secale* turns into *Hordeum*, and *Hordeum* into *Avena* and finally *Avena* into *Bromus*.[4] But more recent men have examined this belief, as it is contrary to the nature of reproduction, and believe that all things are similar to their parents and that fierce eagles cannot produce the peaceful dove. But I shall leave my discussion of the ancients on *Secale*, *Hordeum*, and *Avena* unfinished,

---

3   Editors note: Either Linnaeus means that the progeny are expected to produce monstrosities or at least irregular (i.e. abnormal) variants, or he intended to say, "which previously produced irregular flowers" (meaning non radially symmetrical, comp. Sect. VIII.4).

4   Ole Worm describes the head of grain from the latter as *Secalina*, and from the former as *Hordeacea in museo 150*. but perhaps it was *Hordeum* with all hermaphroditic flowers, and decorticated seeds. *Hort. ups. 23.*
John Gerard mentions a head of *Triticum* (wheat) around whose center were formed a number of *Avena* grains, complete from every side *in historia pl. 65.*
From these Joannes Raius concludes that a transformation of plants is possible but only between cognate and related species *in Cat. Ext. 8.*

and affirm only this that it would still be far greater a transformation in those than a Linaria would undergo to turn into a Peloria.

It still escapes me what reason the Linaria would possibly change into the Peloria. When something like this happens in the animal kingdom, it is due to an unnatural mating of two species. From this something intermediary is born, a mix from either side, examples of which can be seen in mules and in a few other animals. But these hybrids cannot reproduce. Nature forbids that there be more species of mammal than there were in the beginning. Thus the canary and a female *Acanthus* produce offspring, and they are even fertile in the first generation, but all the grandchildren are sterile. In the plant kingdom as far as odor, taste, and color go, it is hardly unusual to find varieties. Experience in tulips teaches us this. Tulip flowers have been pollinated by flowers of another color, and the seeds produced by these made multicolored flowers. Likewise, white female *Brassica* frequently produces common blue Brassica. This happens if the white *Brassica* grows in a location where the other is flowering.

But here it is a matter of different species in the plant kingdom being crossed, and in this situation our experience has found few, or rather, no examples of vestigial characteristics from previous times. And yet I cannot understand how *Peloria* could have come to be except by a fertilization of this type. Since if the area, climate, or kind of sustenance had produced this change, we would see flowers on the same stem, some corresponding more, some less to the structure of *Linaria*. This does not happen, since we find just as exact a likeness in the flowers of all the individual Peloria plants as in the Linaria itself. But what plant could have pollinated the Linaria to produce the Peloria escapes me. Only someone who has studied plants that flower in the same place and time as the Linaria could say. But it should also be noted that the throat of the flower on a Linaria is usually closed, so that it would be very difficult for it to receive the pollen of another flower to pollinate the pistil, unless the lips of the corolla were first torn and eaten by insects.

At first glance it seems a contradiction in the plant kingdom for new species, certainly new genera, to be a result of a mix of different species. But at the same time my observations do not convince me that it cannot be so. Why are all the *cacti* in America? Why so many species of *Aloe* and *Geranium* at the Cape of Good Hope? *Saxifraga petalis lineatis* Hall. T. 8. as it were came from *Parnassia* and *Saxifraga* Breyn. cent. t. 48. It seems as if *Hyoscyamus* Hort. ups. 44. n. 2. came from a father *Physalis* and a mother *Hyoscyamus*. *Primula foliis cordatis* Gmel. seems as if it came from a father *Cortusa* and a mother *Primula auriculae ursi*. Did the *Tragopogon* Hort. Ups. 243. n. 3. come from a father *Lapsana Rhagadiolus*, Hort. ups. 245 n. 2. and a mother *Tragopogon purpureocaeruleo*, Hort. ups. 243. n. 2? Was *Poterium agrimonoides* produced from father *Agrimonia* and a mother *Sanguisorba*, Hort. ups. 288. n. 1? Surely the *Datisca* came from a male *Cannabus* and a female *Reseda luteola*. This is an easily held opinion for one who has compared the flowers. Many varieties of many species should be looked at closely. Observation and time will determine what is certain, as for me I propose these possibilities not as disproven, but as problematic, so that others will inquire into the matter in more detail.

The most illustrious Gmelin in a letter dated May 17, 1745: "I saw in Holmes' Journal that you had published a botanical treatise on *Peloria*, and I cannot resist telling you that it had entered my mind already for a year that sometimes new plants come from a mixing of different species or genera, such as a mule comes from a donkey and a horse in the animal kingdom. And it occurs in the plant kingdom just as rarely as it does in the animal kingdom. I now own five or six Delphinia in the Saint Petersburg Garden, whose differences I am able to point out, although I only removed two species from Siberia. Certainly there are many other things in botany still difficult to explain that could be explained by this theory if it were adopted."

In *Act. Paris.* in the year 1719 Jean Marchánt demonstrated a plant, grown in his own garden in July of 1715, unknown both to himself and all other botanists, which remained intact until the end of December. He was easily able to attribute it to the *Mercurialis* genus, and he called it *Mercurialis foliis capillaceis*. The following year in the month of April, six other plants grew in the same place, two of which seemed similar to the first, but the rest quite different. So, he established a new species from them and called it *Mercurialis foliis in varias et inqaequales lacinias quas dilaceratis*. Jean Marchánt discussed at length in the *Act. Paris.* the way these were produced. But the praeses after seeing a glued plant understood that it was the same as the *Mercurialis caule brachiato, foliis glabris*, Hort. Cliff. 461, in flower, odor, stem, etc., except that its leaves were incised. And this is not unusual in the plant kingdom and can result from a difference in its native soil alone, which has been observed in *Pimpinella* and others.

If it can be clearly established that the Peloria is a hybrid species produced from a Linaria and another plant, a new truth in the plant kingdom would emerge, and that much more advanced than in the animal kingdom, in as much as in that kingdom hybrid offspring lack the ability to reproduce (e.g., mules, and other animals of that type). But the Peloria seems to be able to reproduce, since it has fully-formed seed, and it multiplies itself freely and abundantly in its native location. It is only to be investigated by further experiment whether the Linaria is ever produced from the seed of the Peloria. But if it never happens, as seems probable from what has already been observed, but remains consistent, then this amazing conclusion would follow: that it is very much possible *for new species to appear in the plant kingdom, that genera differing in their reproduction may enjoy one and the same nature and effect; or rather, that one and the same genus can have different methods of flowering.* And this would disprove a fundamental principle of flowering, which is also a fundamental principle of the entire botanical science, and the natural classes of plants would break down. Indeed, all who are learned in the botanical science would marvel with good cause at nature's extremely shocking flowering in this Peloria.

Figure

1. Stem of *Peloria* in its actual size with its racemus and flowers.
2. The flower of *Peloria* in its actual size seen from the rear.
    a. calyx
    bb. Nectaries
    c. corolla tube
    d. limb
3. The same flower seen from the front
    a. calyx
    bbb. Nectaries
4. The same flower seen from the side
    a. calyx
    bb. Nectary, cut crosswise so that the inside cavity is visible.
    c. corolla tube
    d. limb
5. The flower of *Peloria* cut lengthwise so that its internal parts are visible. From its base the flower's five uniform stamens with its pistil are visible.
    a. calyx
    b. Nectaries whose orifices open towards the cavity in five foramina.
    c. corolla tube
    d. limb
6. The flower of *Linaria* as borrowed from the illustrations of Tournefort which he has expanded so that the difference of *Peloria* from *Antirrhinum* is more obvious.

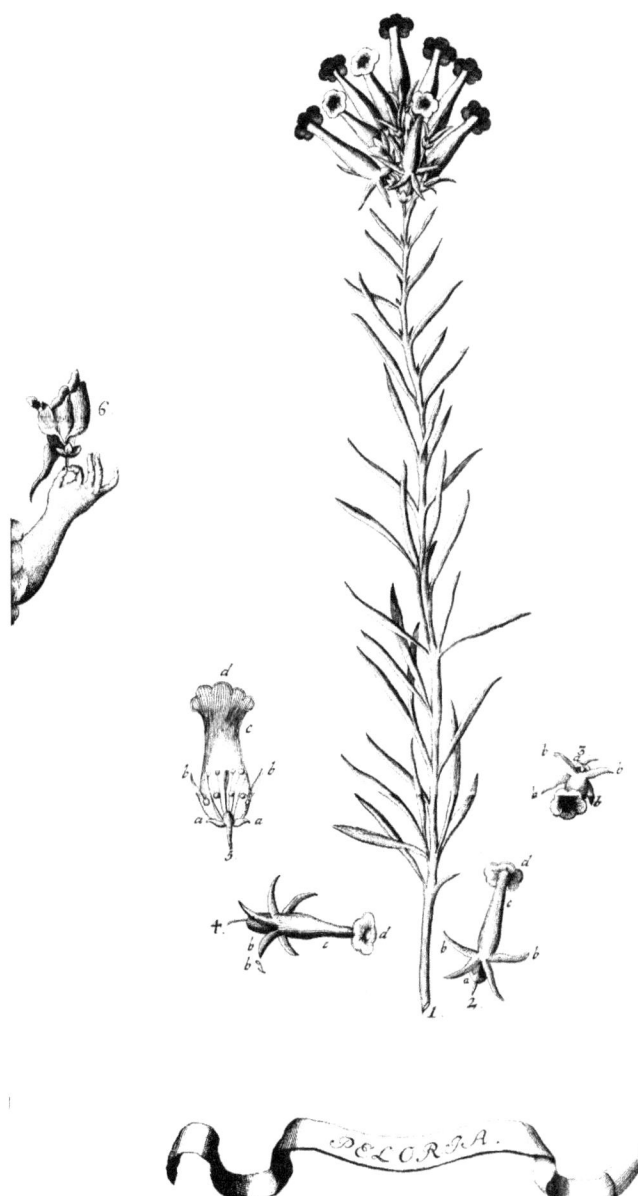

3. William Herbert

(1778–1847)

Herbert, W. 1837. On crosses and hybrid intermixtures in vegetables. In: *Amaryllidaceae*. J. Ridgway and Sons, London. Our extract is from pp. 335-348.

The first experiments, with a view to ascertain the possibility of producing hybrid vegetables, appears to have been made in Germany, by Kolreuter, who published reports of his proceedings in the Acts of the Petersburgh Academy between 50 and 60 years ago. Lycium, digitalis, nicotiana, datura, and lobelia, were the chief plants with which he worked successfully, and as I have found nothing in his reports to the best of my recollection opposed to my own general observations, it is unnecessary to state more concerning his mules than the fact, that he was the father of such experiments. They do not seem to have been at all followed up by others, or to have attracted the attention of cultivators or botanists as they ought to have done; and nothing else material on the subject has fallen under my notice of earlier date than Mr. Knight's report of his crosses of fruit-trees, and my own of ornamental flowers, in the Transactions of the Horticultural Society of London. Those papers attracted the public notice, and appear to have excited many persons both in this country and abroad to similar experiments.

In the year 1819, having for some years previous paid attention to the production of hybrid vegetables, but ignorant of the experiments of Kolreuter, I was induced, rather against my own inclination, to address some detailed observations on the subject to the Horticultural Society, which were published in the transactions of that body. It was, I say, against my inclination, because I was fully aware, that a much longer course of experiments was necessary, in order to obtain any results sufficiently certain to give stability to my views. It is, however, satisfactory to find at the present day, after the attention of botanists and cultivators has been fully called to the subject during the space of many years, and a multitude of experiments carried on by a variety of persons, that, although our knowledge of its mysteries is still very limited, my general views have been fully verified, and my anticipations confirmed in a manner which I was scarcely sanguine enough to have expected. Soon after the publication of that communication to the Society, I was accosted by more than one botanist in the words, "I do not thank you for your mules," and other expressions of like import, under an impression that the intermixture of species which had been commenced, and was earnestly recommended to cultivators, would confuse the labours of botanists, and force them to work their way through a wilderness of uncertainty; whereas it was evident to myself, that it would on the contrary afford a test whereby the accuracy of their distinctions might be more satisfactorily investigated, many of the errors of their system eradicated, and its details established upon a more solid foundation, and less upon the judgment or caprice of individuals. The alarm, which some botanists had taken inconsiderately, appears to have subsided, and admissions have been already made by some of the most distinguished, which, if the consequences that flow from them are considered without prejudice, must lead to much more extensive avowals, and a final assent to the principle of my statements concerning specific and generic distinctions. A number of attempts had been made by the President of the Horticultural Society to produce new varieties of fruit,[1] by impregnating the flowers with the pollen of other individuals, and the success of his proceedings was communicated to the public, both by his letters to the Society, and by the more substantial production of the fruits he had raised; but it must be evident, that less could be expected in the raising of new fruit-bearing plants by intermixture, because the hybridising process is to a certain degree inimical to fertility in the offspring; and that the flower-garden was more likely to be adorned, than the kitchen-garden replenished, by the intermixture of species. The President adopted in his writings a principle or dogma, which seemed to be then much relied upon by botanists, that the production of a fertile cross was proof direct that the two parents were of the same species, and he assumed as a consequence, that a sterile offspring was nearly conclusive evidence that they were of different species; and this dictum was advanced without suggesting any alteration in the definition of the term species, but leaving it to imply what it had before universally signified in the language of botanists. Having, in fact, the same fundamental opinion, that the production of a fertile intermixture, designated the common origin of the parents, I held also, what experience has since in a great measure confirmed, that the production of any intermixture amongst vegetables, whether fertile or not, gave reason to suspect that the parents were descended from one common stock, and shewed that they were referable to one genus; but that there was no substantial and natural difference between what botanists had called species, and what they had termed varieties; the distinction being merely in degree, and not absolute; so that, without first reforming the terms used in botany, and ascertaining

---

1 There is a paper in the Philos. Transact. concerning the production of apples, by crossing the pollen, by Benj. Cooke.

more precisely what was meant by a species, those who argued on the subject were fighting the air; and I suggested, as my view, that the birth of an intermixture afforded presumptive evidence that the parents were of one genus, meaning thereby kind or descent, and implying such an affinity as to enable them to breed together, and to induce a probability that they had diverged from one original created type. The real point in discussion at that period was, whether there did exist a positive and invariable line of fertility or sterility in all mixed vegetable productions, founded upon an original identity or diversity in the parental stocks; aud [sic—and] whether it was possible for two plants, which were considered according to the general system of botanists to be distinct species, to produce a fertile cross, without proving an error of the subdivision in that particular case. Further experiments have shewn, that the sterility or fertility of the offspring does not depend upon original diversity of stock; and that, if two species are to be united in a scientific arrangement on account of a fertile issue, the botanist must give up his specific distinctions generally, and entrench himself within the genera. It has been objected that if any plants, now different, had descended from one original type, we might expect to find new forms and combinations daily arising round us by the process of nature, as well as by artificial agency; whereas the catalogue of European vegetables does not appear to be increased by the production of new plants in a wild[2] state; but it is most probable, that if the Almighty created the original types capable of permanent variations under different circumstances, perhaps of soil or climate, those variations were worked at a very early period, on the first diffusion of seeds into every different portion of the world, especially by the operation of the flood, and may have in part resulted from the changes of climate which accompanied it and shortened the life of man. We must recollect, that although the different races of dogs, which all freely interbreed, are universally admitted to have come from one type, though now outwardly more unlike to each other than numberless distinct species of other animals, we know not what the similitude of that type was; we have no record concerning the original wild dog, nor whether there existed immediately before or after the deluge any dogs in an undomesticated state; nor have we any knowledge of the time or place when any one of the several races. as greyhound, terrier, spaniel. bull-dog, &c. took its birth: nor is there a single known instance of two parent dogs of the same race, giving birth to individuals of a new race, or materially dissimilar to themselves, except where they are mongrels, and one of the ancestral

---

2 Ranunculus, Anemone, Hypericum, Scleranthus, Drosera, Potentilla, Geum, Medicago, Galium, Centaurea, Stachys, Rhinanthus, Digitalis, Verbascum, Gentiana, Mentha, Quercus, Salix, and Narcissus, are however a long list of Genera enumerated by Schiede, 1825, and Lasch Linn. 1829, as having produced spontaneous hybrids, to which Crinum may be added.

types reappears more strongly than the other. Neither have we any information concerning the origin of the different races of mankind, which are as different in appearance as the species of vegetables; we have not seen any new race arise within the period of historical certainty; and whatever we do know concerning them, refers the time of their branching out from the common stock to very remote antiquity, at a period antecedent to or coeval with the dispersion of mankind over the globe. If it had been otherwise, the various races would have been blended, instead of occupying different localities. It is probable that the various races of dogs owe their origin to a very early period; to the days, when the effects arising from change of situation, were first experienced by the several created members of the animal and vegetable kingdom: and it is no more essential to believe that individuals of every one of the present species of fox, or antelope, or finch (many of which are more like to each other than the greyhound is to the terrier, though they do not intermingle), entered with their present respective aspects into the ark, than that all the calceolarias on the mountains of Chili, or all the mezembryanthemums on the wastes of Southern Africa, exhibited their present peculiarities in the days of the patriarch. It was perhaps part of the wise scheme of Providence, for the purpose of peopling the world with the immense diversity of forms that occupy it, to give each created race a disposition to branch into diversities, acquiring constitutional peculiarities, which should keep them more or less separated; and the same phænomenon is observable in the languages of man, which are infinitely numerous; yet there is no reason to believe that many languages were given to man on the confusion of tongues; on the contrary, the cloven tongues that gave back the power of universal speech, imply that they were few; but from these have branched out innumerable languages, which cannot be reunited, and no person can show when or how any one of them arose, though we may trace the mingling of one with another in the later years of the world. One thing seems pretty certain, amongst the mysteries in which this subject is enveloped, that the differences worked, whether in plants or animals, in a state of domesticity, do not effect so great a constitutional separation inducing an indisposition to reunite and produce a prolific offspring, as the changes which have been wrought by nature in the wilderness.

I have said in the preliminary observations on Amaryllidaceæ, that a perfect analogy between animals and vegetables in their generations is not apparent; but I do not mean to assert, that, if this subject can ever be thoroughly bottomed, it may not be found to exist. A reformation of Zoology is in progress; for example, in Ornithology, the Linnæan genus Motacilla was after a time confined to the wagtails, a large group being detached as Silviæ; but later observers found that group to consist of several families, and have since correctly distinguished at least the robins, the redstarts, the nightingales, the hedge warblers, the fruit-eating warblers, the sedge warblers, the chats, the troglodyte wrens, and the greenish wrens, as separate genera with their respective diversities; and within those generic limits I suspect that the power of crossing may be confined, and their several species, however now immutably distinct, may have respectively branched out from one stock since the period of the deluge. I have lately had under my observation a dog, whose father was a fox in an innyard at Ripon, and it has singularly the manners as well as the voice of a fox, but it is the parent of many families of puppies: and I feel satisfied that the fox and the dog are of one origin, and suspect the wolf and jackall to be of the same; nor could I ever contemplate the black line down the back of a dun pony without entertaining a suspicion that the horse, unknown in a wild state except where it has escaped from domesticity, may be a magnificent improvement of the wild ass in the very earliest age of the world: bearing in mind, that both in the animal and vegetable creation, the diversities arising from inscrutable causes in the wild races of the forest, are of a more unalterable character than those which spring up under the care and cultivation of man. With respect to animals in their wild state, their union with their own species seems to be mainly guided by voice and smell, and in domesticity that instinctive preference is evidently much weaker, and the will to keep themselves distinct is therefore lessened. The various species of greenish wrens are so similar in plumage, that it requires nice examination to distinguish them, yet they have different notes, manners, and habits of building their nests, even when in the same locality; but we have no certainty that if their predilection for the voice and smell of their own race was weakened, they would not be capable of producing a fertile cross; and we draw our conclusions from a few instances of domestic mules between species which happen to be widely removed from each other, as the pheasant and fowl, the goldfinch and canary bird; whereas we should apply to this subject, concerning which our knowledge is very limited, the consideration of the fact ascertained concerning vegetables, which have no will to interfere with our experiments, that some crosses are sterile and some quite fertile, without any apparent reason, except the greater or less approximation of constitution in the parents: and that the cross-bred plant, which has seemed for a long course of years to be absolutely sterile, becomes under some circumstances productive.

In accordance with the principle above stated, when it was shown that the botanic subdivisions of Rhododendron, Azalea, and Rhodora, comprehended plants which were capable of intermixing, I asserted that the botanist must reconsider and alter his subdivisions, and acknowledge that, notwithstanding their peculiarities, they constituted but one genus or kind. Conformably with this suggestion, Mr.Sweet, in the second edition of his Hortus Britannicus, has since wisely added to Rhododendron the genera Rhodora and Azalea, with the exception of Azalea procumbens, though in his subdivision of the pelargoniums he has not kept in view sufficiently that certain and unalterable guide. The true meaning of species, not as the word used to be explained by botanists, but as it is in fact used in all botanical arrangements, appears to be, the subdivision of the genera or kinds into branches, which naturally maintain themselves distinct even when approximated, though they may be more or less capable of artificial or accidental intermixture; while a local variety will reproduce itself when isolated under particular circumstances of soil and climate; and a seminal variety will not with equal certainty reproduce itself in the same form anywhere, being more ready to intermingle with others of like origin. In fact, there is no real or natural line of difference between species and permanent or descendible variety, as the terms have been applied by all botanists; nor do there exist any features on which reliance can be placed to pronounce whether two plants are distinguishable as species or varieties. Any person, who attends to the subject, will perceive that no botanist has laid down any precise rules by which that point of inquiry can be solved, and that the most variable, contradictory, and unsubstantial features have been taken by different persons, and by the same person on different occasions, to uphold the distinctions they proposed to establish; the truth being that such distinctions are quite arbitrary, and that, if two plants are found capable of interbreeding, when approached by the hand of man, they are as much one as if they were made to intermix more readily and frequently by the mere agency of the wind, or assiduity of insects; and are not separable with more truth by any positive difference, than the varieties which cannot be prevented from crossing with each other when in the same vicinity. It remained to be ascertained whether there did exist a real, natural, and indefeasible difference between plants which could produce a fertile and those which could produce only a sterile offspring by blending their races. It was my opinion that fertility depended much upon circumstances of climate, soil, and situation, and that there did not exist any decided line of absolute sterility in hybrid vegetables, though from reasons, which I did not pretend to be able to develope, but undoubtedly depending upon certain affinities either of structure or constitution, there was a greater disposition to fertility in some than in others. Subsequent experiments have confirmed this view to such a degree as to make it almost certain that the fertility of the hybrid or mixed offspring depends more upon the constitutional than the closer botanical affinities of the parents. The most striking and unanswerable proof of this fact was afforded by the genus Crinum, which is spread round the whole belt of the globe, within the tropics and within a certain distance from them, under a great variety of circumstances affecting the constitution of individuals, which nevertheless readily intermix, when brought together by human agency. The plant called Crinum Capense (formerly Amaryllis longifolia), impregnated by either Crinum Zeylanicum or scabrum, both at that time also called Amaryllis, produced offspring, which during sixteen years proved sterile, probably because, notwithstanding their botanical affinity, the first is an extra-tropical aquatic plant, and the two latter tropical plants which affect drier habitations and readily rot, at least in this climate, in a wet situation. The same C. Capense, impregnated by Crinum pedunculatum, canaliculatum, or defixum, produces a fertile cross, though they are so dissimilar as to have been placed in different genera, and the author was formerly reproached by botanists as having committed an absurdity when he insisted upon uniting them. The reason of the fertility of their joint produce seems to be, that they are all aquatic or swamp plants; and it may be further observed that the crosses with the two former, the plants being all extra-tropical, are much more fertile than that between C. Capense and defixum, because the latter is a tropical plant. The mules between Scabrum and Capense having continued so many years with every appearance of absolute sterility, without any change of situation or treatment, at last produced one good seed in 1834 and another in 1835. These facts were of such an overbearing nature, that it became impossible for those, who had charged the author with absurdity for uniting the parents under the genus Crinum (to which even certain other plants were then asserted to be more nearly allied than the species at that time called Amaryllis), to contend any longer that they, producing a fertile offspring, were of different genera, and they will probably be never again disunited in any botanical work; but the facts furnish much ground for the serious consideration of men of science. It happens (as if expressly designed to overthrow the theory, that the identity of species is proved by fertility or sterility in the mixed issue), that, while C. Capense, Zeylanicum, and scabrum, are very similar in their general appearance, and yield an offspring which has been found quite sterile except in the case of the two seeds above mentioned, C. Capense and pedunculatum are as unlike as perhaps any two species of any known genus; and if it were asserted that C. Capense and pedunculatum are one species, and C. Capense and scabrum two species, the assertion would appear, to any person looking at the plants, too preposterous to require a serious answer.

In further confirmation of the fact that the sterility depends on constitutional discrepancy, or difference of what medical men call idiosyncrasy, may be adduced the curious plant figured in the Botanical Magazine under the name of Crinum submersum, which was found by my collector in a pond or flooded spot not far from Rio Janeiro, in company with a small variety of C. erubescens, and appeared to be exactly intermediate between that aquatic plant and C. scabrum, which grows on high ground amongst the woods. It is absolutely sterile, the anthers being always shrivelled and the pollen dry, and it is not materially different from the mules raised in our stoves between C. scabrum and a larger variety of C. erubescens, the latter being of course a finer mule, but with exactly the same barrenness of the anthers. C. submersum is certainly a natural cross, in consequence of the pollen of C. scabrum having been brought to the lake by some humming-bird or insect which touched the stigma of the aquatic species. The same sterility has been found in C. amabile and C. angustum, which are undoubtedly mules accidentally produced between dry-land and swamp-species, the former probably between C. Zeylanicum and procerum, the latter between C. Zeylanicum and bracteatum; as also C. longiflorum (Amaryllis longiflora of the Botanical Register), which is an accidental cross between C. Capense and erubescens, one variety of it having been produced at Demerara, the other in Jamaica. The fact being established with respect to one genus, that the species which have most botanical affinity and general likeness, if they delight in a different state of soil or of atmosphere, produce a barren cross, while the most dissimilar, if they possess the same constitutional predilections, give birth to a fertile plant, cannot remain as an isolated circumstance, but must be considered by every unprejudiced and philosophical mind with reference to the whole vegetable creation. I have lately heard it admitted in conversation by an eminent botanist, that he had almost arrived at the conviction that there was but one rose, meaning that there seemed to be no natural impediment to the fertile intercourse of the great variety of plants which constitute the known species of that extensive genus. Let it be observed, if the fact is so, the reason is apparent enough; that, although some roses will endure a little more cold than others, there is a sameness of constitution throughout the genus, which affects a dry soil and a temperate atmosphere. The genus Calceolaria embraces plants very dissimilar to the eye of the botanist, as well as of the unlearned observer, of which some are absolutely stemless, and bear only leaves and flower-stalks, while others are shrubby, and acquire a strong woody stem some feet in height; yet there appears to be no limit whatsoever to their intermixture, and their produce may be crossed again indefinitely. Are we, then, to come to the result that there is but one Calceolaria, oversetting not only the nicer distinctions of botanical science, but the difference between herb and shrub? The African Gladioli, excepting those which, like the European, present their flowers in front of the stalk, have been intermixed by me without any difficulty occurring, and the crosses of the most dissimilar have proved abundantly fertile, and four or five sorts have been blended in successive generations. Some of the complicated crosses have produced seed less freely, and one treble cross (Hirsuto-Cardinali-blandus) has as yet produced none that has vegetated, probably because the last male, G. hirsutus, is of a constitution much less suited to our climate than the other two. Are we then to come to the result, that these dissimilar species are all one natural Gladiolus? There is no outward sign of barrenness in G. hirsuto-Cardinali-blandus, which will probably bear seed under favourable circumstances; that there is no insurmountable natural impediment may be proved thus; the offspring of G. versicolor by hirsutus, of blandus by versicolor, and of Cardinali-blandus by tristis, have all borne seed, shewing that G. hirsutus is not of a separate race, and that the triple cross is not an impediment. I have crosses raised by me between the yellow Linaria genistifolia and the purple purpurea, and also between Penstemon angustifolium and pulchellum, both perfectly fertile and sowing themselves about the garden, and, from my having given them many years ago to more than one nurseryman, become common. It is scarcely possible to assert that these very unlike plants are respectively one, and at the same time to distinguish them from the rest of their own genera, especially the former. That whole portion of Amaryllideæ which constitutes the genus Hippeastrum, and was confounded by botanists with a portion of the genus Crinum, not only interbreed freely, but produce offspring invariably fertile, because they are all of like constitution, and impatient of excessive moisture, though some will bear more cold than others. Amongst the Pelargoniums a similar convertibility has been found to exist within certain limits, which, if duly observed, will be sure guides to ascertain the genera, into which they ought to be subdivided, and by which the botanist, who is desirous that his labours should not be overturned hereafter, must be in a great measure ruled in classing them. Amongst the Cacti or Cerei the prickly angular speciosissimus, the flexible flagelliformis or whip-plant, and the flat unarmed phyllanthocides, are nearly the most dissimilar, yet they have produced mixed offspring, which readily bears eatable fruit of intermediate appearance, colour, and flavour. The fruit of the speciosissimus is large, green, and well-flavoured, round oblong; that of phyllanthocides small, purple, and very inferior; the mule from the former has purple fruit of a medium size and taste. The cross from the former by flagelliformis is now ripening here a short angular fruit, quite unlike that of the mother plant. The fertility of these crosses, and readiness to vary the appearance and taste of the fruit, though derived from such very dissimilar parents, is one of the most striking results of our experiments. I have had no opportunity of attempting to cross them with the plants called echino-cacti, but I do not see a single point in the generic character given of those plants which can uphold it, and I believe them to be of one genus with Cereus, and capable of intermixing; but I have had no opportunity of examining the flower of any of the plants called Echinocactus myself. Amongst melons I have had the Cucumis osmocarpus from Mexico, bearing a small egg-shaped white fruit and a small flower and leaf, very different from the Cucumis melo, fertilized accidentally by its pollen, thus occasionally producing fruit of twice the natural size with red flesh. Lobelia speciosa is a cross between L. siphylitica and fulgens, yet it reproduces itself abundantly.

The more these facts are considered, and the more they are multiplied, as they will be by the daily experiments of cultivators in other genera, the more strongly will my original suggestions impress themselves upon every botanist, who will look on the subject without prejudice, that the genera of plants are the real natural divisions; that no plants which interbreed can belong to separate genera; that any arrangement, which shall have parted such plants, must be revised; that any discrimination between species and permanent varieties of plants is artificial, capricious, and insignificant; that the question which is perpetually agitated, whether such a wild plant is a new species or a variety of a known species, is waste of intellect on a point which is capable of no precise definition, and that the only thing to be decided by the botanist in such cases is whether the plant is other than an accidental seedling, and whether there are features of sufficient dissimilarity to warrant a belief that they will be reproduced, and to make the plant deserve on that account to be distinguished by name amongst its fellows. The effect, therefore, of the system of crossing, as pursued by the cultivator, instead of confusing the labours of the botanist, will be to force him to study the truth, and take care that his arrangement and subdivisions are conformable to the secret laws of nature; and will only confound him when his views shall appear to have been superficial and inaccurate; while on the other hand it will furnish him an irrefragable confirmation when they are based upon reality. To the cultivators of ornamental plants the facility of raising hybrid varieties affords an endless source of interest and amusement. He sees in the several species of each genus that he possesses the materials with which he must work, and he considers in what manner he can blend them to the best advantage, looking to the several gifts in which each excels, whether of hardiness to endure our seasons, of brilliancy in its colours, of delicacy in its markings, of fragrance, or stature, or profusion of blossom, and he may anticipate with tolerable accuracy the probable aspect of the intermediate plant which he is permitted to create; for that term may be figuratively applied to the introduction into the world of a natural form which has probably never before existed in it. In constitution the mixed offspring appears to partake of the habits of both parents; that is to say, it will be less hardy than the one of its parents which bears the greatest exposure, and not so delicate as the other; but if one of the parents is quite hardy and the other not quite able to support our winters, the probability is that the offspring will support them, though it may suffer from a very unusual depression of the thermometer or excess of moisture, which would not destroy its hardier parent. Such is the case with the beautiful mule Rhododendron Altaclaræ, of which the mother was a cross between Ponticum and Catawbiense, and the father the Nepal scarlet arboreum. We now possess a further cross by the impregnation of Altaclaræ by arboreum, which will probably come so near the father in its colour, that if, as expected, it should be able to endure our winters, we shall have nearly attained the result, which would be otherwise most likely impracticable, of acclimating the magnificent Nepal plant; for it does not appear that in reality any plant becomes acclimated under our observation, except by crossing with a hardier variety, or by the accidental alteration of constitution in some particular seedling; nor that any period of time does in fact work an alteration in the constitution of an individual plant, so as to make it endure a climate which it was originally unable to bear; and, although we are told that laurels were at first kept in hothouses in this country, it was not that they were less capable of supporting our seasons than at present, but that the cultivators had not made full trial of their powers of endurance. The notion of Mr. Sweet that the roots produced by cuttings are hardier than those of seedling plants is probably fanciful, if he meant permanently so, which alone would be of importance. They may be tougher at the first period of propagation, while the seedling is in its infancy, but that, if not permanent, could have no effect in acclimating a plant. In truth it is not the root that is tougher, but the nucleus or base of the cutting from which the roots issue, and in which the life resides, which is tougher than in a young seedling at the first. All his other experiments only tended to shew that some half-hardy plants would live through an English winter in very dry and sheltered situations, or during two or three years, till a more inclement season cut them off, but not that by any process of his they had become hardier; the word acclimating seems, therefore, to have been misapplied in his paper in the Transactions of the Horticultural Society. For the purpose of obtaining a large or a brilliant corolla, it will be probably found in the long run best to use the pollen of the species which excels in those points, because the corolla, in truth, belongs to the male portion of the flower, the anthers being usually either borne upon it, or in some manner connected with it by a membrane; but upon the whole an intermediate appearance may be generally expected, but with a great disposition to sport, especially in the seminal produce of the fertile crosses, as in plants which are apt to break into cultivated varieties.

4. Louis Agassiz

(1807–1873)

Agassiz, L. 1850. Geographical distribution of animals. *The Christian Examiner and Religious Miscellany* 48:181-204.

The greatest obstacles in the way of investigating the laws of the distribution of organized beings over the surface of our globe, are to be traced to the views generally entertained about their origin. There is a prevailing opinion, which ascribes to all living beings upon earth one common centre of origin, from which if is supposed they, in the course of time, spread over wider and wider areas, till they finally came into their present state of distribution. And what gives this view a higher recommendation in the opinion of most men is the circumstance, that such a method of distribution is considered as revealed in our sacred writings. We hope, however, to be able to show that there is no such statement in the book of Genesis; that this doctrine of a unique centre of origin and successive distribution of all animals is of very modern invention, and that it can be traced back for scarcely more than a century in the records of our science.

There is another view, to which, more recently, naturalists have seemed to incline; namely, the assuming several centres of origin, from which organized beings were afterwards diffused over wider areas, in the same manner as according to the first theory, the difference being only in the assumption of several centres of dispersion instead of a single one.

We have recently been led to take a very different view of the subject, and shall presently illustrate the facts upon which the view rests. But before we undertake to introduce more directly this subject, there is another point which requires preliminary investigation, which seems to have been entirely lost sight of by all those, without exception, who have studied the geographical distribution of animals, and which seems to us to be the keystone of the whole edifice, whenever we undertake to reconstruct the primitive plan of the geographical distribution of animals and plants. The distribution of organized beings over the surface of our globe in its present condition cannot be considered in itself, and without an investigation, at the same time, of the geographical distribution of those organized beings which have existed in former geological periods, and had become extinct before these of the present creation were called into being. For it is well ascertained now that there is a natural succession in the plan of creation, an intimate connection between all the types of the different periods of the creation from its beginning up to this day; so much so, that the present distribution of animals and plants is the continuation of an order of things which prevailed for a time at an earlier period, but which came to an end before the existing arrangement of things was introduced.

The animal kingdom, as we know it in our days, is therefore engrafted upon its condition in earlier periods, and it is to the distribution of animals in these earlier periods that we must look, if we would trace the plan of the Creator from its commencement to its more advanced development in our own time.

If there is any truth in the view that animals and plants originated from a common centre, it must be at the same time shown that such an intimate connection between the animals existed at all periods, or, at least, we should, before assuming such a view for the animals living in our days, discover a sufficient reason for ascribing to them another mode of dispersion than to the animals and plants of former periods. But there is such a wonderful harmony in all the great processes of nature, that, at the outset, we should be carefully on our guard against assuming different modes of distribution for the organized beings of former periods, and for those which at present cover the globe. Should it be plain that the animals and plants did not originate from a common centre at the beginning of the creation, and during the different successive geological periods, we have at once a strong indication that neither has such been the case with the animals of the present day. And, on the other hand, if there were satisfactory evidence that the animals and plants now living originated from a common centre, we should consider the matter carefully, before trusting to the views derived from geological facts. Let us, therefore, examine first the value of the evidence on both sides.

We have already expressed, and we repeat here, our earnest belief that the view of a unique centre of origin and distribution rests chiefly upon the supposed authority of the Mosaic record, and is in no way sustained by evidence derived from investigations in natural history. On the contrary, wherever we trace the animals in their present distributions, we find them scattered over the surface of our globe in such a manner, according to such laws, and under such special adaptations, that it would baffle the most fanciful imagination to conceive such an arrangement as the mere result of migrations, or of the influence of physical causes over the dispersion of both animals and plants. For we find that all animals and plants of the arctic zones agree in certain respects and are uniform over the three continents which verge towards the northern pole, whilst those of the temperate zone agree also in certain respects, but differ somewhat from each other within definite limits, in the respective continents. And the differences grow more and more prominent as we approach the tropical zone, which has its peculiar Fauna and Flora in each continent; so much so, that it is impossible for us to conceive such a normal arrangement, unless it be the result of a premeditated plan carried out voluntarily according to predetermined laws.

The opinion which is considered as the Biblical view of the case, and according to which all animals have originated in a common centre, would leave us at a loss for any cause by which to account for the special dispersion of animals and plants beyond the mere necessity of removing from the crowded ground to assume wider limits, as their increased number made it constantly more and more necessary and imperative. According to this view, the animals of the arctic zone, as well as those of the tropics,—those of America, as well as those of New Holland,— have been first created upon the high lands of Iran, and have taken their course in all directions to settle where they are now found to be strictly limited. It does not appear how such migrations of polar animals could have taken place over the warmer tracts of land which they had to cross, and in which they cannot even be kept alive, in our days, with the utmost precautions; nor how the terrestrial animals of New Holland, which have no analogues in the main continents, could have reached that large island, nor why they should have all moved thither. And, indeed, it is impossible, with such a theory, to account, either for the special adaptation of types to particular districts of the earth's surface, or for the limited distribution of so many species which are found only over narrow districts in their present arrangement. It is inconsistent with the structure, habits, and natural instincts of most animals, even to suppose that they could have migrated over any great distances. It is in complete contradiction with the laws of nature, and all we know of the changes our globe has undergone, to imagine that the animals have actually adapted themselves to their various circumstances during their migration, as this would be ascribing to physical influences as much power as to the Creator himself.

And, again, the regular distribution, requiring precise laws, as we find it does, cannot be attributed either to the voluntary migration of animals, or to the influence of physical causes, when we see so plainly that this distribution is in accordance with the geographical distribution of animals and plants in former geological periods. But about this presently. We will only add, that we cannot discover in the Mosaic account any thing to sustain such a view, nor even hints leading to such a construction. What is said of animals and plants in the first chapter of Genesis, what is mentioned of the preservation of these animals and plants at the time of the deluge, relates chiefly to organized beings placed about Adam and Eve, and those which their progeny had domesticated, and which lived with them in closer connection. That Adam and Eve were neither the only nor the first human beings created is intimated in the statement of Moses himself, where Cain is represented to us as wandering among foreign nations after he was cursed, and taking a wife from the people of Nod, where he built a city, certainly with more assistance than that of his two brothers. Thus we maintain that the view of mankind as originating from a single pair, Adam and Eve,—and of the animals and plants as having originated from one common centre, which was at the same time the cradle of humanity,—is neither a Biblical view nor a correct view, nor one agreeing with the results of science, and our profound veneration for the Sacred Scriptures prompts us to pronounce the prevailing view of the origin of man, animals, and plants as a mere human hypothesis, not entitled to more consideration than belongs to most theories framed in the infancy of science. It is not for us,—for we have not the knowledge necessary for undertaking such an investigation,—it is not for us to inquire further into the full meaning of the statements of Moses. But we are satisfied that he never meant to say that all men originated from a single pair, Adam and Eve, nor that the animals had a similar origin from one common centre or from single pairs.

Let us now look at the results of geological investigations respecting the origin of earlier races of animals and plants. It is satisfactorily ascertained at present, that there have been many distinct successive periods, during each of which large numbers of animals and plants have been introduced upon the surface of our globe, to live and multiply for a time, then to disappear and be replaced by other kinds. Of such distinct periods, such successive creations, we know now at least about a dozen, and there are ample indications that the inhabitants of our globe have been successively changed at more epochs than are yet fully ascertained. But whether the number of these distinct successive creations be twelve or twenty, the fact stands in full light and evidence, that animals and plants which lived during the first period disappeared, either gradually or successively, to make room for others, and this at often-repeated intervals; and that the existence of animals and plants which live now is of but recent origin, is equally well ascertained.

There is another series of phenomena, not less satisfactorily established, which go to show that the extent of dry land rising above the surface of the ocean has neither been equally extensive at all times, nor has it had the same outline at all periods. On the contrary, we know that, early in the history of our globe, there has been a period, when but few low groups of islands existed above the surface of the ocean, which, through successive elevation and depression, have gradually enlarged and modified the extent and form of the mainland.

Again, in examining the remains of organized beings preserved in the different strata constituting the solid crust of our globe, we find that at each period animals and plants were distributed in the ocean and over the mainland in a particular manner, characteristic of every great epoch. A closer uniformity in their distribution is found in the earlier deposits, so much so that the oldest fossils discovered in the southern extremity of Africa, on the eastern and southern shores of New Holland and in Van Diemen's Land, in North America, or in various parts of Europe, are almost identical, or at least so nearly related, that they resemble each other much more than the animals and plants which at present live in the same countries; showing that uniformity in the aspect of the surface of the globe, as well as in the nature of animals and plants, was at first the prevailing rule, and that, whatever was the primitive region of these animals and plants, their types occupied much more extensive districts than any race of living beings during later periods. Are we to infer from this fact, that, at that period, these animals and plants originated from one common centre, and were distributed equally all over the globe? By no means. Though slight, we find nevertheless such differences among them in distant parts of the world as would rather sustain the view of an adaptation in the earliest creations to more uniform circumstances, than that of one centre of origin for all animals and plants of those days. During later periods, indeed, we find from geological evidence that large islands had been formed, more extensive tracts of land elevated above the surface of the ocean, and the remains both of the animals and plants derived from these different regions present already marked differences when we compare them with each other,—varieties similar to those which exist between the respective continents at present, though perhaps less marked. Shall we here again assume that animals and plants originated from another centre, or from the same centre as those of former periods, to migrate over those different parts of the world, through the sea as well as over land? It is impossible to arrive at such a conclusion, when we consider the distribution of fossil remains in the more recent geological deposits, or in those strata which were formed during the latest geological periods, immediately before the present creation. For we find in these comparatively modem beds a distribution of fossil remains which agrees in a most remarkable manner with the present geographical arrangement of animals and plants. For instance, the fossils of modem geological periods in New Holland are of the same types as most of the animals now living there. Again, the recent fossils of Brazil belong to the same families as those prevailing at present in Brazil; though, in both cases, fossil species are distinct from living ones. If, therefore, the organized beings of the recent geological periods had arisen from one central point of distribution, to be dispersed and finally to become confined to those countries where their remains are found in a fossil condition, and if the animals now living had also spread from a common origin over the same districts, and had then been circumscribed within equally distinct limits, we should be led to the unnatural supposition, that animals of two distinct creations, differing specifically throughout, had taken the same lines of migration, had assumed finally the same distribution, and had become permanent in the same regions, without any other inducement for their removal and final settlement than the mere necessity of covering more extensive ground after they had become too numerous to remain any longer together in one and the same district. This were to ascribe to the animals themselves, or to the physical agents under which they lived, and by which they may be influenced, as much wisdom, as much providential forethought, as is evinced throughout nature, both in the distribution of animals and in their special adaptation to particular portions of the globe in which they are closely circumscribed at present, and to which they were limited under similar circumstances during those periods which preceded immediately the present arrangement of things. Now these facts in themselves leave not the shadow of a doubt, in our mind, that animals were primitively created all over the world, within those districts which they were naturally to inhabit for a certain time. The next question is, Were these organized beings created in pairs, as is generally thought and believed? The opinion, that all animals must be referred to one single, primitive pair, is derived from evidence worthy of consideration, no doubt, but the value of which may fairly be questioned by naturalists; since this point, at least if we except Adam and Eve, is entirely of human construction, and only assumed because it is thought to show a wise economy of means in the established order of things which exists. It is supposed, that, if one pair were sufficient, there is no reason why the Creator should have introduced at one time a greater number of each kind, as economy of means is always considered an indication of high wisdom. But are not these human considerations? And if they are, and if we are entitled to question their value, let us see how they answer the object which was intended, namely, the peopling of the whole world with various races of organized beings.

Whenever we consider the economy of nature, we observe great varieties in the habits of different animals. There are, indeed, some which live constantly in pairs, and which by nature are designed to perpetuate their races in that way, and to spread generation after generation over their natural boundaries, thus mated. But there are others to which it is equally natural to live in herds or shoals, and which we never find isolated. The idea of a pair of herrings or of a pair of buffaloes is as contrary to the nature and habits of those animals, as it is contrary to the nature of pines and birches to grow singly and to form forests in their isolation.

But we can go further. There are animals in which the number of individuals of different sexes is naturally unequal, and among which there are either constantly more males or constantly more females born, as the result of their peculiar nature and habits in the creation. A beehive never consists of a pair of bees, and never could such a pair preserve the species, with their habits. For them it is natural to have one female and many males devoted to it, and thousands of neutral bees working for them. And this is the natural original mode of existence among that species of animals, which it would be utterly contrary to the laws of nature to consider as derived from a single pair. There are a number of birds, on the contrary, in which only a few males are universally found with many females living together in companies, such as the pheasants, and our domesticated fowls. It were easy to multiply examples in order to show that a creation of all animals in pairs would have been contrary to their very nature, as we observe it in all. To assume that they have changed this nature would be to fall back upon the necessity of ascribing to physical influences a power which they do not possess,— that of producing changes in the very nature of organized beings, and of modifying the primitive plan of the Creator.

Again, there are animals which, by nature, are impelled to feed upon other animals. Was the primitive pair of lions to abstain from food until the gazelles and other antelopes had sufficiently multiplied to preserve their races from the persecution of these ferocious beasts? Were all animals, and the innumerable tribes of ferocious fishes which live upon smaller ones, to abstain from food till these had been multiplied to a sufficient extent to secure their preservation? Or were, perhaps, the carnivorous animals created only at a later period? But we find them everywhere together. They constitute natural, harmonious groups with the herbivorous tribes, both in the waters and on land, preserving among each other such proportions as will maintain for ages an undisturbed harmony in the creation.

Again, we find animals and plants occurring in distinct districts, unconnected with each other, in such ways that it would seem almost impossible for either to migrate from any point of their natural circle of distribution over its whole surface. Have, for instance, such animals as are found identical both in America and Europe been created either in Europe or in America, and wandered from one of the continents over to the other? Have those species which occur only in the far north, and upon the higher summits of the Alps, been created either in the Alps or in the north, and wandered from one place to the other? We are at a loss for substantial arguments for believing that either one or the other place has been the primitive location of such animals, or for denying their simultaneous creation in both.

Evidence could be accumulated to show, we will not say the improbability only, but even the impossibility, of supposing that animals and plants were created in single pairs, and assumed afterwards their present distribution. But the facts mentioned will be sufficient to introduce our argument, and from all we know of the laws of nature and of the distribution of animals, we conclude that they could neither originate from a single pair, nor upon a single spot. And as for plants, we would ask naturalists whether it were not superfluous to create more than a single stock of most plants, as vegetables, with a few exceptions, may multiply extensively from a single stem. But if it is granted that animals could not originate from single pair, nor upon a single spot, what is the more natural view to take of the subject?

Without entering fully into this question, we may as well state that we have been gradually led to the conclusion, that most animals and plants must have originated primitively over the whole extent of their natural distribution. We mean to say that, for instance, lions, which occur over almost the whole of Africa, over extensive parts of Southern Asia, and were formerly found even over Asia Minor and Greece, must have originated primitively over the whole range of these limits of their distribution. We are led to these conclusions by the very fact, that the lions of the East Indies differ somewhat from those of Northern Africa; these, again, differ from those of Senegal. It seems more natural to suppose that they were thus distributed over such wide districts, and endowed with particular characteristics in each, than to assume that they constituted as many species; or to believe that, created anywhere in this circle of distribution, they have gradually been modified to their present differences in consequence of their migration. We admit these differences to be primitive and contemporaneous, from the fact, that there are other animals of different genera extending over the same tracts of land which have different representatives in each, circumscribed within narrower bounds, and this particular combination in each special district of the wider circle covered by the lion seems, in our opinion, the strongest argument in favor of the view that the particular districts of distribution have been primitively ascribed, with definite limits, to each species. Why should the antelopes north of the Cape of Good Hope differ from those of Arabia, or those of the Senegal, or those of the Atlas, or those of the East Indies, if they were not primitively adapted with their special modifications to those districts, when we see the lion cover the whole range? And why should the varieties we notice among the lions within these boundaries not be primitive, though not constituting distinct species, when we see the herbivorous species of the same genus differ front one district to another? And why should the differences in that one species of lion be the result of changes in its primitive character, arising from its distribution into new districts, when we see that the antelopes are at once fixed as distinct species over the same ground?

This argument cannot be fully appreciated by those who are not extensively acquainted with natural history, but we may, perhaps, make it plainer by alluding to some other similar facts. Our fresh waters teem everywhere with animals and plants. Fishes and mollusca are among the most prominent of their animals. Let us compare for a moment the different species which occur in the Danube, in the Rhine, and in the Rhone, three hydrographic basins entirely unconnected with each other throughout their whole extent. They spring from the same mountain chain, as we may take the Inn as the source of the Danube. These three great rivers rise within a few miles of each other. Nevertheless, most of their fishes differ, but there are some which are common to the three. We find the pickerel, the European pickerel, in the three basins. The eel is also common to them all. One kind of trout occurs in the three. But how strange the distribution of some others!—for instance, the perches. In the Rhine we find Perca fluviatilis, and Acerina cernua; in the Rhone, Perca fluviatilis and Aspro vulgaris; in the Danube, Perca vulgaris, Lucioperca Sandra, Acerina cernua, A. Schraitzer, Aspro vulgaris, and A. Zingel. If these animals had not originated in these rivers separately, why should not such closely allied species, some of which occur in the three basins, have all spread equally into them? and if they originated in the separate basins, we have within close limits a multiple origin of the same species.

And that this multiple origin must be admitted as a fact is shown by the following further evidence. Among the carps we find, for instance, Barbus, Gobio, Carpio, common to the three. But the Danube has three Gobios, whilst the others have but one, one of the Danube being identical with the one of the other two rivers. The most striking fact, however, occurs in the genus Leuciscus. Leuciscus Dobula is common to the three, but in addition to it, the Danube has several species which occur neither in the Rhine nor in the Rhone. The basin of the Rhone, again, has several species which occur neither in the Danube nor in the Rhine; and in the Rhine there are species which belong neither to the Rhone nor to the Danube. Now we ask, Could all these species of Leuciscus have been created in one of the basins,—in the Danube, for instance,—and have migrated in such a. way, that a certain number of the species should remain solely in the Danube, while some others left the Danube altogether to settle finally only in the Rhone, and others to settle only in the Rhine; that one :accompanying those species peculiar to the Rhone remained in the Danube with those species peculiar to it, and settled also in the Rhone with those species peculiar to that river, and also in the Rhine with the species peculiar to the Rhine? And whether we assume the Rhone as the primitive centre, instead of the Danube or the Rhine, the argument holds equally good. We have one species common to the three rivers, and several species peculiar to each, which could never have migrated (if migration took place) in such a manner as to assume their present combinations. But if, on the contrary, we suppose that all the species originated in the rivers where they occur, then we have again a multiple origin of that species which is common to the three, for it were wonderful if that one alone had migrated, when they are all so closely allied. Here, again, we arrive at the conclusion, that the same species can have a multiple origin, in the same manner as, from the considerations alluded to before, we have decided that species do not originate from single pairs, but in their natural proportion with the other species with which they live simultaneously over the whole ground which they cover. And this is the view which we take of the natural distribution of animals, that they originated primitively over the whole extent of their natural distribution; that they originated there, not in pairs, but in large numbers, in such proportions as suits their natural mode of living and the preservation of their species; and that the same species may have originated in different unconnected parts of the more extensive circle of their distribution. We are well aware that there are very many species which are known to have spread beyond what we would call their natural limits; species which did not occur in North America before the settlement of the whites, that are now abundant here over very extensive tracts of country; other species which have been introduced from America into Europe, and also into other parts of the world, in different ways. But these are exceptional facts; and, what is more important, these changes in the primitive distribution of organized beings, both animals and plants, have taken place under the influence of man,—under the influence of a being acting not merely from natural impulses, or under the pressure of physical causes, but moved by a higher will. So that these apparent exceptions to the rule would only go to confirm it; as, within the limits of these secondary changes, we see a will acting, just as we consider that the primitive distribution of all organized beings has been the result of the decrees of the Creator, and not the result of mere natural influences.

Having thus led the way to what we would consider as a fairer ground for investigating the natural geographical distribution of animals and plants, let us now examine the natural lines which seem to regulate this distribution. Nothing can be more striking to the observer than the fact, that animals, though endowed with the power of locomotion, remain within fixed bounds in their geographical distribution, although an unbounded field for migration is open to them in all directions, over land, through the air, and through the waters. And no stronger argument can be introduced to show that living beings are endowed with their power of locomotion to keep within genial boundaries, rather than to spread extensively. There is another fact which shows that animals are made to remain within these natural limits. We would allude especially to the difficulty we experience whenever we attempt to transport animals from their native country into other countries, even if we secure for them as nearly as can be the same conditions in which they used to live. Again, observe the changes which animals undergo when they are once acclimatized to countries different from their native land. There can be no more striking evidence of this than the endless variety of our domestic animals, and there is no subject which more requires a renewed and careful investigation than this. We do not, however, feel competent to introduce this point more fully to the notice of our readers. Some facts bearing upon the question may best be mentioned in a reference to the different animals which man has thus made subservient to his social condition. We shall here allude only to the laws of distribution of wild animals in their natural condition.

It has already been stated, that the present distribution of animals agrees with the distribution of extinct types belonging to earlier geological periods, so that the laws which regulate the geographical distribution of animals seem to have been the same at all times, though modified in accordance with the successive changes which the animal kingdom has undergone from the earliest period of its creation to the present day. The universal law is, that all animals are circumscribed within definite limits. There is not one species which is uniformly spread all over the globe, either among the aquatic races, or among the terrestrial ones. Of the special distribution of man, who alone is found everywhere, we shall speak hereafter. The special adaptation of animals to certain districts is not merely limited to the individual species. We observe a similar adaptation among genera, entire families, and even whole classes. For instance, all Polypi, Medusæ, and Echinoderms, that is to say all Radiata without exception, are aquatic.[1] That large group of animals has not a single terrestrial representative upon any point of the surface of the globe; and during all periods of the history of our earth, we find that they have always been limited to the liquid element. And they are not only aquatic, they are chiefly marine, as but exceedingly few of them are found in fresh waters. Among Mollusca we find almost the same adaptation. Their element also is the sea. The number of fresh-water species is small compared with that of marine types; and we find terrestrial species in only one of their classes. In former periods, also, Mollusca were chiefly marine; fluviatile and terrestrial types occurring only in more recent periods.

With the Articulata we find another state of things. Two of their classes, the worms and Crustacea, are chiefly marine, or at least aquatic, as we have a number of fresh-water worms, and some fresh-water Crustacea. But insects are, for the most part, chiefly terrestrial, feeding upon terrestrial plants, at least in their full-grown condition; though a large number of these animals are fluviatile, and even some marine, during their earlier periods of life. In the Vertebrata, the adaptations are more diversified. Only one class of these animals is entirely aquatic, the fishes; and the number of the marine species is far greater than that of the fresh-water kinds. Among reptiles there are many which are aquatic, either throughout life, or through the earlier period of their existence. But, as if animal life rose to higher organization as it leaves the ocean to inhabit dry land or fresh waters, we find that the greater number of the aquatic

---

[1] The following statements have been strictly considered, and are made in reference to a revised classification of the animal kingdom, the details of which must, however, be omitted here, as they would extend this article beyond our allotted bounds.

reptiles are fluviatile, and but a few marine. This fact agrees wonderfully with the natural gradation of the classes already mentioned. The lower type of animals, the Radiata, is almost exclusively marine. Among Mollusca we have a greater number of marine types, a large number of fluviatile species, and fewer terrestrial, and these are the highest in their class. Again, among Articulata the lower classes, worms and Crustacea, are marine, or at least fluviatile, whilst the highest class, that of insects, is chiefly terrestrial, or fluviatile during the earlier periods of their growth. Among the Vertebrata we see the lowest form, that of fishes, entirely aquatic, and the same rule applies partially to the reptiles; but as the class rises, the number of the fluviatile species is greater than that of the marine types. Next, among birds, which by their structure are exclusively adapted to live in the atmospheric air, we find the larger number to be terrestrial, and only the lower ones to live upon water, or dive occasionally into it, always seeking the surface, however, to breathe and to perform their most important vital functions. It is, nevertheless, not a little strange, that this class should by nature be adapted to rise into the air, just as if the first tendency towards liberating them from the aquatic element had been carried to an excess, and gave them a relation to the earth which no other class, as a whole, holds to that degree, except, perhaps, the insects, which are placed among the Articulata in the same relation to the lower classes and the natural element, which the class of birds maintains among Vertebrata. The highest class of Vertebrata affords us examples of these three modes of adaptation, the lowest of these being entirely aquatic, and even absolutely marine; next we have fluviatile types of the large terrestrial Mammalia in the family of Manatees, again a swimming family among Carnivora, another flying, most of them, however, walking upon their four extremities on solid ground, but at the head of all man, standing upright, to look freely upwards and to contemplate the whole universe.

This wonderful adaptation of the whole range of animals, as it exists at present, shows the most intimate connection with the order of succession of animals in former geological periods. The four great types, Radiata, Mollusca, Articulata, and Vertebrata, were introduced at the beginning simultaneously. However, the earliest representatives of these great types were all aquatic. We find in the lowest beds which contain fossils, Polypi, together with star-fishes, bivalve shells, univalves, chambered shells, cases of worms, and Crustacea, being representatives of at least seven out of nine classes of invertebrate animals, if we are not allowed to suppose that Medusæ existed also, and if insects were still wanting for a time. But in addition to these, fishes among Vertebrata are introduced, but fishes only, all of which are exclusively marine. At a somewhat later period insects come in. We find next reptiles in addition to fishes, the lower classes, or invertebrates, continuing to be represented through all subsequent epochs, but by species changing gradually at each period, as all classes do after they have once been introduced. The first representatives among reptiles are marine, next huge terrestrial ones, some, perhaps, flying types, and with them, and perhaps even before them, birds, allied to the wading tribes. Still later Mammalia, beginning again with marine and huge terrestrial types, followed by the higher quadrupeds. And last only, Man, at the head of the creation in time as well as in eminence, by structure, intelligence, and moral endowments.

Besides the general adaptation of animals to the surrounding media, there is a more special adaptation, which seems not less important, though it is perhaps less striking. Animals, as well as plants, do not live equally at all depths of the ocean, or at all heights above its surface. There must be a deep influence upon the geographical distribution of animals in a vertical direction derived from atmospheric pressure above the surface of the waters, and from the pressure of the water itself at greater and greater depths,—the level of the ocean, or a small elevation above its surface, or a shallow depth under its surface, being the field of the most extensive and intensive development of animal life. And it is not a little remarkable that in the same classes we should find lower types at greater depths in the ocean, and also lower types at greater heights above. We will quote a few examples, to show how much we may expect from investigations pursued in this direction, for at present we have but little information which can aid us in ascertaining the relationship between atmospheric and hydrostatic pressure and the energies of animal life.

Among Polypi, the higher forms, such as Actiniæ, are more abundant in shallow water than the lower coral-forming types. Among Medusæ, the young are either attached to the bottom, or grow from the depth, while the perfect free forms of these animals come to the surface. Among Echinoderms, the Crinoids are deep-water forms; free star-fishes and Echini, and above all Holothuriæ, living nearer the surface. Among Mollusca, the Acephala, which are lowest, have their lower types,—the Brachiopods, entirely confined to deep waters; the Monomyarians appear next, and above them the Dimyarians; among these latter, the highest family, the Nayades, rises above the level of the ocean into the fresh waters, and extends even to considerable heights above the sea, in lakes and rivers. A number of examples of all classes should be mentioned to show that this is the universal case; as, for instance, among Crustacea the Macrura are in general species of deeper water than the true crabs, of which some come even upon dry land. Again, on the slopes of our mountains, the highest forms among Mammalia which remain numerous are the Ruminants and Rodents. There are no Carnivora living in high regions. Among birds of prey, we have the vultures, rising above the highest summits of mountains, while eagles and falcons hover over the woods and plains, by the water-sides, and along the sea-shores. Among reptiles, salamanders, frogs, and toads occur higher than any turtles, lizards, &c. But the same adaptation may be traced with reference to the latitudes under which animals are found. Those of the higher latitudes, the arctic and antarctic species, resemble both the animals of high, prominent mountain chains, and those of the deep-sea waters, which there meet in the most unexpected combinations (and it is surprising to see how extensively this is the case); while, in lower latitudes, towards the tropics, we find everywhere the higher representatives of the same families. For instance, among Mammalia we observe monkeys only in warm latitudes, and they die out in the warmer parts of the temperate zone. The great development of Digitigrades—lions, tigers, &c.—takes place within the tropics, smaller species, like wolves and foxes, weasels, &c., occurring in the north, whilst the Plantigrades, which come nearer and nearer to the seal, follow an inverse progression, the largest and most powerful of them being the arctic ice-bear, which meets there his family relations, the Pinnipedia, that are so numerous in the polar regions. Again, the families of Ruminants and Pachyderms seem to form an exception, for though belonging to the lower types of Mammalia, they prevail in the tropical zone; but let us remember that they were among the earlier inhabitants of our globe, and the fact of their occurring more extensively in warm climates is rather a reminiscence of the plan of creation in older times, than an adaptation to the law regulating at present the distribution of organized beings. The gradation of animals among birds being less satisfactorily ascertained, we do not venture to say any thing respecting their geographical distribution in relation to climates. But among reptiles, we cannot overlook the fact, that the crocodiles, which are the highest in structure, are altogether tropical, and the Batrachians, which rank lowest, especially the salamandroid forms, are rather types of the colder temperate zone, than of the warm, &c. From these facts it is plain that the geographical distribution of all groups has a direct reference to atmospheric and hydrostatic pressure on one side, and. also to the intensity of light and heat over the surface of the globe.

The special adaptation of minor groups begins very early in the history of our globe, and extends at present all over its surface. In the same manner as animals are adapted to natural limits in their large primitive groups which we call classes, we find also the minor divisions more closely adapted to particular circumstances of the physical condition of all parts of the globe. Among Mammalia, the great type of Marsupialia is placed in New Holland, and extends little beyond that continent into the adjacent islands. A very few representatives of that family are found in America. Asia, Africa, the colder parts of North America, and its southern extremity, are entirely deprived of this type. The family of Edentata again has its centre of development in South America, where the sloth, dasypus, ant-eaters &c., form characteristic types, of which a few analogues occur in Africa along its southern extremity and western coast. Now it is a fact upon which we cannot insist too strongly, that the same districts of New Holland and South America were, during an earlier geological period comparatively recent, the seat of an equally wide development of the same animals in the same extensive proportions as at present. We need only refer to the beautiful investigations of Dr. Lund, upon the fossil Mammalia of Brazil, and to those no less important of Professor Owen, upon the fossil remains of Mammalia of New Holland, to leave not a shadow of a doubt upon this adaptation, which indicates distinctly these two regions, at two distinct periods remote from each other, as the points of development of two distinct families, which have never spread over other parts of the globe at any period since the time of their existence, indicating there at least two distinct foci of creation, with the same characters, at two successive epochs; a fact, which, in our opinion, can never be reconciled to the idea of a unique centre of origin of the animals now living. But though other families have never been and are not now localized in so special a manner, we nevertheless find them circumscribed within certain limits, in particular districts, or, at least, in particular zones.

As already mentioned, the monkeys are entirely tropical. But here, again, we notice a very intimate adaptation of their types to the particular continents, as the monkeys of tropical America constitute a family altogether distinct from the monkeys of the Old World, there being not one species of any of the genera of Quadrumana, so numerous on this continent, found either in Africa or in Asia. The monkeys of the Old World, again, constitute a natural family by themselves, extending equally over Africa and Asia; but the species of Africa differ from those of Asia; and there is even a close representative analogy between those of different parts of these two continents, the orangs of Africa, the chimpanzee and gorilla, corresponding to the red orang of Sumatra and Borneo, and the smaller long-armed species of continental Asia. And what is not a little remarkable is the fact, that the black orang occurs upon that continent which is inhabited by the black human race, whilst the brown orang inhabits those parts of Asia over which the chocolate-colored Malays have been developed. There is again a peculiar family of Quadrumana confined to the island of Madagascar, the Makis, which are entirely peculiar to that island and the eastern coast of Africa opposite to it, and to one spot on the western shore of Africa. But in New Holland and the adjacent islands there are no monkeys at all, though the climatic conditions seem not to exclude their existence any more than those of the large Asiatic islands, upon which such high types of this order are found. And these facts more than any other would indicate that the special adaptation of animals to particular districts of the surface of our globe is neither accidental, nor dependent upon physical conditions, but is implied in the primitive plan of the creation itself. Whatever classes we may take into consideration, we shall find similar adaptations, and though, perhaps, the greater uniformity of some families renders the difference of the types in various parts of the world less striking, they are none the less real. The Carnivora of tropical Asia are not the same as those of tropical Africa or those of tropical America Their birds and reptiles present similar differences. The want of an ostrich in Asia, when we have one, the largest of the family, in Africa, and two distinct species in Southern America, and two cassowaries, one in New Holland and another in the Sunda Islands, shows this constant process of analogous or representative species repeated over different parts of the world to be the principle regulating the distribution of animals, and the fact that these analogous species are different, again, cannot be reconciled to the idea of a common origin, as each type is peculiar to the country where it is now found. These differences are more striking in tropical regions than anywhere else. The rhinoceros of the Sunda Islands differs from those of Africa, and there is none in America. The elephant of Asia differs from that of Africa, and there is none in America. One tapir is found on the Sunda Islands, there is none in Africa, but we find one in South America, &c. Everywhere special adaptation, particular forms in each continent, an omission of some allied type here, when in the next group it occurs all over the zone.

As we ascend into the temperate zone, we find, however, the similarity greatly increased. The difference between the species of the same family in temperate Asia, temperate Europe, and temperate America is much less than between the corresponding animals of the tropical zone, and no doubt it is to this great assemblage of more uniform animals, living originally within the main seat of human civilization, that we must ascribe the idea of their common origin, which has so long prevailed and been so serious an obstacle to a real insight into these natural phenomena. What, indeed, could be more natural for man, when for the first time reflecting upon nature around him,—when seeing, as far as he could extend his investigations, all things alike,—than to imagine that every thing arose from a common centre, and spread with him over the world, as it has been the fate of the white race, and of that only, to extend all over the globe, and that, influenced by the phenomena of the zone in which he lived, and wandered, and from which he extended farther, he took it for granted that all animals followed the same laws? But now that we know the whole surface of our globe so satisfactorily, there can no longer be a question about the difference between animals and plants in the lower latitudes in all continents. Besides, we see them equally striking in the southernmost extremities of the three great continents, so that there can no longer be any doubt about the primitive adaptation of these various types to the continents where they live, as we do not find single one naturally diffused everywhere over all continents. Notwithstanding therefore, the slighter differences we notice between the animals of different continents in the temperate zone, we are thus led step by step to ascribe to them also a special origin upon those continents where they now occur.

But as soon as we rise to the highest latitudes, the uniformity becomes so close, that there is no longer any marked difference noticed between the animals about the arctic regions, either in America, Europe, or Asia; and we are naturally led to restrict the idea of a common centre of origin, or at least of a narrow circle of primitive development, to those animals which spread equally over the icy fields extending around the northern pole upon the three continents which meet in the north. The phenomena of geographical distribution which we observe there among the terrestrial animals are repeated in the same manner among the aquatic ones. The fishes in the arctic seas do not materially differ on the shores of Europe, Asia, and America, and through the Northern Atlantic and through Behring's Straits they extend more or less towards the colder temperate zone, or migrate into it at particular seasons of the year, as do most birds of the arctic regions also. But in the temperate zone we begin to find more and more marked differences between the inhabitants of different continents, and even between those of the opposite shores of the same ocean; as, for instance, the fishes of Europe (some of the northern species excepted) are not identical with those of the temperate shores of North America, notwithstanding the very open field left for their uniform distribution across the Atlantic. Such is also the case between the fishes of Western Africa and those of Central America, and between those of the southern extremities of these continents. The fishes of the Indian Ocean and the fishes of the Pacific vary greatly, and, though some families have a wider range, there are many which are circumscribed within the narrowest limits. It is one of the most striking phenomena in the geographical distribution of aquatic animals, to find entire families of fishes completely circumscribed within particular groups of islands, such, for instance, as the Labyrinthici, which are peculiar to the Sunda Islands, and the family of Goniodonts, which are found only in the rivers of South America.

A similar narrow limitation occurs also among the terrestrial animals, as the family of Colubris is entirely circumscribed within the boundaries of the warmer parts of the American continent. The appearance during the warmer season of the year of a few species of that family in the Northern States does not make this case less strong. Examples might be multiplied without end to show everywhere special adaptation, narrow circumscription, or representative adaptation of species in different parts of the world; but those mentioned will be sufficient to sustain the argument that animals are naturally autochthones wherever they are found, and have been so at all geological periods; that in northern regions they are most uniform; that their diversity goes on increasing through the temperate zone till it reaches its maximum in the tropics; that this diversity is again reduced in the aquatic animals towards the antarctic pole, though the physical difference between the southernmost extremities of America, Africa, and New Holland seems to have called for an increased difference between their terrestrial animals.

We are thus led to distinguish special provinces in the natural distribution of animals, and we may adopt the following division as the most natural. First, the *arctic province*, with prevailing uniformity. Second, the temperate zone, with at least three distinct zoölogical provinces: the *European temperate zone* west of the Ural Mountains, the *Asiatic temperate zone* east of the Ural Mountains, and the *American temperate zone*, which may be subdivided into two, the *eastern* and the *western*, for the animals east and west of the Rocky Mountains differ sufficiently to constitute two distinct zoölogical provinces. Next, the tropical zone, containing the *African zoölogical province*, which extends over the main part of the African continent, including all the country south of the Atlas and north of the Cape Colonies; the *tropical Asiatic province*, south of the great Himalayan chain, and including the Sunda Islands, whose Fauna has quite a continental character, and differs entirely from that of the islands of the Pacific, as well as from that of New Holland; the *American tropical province*, including Central America, the West Indies, and tropical South America. New Holland constitutes in itself a special province, notwithstanding the great differences of its northern and southern climate, the animals of the whole continent preserving throughout their peculiar typical character. But it were a mistake to conceive that the Faunæ or natural groups of animals are to be limited according to the boundaries of the mainlands. On the contrary, we may trace their natural limits into the ocean, and refer to the temperate European Fauna the eastern shores of the Atlantic, as we refer its western shores to the American temperate Fauna. Again, the eastern shores of the Pacific belong to the western American Fauna, as the western Pacific shores belong to the Asiatic Fauna. In the Atlantic Ocean there is no purely oceanic Fauna to be distinguished, but in the *Pacific* we have such a Fauna, entirely marine in its main character, though inter-spread with innumerable islands extending east of the Sunda Islands and New Holland to the western shores of tropical America. The islands west of this continent seem, indeed, to have very slight relations in their zoölogical character with the western parts of the mainland. South of the tropical zone, we have the *South American temperate Fauna*, and that of the *Cape of Good Hope*, as other distinct zoölogical provinces. Van Diemen's Land, however, does not constitute a zoölogical province in itself, but belongs to the province of New Holland, by its zoölogical character. Finally, the antarctic circle incloses a special zoölogical province, including the *antarctic Fauna*, which, in a great measure, corresponds to the arctic Fauna in its uniformity, though it differs from it having chiefly a maritime character, while the arctic Fauna has an almost entirely continental aspect.

The fact that the principal races of man, in their natural distribution, cover the same extent of ground as the great zoölogical provinces, would go far to show that the differences which we notice between them are also primitive; but for the present we shall abstain from further details upon a subject involving so difficult problems as the question of the unity or plurality of origin of the human family, satisfied as we are to have shown that animals, at least, did not originate from a common centre, nor from single pairs, but according to the laws which at present still regulate their existence.

5. Asa Gray

(1810–1888)

Gray, A. 1860. Review of Darwin's theory on the origin of species by means of natural selection. *The American Journal of Science and Arts,* Second Series 29(66):153-184.

Fully to understand the foregoing Essay of Dr. Hooker,[1] it should be read in the light of Mr. Darwin's book. The Essay is a trial of the Theory,—an attempt by one inclined in its favour to see how the theory will work, when applied to the flora of a large and most peculiar province of the world.

This book is already exciting much attention. Two American editions are announced, through which it will become familiar to many of our readers, before these pages are issued. An abstract of the argument,—for "the whole volume is one long argument," as the author states,—is unnecessary in such a case; and it would be difficult to give by detached extracts. For the volume itself is an abstract, a prodromus of a detailed work upon which the author has been laboring for twenty years, and which "will take two or three more years to complete." It is exceedingly compact; and although useful summaries are appended to the several chapters, and a general recapitulation contains the essence of the whole, yet much of the aroma escapes in the treble distillation, or is so concentrated that the flavor is lost to the general, or even to the scientific reader. The volume itself,—the proof-spirit—is just condensed enough for its purpose. It will be far more widely read, and perhaps will make deeper impression than the elaborate work might have done, with its full details of the facts upon which the author's sweeping conclusions have been grounded. At least it is a more readable book: but all the facts that can be mustered in favor of the theory are still likely to be needed.

Who, upon a single perusal, shall pass judgment upon a work like this, to which twenty of the best years of the life of a most able naturalist have been devoted? And who among those naturalists who hold a position that entitles them to pronounce summarily upon the subject, can be expected to divest himself for the nonce of the influence or [*sic*–of]

---

[1] This article was intended to follow the remaining part of the essay of Dr. Hooker, commenced in our January number; the continuation of which we are obliged to defer, for want of room.–Eds.

received and favorite systems? In fact, the controversy now opened is not likely to be settled in an off-hand way, nor is it desirable that it should be. A spirited conflict among opinions of every grade must ensue, which,— to borrow an illustration from the doctrine of the book before us—may be likened to the conflict in nature among races in the struggle for life, which Mr. Darwin describes; through which the views most favored by facts will be developed and tested by 'Natural Selection,' the weaker ones be destroyed in the process, and the strongest in the long run alone survive.

The duty of reviewing this volume in the American Journal of Science would naturally devolve upon the principal Editor, whose wide observation and profound knowledge of various departments of natural history, as well as of geology, particularly qualify him for the task. But he has been obliged to lay aside his pen, and to seek in distant lands the entire repose from scientific labor so essential to the restoration of his health,—a consummation devoutly to be wished, and confidently to be expected. Interested as Mr. Dana would be in this volume, he could not be expected to accept its doctrine. Views so idealistic as those upon which his "Thoughts upon Species"[2] are grounded, will not harmonize readily with a doctrine so thoroughly naturalistic as that of Mr. Darwin. Though it is just possible that one who regards the kinds of elementary matter, such as oxygen and hydrogen, and the definite compounds of these elementary matters, and their compounds again, in the mineral kingdom, as constituting species, in the same sense, fundamentally, as that of animal and vegetable species, might admit an evolution of one species from another in the latter as well as the former case.

Between the doctrines of this volume and those of the other great Naturalist whose name adorns the title-page of this Journal, the widest divergence appears. It is interesting to contrast the two, and, indeed, is necessary to our purpose; for this contrast brings out most prominently, and sets in strongest light and shade the main features of the theory of the origination of species by means of Natural Selection.

The ordinary and generally received view assumes the independent, specific creation of each kind of plant and animal in a primitive stock, which reproduces its like from generation to generation, and so continues the species.[3] Taking the idea of species from this perennial succession of essentially similar individuals, the chain is logically traceable back to a local origin in a single stock, a single pair, or a single individual, from which all the individuals composing the species have proceeded by natural generation. Although the similarity of progeny to parent is

---

2 Article in this Journal, vol. xxiv., p. 305.
3 "Species tot sunt, quot diversas formas ab initio produxit Infinitum Ens; quæ formæ, secundum generationis inditas leges, produxere plures, at sibi semper similes."— *Linn. Phil. Bot.*, 99, 157.

fundamental in the conception of species, yet the likeness is by no means absolute: all species vary more or less, and some vary remarkably—partly from the influence of altered circumstances, and partly (and more really) from unknown constitutional causes which altered conditions favor rather than originate. But these variations are supposed to be mere oscillations from a normal state, and in nature to be limited if not transitory; so that the primordial differences between species and species at their beginning have not been effaced, nor largely obscured, by blending through variation. Consequently, whenever two reputed species are found to blend in nature through a series of intermediate forms, community of origin is inferred, and all the forms, however diverse, are held to belong to one species. Moreover, since bisexuality is the rule in nature (which is practically carried out, in the long run, far more generally than has been suspected), and the heritable qualities of two distinct individuals are mingled in the offspring, it is supposed that the general sterility of hybrid progeny, interposes an effectual barrier against the blending of the original species by crossing.

From this generally accepted view the well-known theory of Agassiz and the recent one of Darwin diverge in exactly opposite directions.

That of Agassiz differs fundamentally from the ordinary view only in this, that it discards the idea of a common descent as the real bond of union among the individuals of a species, and also the idea of a local origin,—supposing, instead, that each species originated simultaneously, generally speaking, over the whole geographical area it now occupies or has occupied, and in perhaps as many individuals as it numbered at any subsequent period.

Mr. Darwin, on the other hand, holds the orthodox view of the descent of all the individuals of a species not only from a local birthplace, but from a single ancestor or pair; and that each species has extended and established itself, through natural agencies, wherever it could; so that the actual geographical distribution of any species is by no means a primordial arrangement, but a natural result. He goes farther, and this volume is a protracted argument intended to prove that the species we recognize have not been independently created, as such, but have descended, like varieties, from other species. Varieties, on this view, are incipient or possible species: species are varieties of a larger growth and a wider and earlier divergence from the parent stock: the difference is one of degree, not of kind.

The ordinary view—rendering unto Cæsar the things that are Cæsar's—looks to natural agencies for the actual distribution and perpetuation of species, to a supernatural for their origin.

The theory of Agassiz regards the origin of species and their present general distribution over the world as equally primordial, equally supernatural; that of Darwin, as equally derivative, equally natural.

The theory of Agassiz, referring as it does the phenomena both of origin and distribution directly to the Divine will,—thus removing the latter with the former out of the domain of inductive science (in which efficient cause is not the first, but the last word),—may be said to be theistic to excess. The contrasted theory is not open to this objection. Studying the facts and phenomena in reference to proximate causes, and endeavoring to trace back the series of cause and effect as far as possible, Darwin's aim and processes are strictly scientific, and his endeavor, whether successful or futile, must be regarded as a legitimate attempt to extend the domain of natural or physical science. For though it well may be that "organic forms have no physical or secondary cause," yet this can be proved only indirectly, by the failure of every attempt to refer the phenomena in question to causal laws. But, however originated, and whatever be thought of Mr. Darwin's arduous undertaking in this respect, it is certain that plants and animals are subject from their birth to physical influences, to which they have to accommodate themselves as they can. How literally they are "born to trouble," and how incessant and severe the struggle for life generally is, the present volume graphically describes. Few will deny that such influences must have gravely affected the range and the association of individuals and species on the earth's surface. Mr. Darwin thinks that, acting upon an inherent predisposition to vary, they have sufficed even to modify the species themselves and produce the present diversity. Mr. Agassiz believes that they have not even affected the geographical range and the actual association of species, still less their forms; but that every adaptation of species to climate and of species to species, is as aboriginal, and therefore as inexplicable, as are the organic forms themselves.

Who shall decide between such extreme views so ably maintained on either hand, and say how much of truth there may be in each? The present reviewer has not the presumption to undertake such a task. Having no prepossession in favor of naturalistic theories, but struck with the eminent ability of Mr. Darwin's work, and charmed with its fairness, our humbler duty will be performed if, laying aside prejudice as much as we can, we shall succeed in giving a fair account of its method and argument, offering by the way a few suggestions, such as might occur to any naturalist of an inquiring mind. An editorial character for this article must in justice be disclaimed. The plural pronoun is employed not to give editorial weight, but to avoid even the appearance of egotism, and also the circumlocution which attends a rigorous adherence to the impersonal style.

We have contrasted these two extremely divergent theories, in their broad statements. It must not be inferred that they have no points nor ultimate results in common.

In the first place they practically agree in upsetting, each in its own way, the generally received definition of species, and in sweeping away the ground of their objective existence in nature. The orthodox conception of species is that of lineal descent: all the descendants of a common parent, and no other, constitute a species; they have a certain identity because of their descent, by which they are supposed to be recognizable. So naturalists had a distinct idea of what they meant by the term species, and a practical rule, which was hardly the less useful because difficult to apply in many cases, and because its application was indirect,—that is, the community of origin had to be inferred from the likeness; that degree of similarity, and that only, being held to be conspecific which could be shown or reasonably inferred to be compatible with a common origin. And the usual concurrence of the whole body of naturalists (having the same data before them) as to what forms are species attests the value of the rule, and also indicates some real foundation for it in nature. But if species were created in numberless individuals over broad spaces of territory, these individuals are connected only in idea, and species differ from varieties on the one hand, and from genera, tribes, &c. on the other only in degree; and no obvious natural reason remains for fixing upon this or that degree as specific, at least no natural standard, by which the opinions of different naturalists may be correlated. Species upon this view are enduring, but subjective and ideal. Any three or more of the human races, for example, are species or not species, according to the bent of the naturalist's mind. Darwin's theory brings us the other way to the same result. In his view, not only all the individuals of a species are descendants of a common parent but of all the related species also. Affinity, relationship, all the terms which naturalists use figuratively to express an underived, unexplained resemblance among species, have a literal meaning upon Darwin's system, which they little suspected, namely, that of inheritance. Varieties are the latest offshoots of the genealogical tree in "an unlineal" order; species, those of an earlier date, but of no definite distinction; genera, more ancient species, and so on. The human races, upon this view likewise may or may not be species according to the notions of each naturalist as to what differences are specific: but, if not species already, those races that last long enough are sure to become so. It is only a question of time.

How well the simile of a genealogical tree illustrates the main ideas of Darwin's theory the following extract from the summary of the fourth chapter shows.

> "It is a truly wonderful fact,—the wonder of which we are apt to overlook from familiarity—that all animals and all plants throughout all time and space should be related to each other in group subordinate to group, in the manner which we

everywhere behold—namely, varieties of the same species most closely related together, species of the same genus less closely and unequally related together, forming sections and sub-genera, species of distinct genera much less closely related, and genera related in different degrees, forming sub-families, families, orders, sub-classes, and classes. The several subordinate groups in any class cannot be ranked in a single file, but seem rather to be clustered round points, and these round other points, and so on in almost endless cycles. On the view that each species has been independently created, I can see no explanation of this great fact in the classification of all organic beings; but, to the best of my judgment, it is explained through inheritance and the complex action of natural selection, entailing extinction and divergence of character, as we have seen illustrated in the diagram.

"The affinities of all the beings of the same class have sometimes been represented by a great tree. I believe this simile largely speaks the truth. The green and budding twigs may represent existing species; and those produced during each former year may represent the long succession of extinct species. At each period of growth all the growing twigs have tried to branch out on all sides, and overtop and kill the surrounding twigs and branches, in the same manner as species and groups of species have tried to overmaster other species in the great battle for life. The limbs divided into great branches, and these into lesser and lesser branches, were themselves once, when the tree was small, budding twigs; and this connexion of the former and present buds by ramifying branches may well represent the classification of all extinct and living species in groups subordinate to groups. Of the many twigs which flourished when the tree was a mere bush, only two or three, now grown into great branches, yet survive and bear all the other branches; so with the species which lived during long-past geological periods, very few now have living and modified descendants. From the first growth of the tree, many a limb and branch has decayed and dropped off; and these lost branches of various sizes may represent those whole orders, families, and genera, which have now no living representatives, and which are known to us only from having been found in a fossil state. As we here and there see a thin, straggling branch springing from a fork low down in a tree, and which by some chance has been favored and is still alive on its summit, so we occasionally see an animal like the Ornithorhynchus or Lepidosiren, which in some small degree connects by its affinities two large branches of life, and which has apparently been saved from fatal competition by having inhabited a protected station. As buds give rise by growth to fresh buds, and these, if vigorous, branch out and overtop on all sides many a feebler branch, so by generation I believe it has been with the great Tree of Life, which fills with its dead and broken branches the crust of the earth, and covers the surface with its ever branching and beautiful ramifications."

It may also be noted that there is a significant correspondence between the rival theories as to the main facts employed. Apparently every capital fact in the one view is a capital fact in the other. The difference is in the interpretation. To run the parallel ready made to our hands:[4]

"The simultaneous existence of the most diversified types under identical circumstances,...the repetition of similar types under the most diversified circumstances,...the unity of plan in otherwise highly diversified types of animals,...the correspondence, now generally known as special homologies, in the details of structure otherwise entirely disconnected, down to the most minute peculiarities,...the various degrees and different kinds of relationship among animals which [apparently] can have no genealogical connection,...the simultaneous existence in the earliest geological periods,...of representatives of all the great types of the animal kingdom,... the gradation based upon complications of structure which may be traced among animals built upon the same plan; the distribution of some types over the most extensive range of surface of the globe, while others are limited to particular geographical areas,...the identity of structures of these types, notwithstanding their wide geographical distribution,...the community of structure in certain respects of animals otherwise entirely different, but living within the same geographical area,...the connection by series of special structures observed in animals widely scattered over the surface of the globe,...the definite relations in which animals stand to the surrounding world, ...the relations in which individuals of the same species stand to one another,...the limitation of the range of changes which animals undergo during their growth,...the return to a definite norm of animals which multiply in various ways,... the order of succession of the different types of animals and

---

4   Agassiz, Essay on Classification; Contrib. to Nat. Hist., i, p. 132, et seq.

plants characteristic of the different geological epochs,...the localization of some types of animals upon the same points of the surface of the globe during several successive geological periods,...the parallelism between the order of succession of animals and plants in geological times, and the gradation among their living representatives,...the parallelism between the order of succession of animals in geological times and the changes their living representatives undergo during their embryological growth,[5]...*the combination in many extinct types of characters which in later ages appear disconnected in different types,*...the parallelism between the gradation among animals and the changes they undergo during their growth,... the relations existing between these different series and the geographical distribution of animals,...the connection of all the known features of nature into one system,—"

In a word, the whole relations of animals, &c. to surrounding nature and to each other, are regarded under the one view as ultimate facts, or in their ultimate aspect, and interpreted theologically;—under the other as complex facts, to be analyzed and interpreted scientifically. The one naturalist, perhaps too largely assuming the scientifically unexplained to be inexplicable, views the phenomena only in their supposed relation to the Divine mind. The other, naturally expecting many of these phenomena to be resolvable under investigation, views them in their relations to one another, and endeavors to explain them as far as he can (and perhaps farther) through natural causes.

But does the one really exclude the other? Does the investigation of physical causes stand opposed to the theological view and the study of the harmonies between mind and nature? More than this, is it not most presumable that an intellectual conception realized in nature would be realized through natural agencies? Mr. Agassiz answers these questions affirmatively when he declares that "the task of science is to investigate what has been done, to enquire if possible *how it has been done*, rather than to ask what is possible for the Deity, since *we can know that only by what actually exists;*" and also when he extends the argument for the intervention in nature of a creative mind to its legitimate application in

---

[5] As to this, Darwin remarks that he can only hope to see the law hereafter proved true (p. 449); and p. 338: "Agassiz insists that ancient animals resemble to a certain extent the embryos of recent animals of the same classes; or that the geological succession of extinct forms is in some degree parallel to the embryological development of recent forms. I must follow Pictet and Huxley in thinking that the truth of this doctrine is very far from proved. Yet I fully expect to see it hereafter confirmed, at least in regard to subordinate groups, which have branched off from each other within comparatively recent times. For this doctrine of Agassiz accords well with the theory of natural selection."

the inorganic world; which, he remarks, "considered in the same light, would not fail also to exhibit unexpected evidence of thought, in the character of the laws regulating the chemical combinations, the action of physical forces, etc., etc."[6] Mr. Agassiz, however, pronounces that "the connection between the facts is *only intellectual;*"—an opinion which the analogy of the inorganic world, just referred to, does not confirm, for there a material connection between the facts is justly held to be consistent with an intellectual—and which the most analogous cases we can think of in the organic world do not favor; for there is a material connection between the grub, the pupa, and the butterfly, between the tadpole and the frog, or, still better, between those distinct animals which succeed each other in alternate and very dissimilar generations. So that mere analogy might rather suggest a natural connection than the contrary; and the contrary cannot be demonstrated until the possibilities of nature under the Deity are fathomed.

But the intellectual connection being undoubted, Mr. Agassiz properly refers the whole to "the agency of Intellect as its first cause." In doing so, however, he is not supposed to be offering a scientific explanation of the phenomena. Evidently he is considering only the ultimate *why,* not the proximate why or *how.*

Now the latter is just what Mr. Darwin is considering. He conceives of a physical connection between allied species: but we suppose he does not deny their intellectual connection, as related to a Supreme Intelligence. Certainly we see no reason why he should, and many reasons why he should not. Indeed, as we contemplate the actual direction of investigation and speculation in the physical and natural sciences, we dimly apprehend a probable synthesis of these divergent theories, and in it the ground for a strong stand against mere naturalism. Even if the doctrine of the origin of species through natural selection should prevail in our day, we shall not despair; being confident that the genius of an Agassiz will be found equal to the work of constructing, upon the mental and material foundations combined, a theory of nature as theistic and as scientific as that which he has so eloquently expounded.

To conceive the possibility of "the descent of species from species by insensibly fine gradations" during a long course of time, and to demonstrate its compatibility with a strictly theistic view of the universe, is one thing: to substantiate the theory itself or show its likelihood is quite another thing. This brings us to consider what Darwin's theory actually is, and how he supports it.

That the existing kinds of animals and plants, or many of them, may be derived from other and earlier kinds, in the lapse of time, is by no

---

6   Op. cit., p. 131.—One or two Bridgewater Treatises, and most modern works upon Natural Theology should have rendered the evidences of thought in inorganic nature not "unexpected."

means a novel proposition. Not to speak of ancient speculations of the sort, it is the well-known Lamarckian theory. The first difficulty which such theories meet with is that, in the present age, with all its own and its inherited prejudgments, the whole burden of proof is naturally, and indeed properly, laid upon the shoulders of the propounders; and thus far the burden has been more than they could bear. From the very nature of the case, substantive proof of specific creation is not attainable; but that of derivation or transmutation of species may be. He who affirms the latter view is bound to do one or both of two things: Either, 1, to assign real and adequate causes, the natural or necessary result of which must be to produce the present diversity of species and their actual relations; or, 2, to show the general conformity of the whole body of facts to such assumption, and also to adduce instances explicable by it and inexplicable by the received view,—so perhaps winning our assent to the doctrine, through its competency to harmonize all the facts, even though the cause of the assumed variation remain as occult as that of the transformation of tadpoles into frogs, or that of *Coryne* into *Sarzia*.

The first line of proof, successfully carried out, would establish derivation as a true physical theory; the second, as a sufficient hypothesis.

Lamarck mainly undertook the first line, in a theory which has been so assailed by ridicule that it rarely receives the credit for ability to which in its day it was entitled. But he assigned partly unreal, partly insufficient causes; and the attempt to account for a progressive change in species through the direct influence of physical agencies, and through the appetencies and habits of animals reacting upon their structure, thus causing the production and the successive modification of organs, is a conceded and total failure. The shadowy author of the Vestiges of the Natural History of Creation can hardly be said to have undertaken either line, in a scientific way. He would explain the whole progressive evolution of nature by virtue of an inherent tendency to development,— thus giving us an idea or a word in place of a natural cause, a restatement of the proposition instead of an explanation. Mr. Darwin attempts both lines of proof, and in a strictly scientific spirit; but the stress falls mainly upon the first; for, as he does assign real causes, he is bound to prove their adequacy.

It should be kept in mind that, while all direct proof of independent origination is attainable from the nature of the case, the overthrow of particular schemes of derivation has not established the opposite proposition. The futility of each hypothesis thus far proposed to account for derivation may be made apparent, or unanswerable objections may be urged against it; and each victory of the kind may render derivation more improbable, and therefore specific creation more probable, without settling the question either way. New facts, or new arguments and a new mode of viewing the question may some day change the whole aspect of the case. It is with the latter that Mr. Darwin now reopens the discussion.

Having conceived the idea that varieties are incipient species, he is led to study variation in the field where it shows itself most strikingly and affords the greatest facilities to investigation. Thoughtful naturalists have had increasing grounds to suspect that a re-examination of the question of species in zoology and botany, commencing with those races which man knows most about, viz. the domesticated and cultivated races, would be likely somewhat to modify the received idea of the entire fixity of species. This field, rich with various but unsystematized stores of knowledge accumulated by cultivators and breeders, has been generally neglected by naturalists, because these races are not in a state of nature; whereas they deserve particular attention on this very account, as experiments, or the materials for experiments, ready to our hand. In domestication we vary some of the natural conditions of a species, and thus learn experimentally what changes are within the reach of varying conditions in nature. We separate and protect a favorite race against its foes or its competitors, and thus learn what it might become if nature ever afforded it equal opportunities. Even when, to subserve human uses, we modify a domesticated race to the detriment of its native vigor, or to the extent of practical monstrosity, although we secure forms which would not be originated and could not be perpetuated in free nature, yet we attain wider and juster views of the possible degree of variation. We perceive that some species are more variable than others, but that no species subjected to the experiment persistently refuses to vary; and that when it has once begun to vary, its varieties are not the less but the more subject to variation. "No case is on record of a variable being ceasing to be variable under cultivation." It is fair to conclude, from the observation of plants and animals in a wild as well as domesticated state, that the tendency to vary is general, and even universal. Mr. Darwin does "not believe that variability is an inherent and necessary contingency, under all circumstances, with all organic beings, as some authors have thought." No one supposes variation could occur under all circumstances; but the facts on the whole imply a universal tendency, ready to be manifested under favorable circumstances. In reply to the assumption that man has chosen for domestication animals and plants having an extraordinary inherent tendency to vary, and likewise to withstand diverse climates, it is asked:

> "How could a savage possibly know, when he first tamed an animal, whether it would vary in succeeding generations, and whether it would endure other climates? Has the little variability of the ass or guinea-fowl, or the

small power of endurance of warmth by the rein-deer, or of cold by the common camel, prevented their domestication? I cannot doubt that if other animals and plants, equal in number to our domesticated productions, and belonging to equally diverse classes and countries, were taken from a state of nature, and could be made to breed for an equal number of generations under domestication, they would vary on an average as largely as the parent species of our existing domesticated productions have varied."

As to amount of variation, there is the common remark of naturalists that the varieties of domesticated plants or animals often differ more widely than do the individuals of distinct species in a wild state: and even in nature the individuals of some species are known to vary to a degree sensibly wider than that which separates related species. In his instructive section on the breeds of the domestic pigeon, our author remarks that:—"at least a score of pigeons might be chosen, which if shown to an ornithologist, and he were told that they were wild birds, would certainly be ranked by him as well defined species. Moreover, I do not believe that any ornithologist would place the English carrier, the short-faced tumbler, the runt, the barb, pouter, and fantail in the same genus; more especially as in each of these breeds several truly inherited sub-breeds, or species as he might have called them, could be shown him." That this is not a case like that of dogs, in which probably the blood of more than one species is mingled, Mr. Darwin proceeds to show, adducing cogent reasons for the common opinion that all have descended from the wild rock-pigeon. Then follow some suggestive remarks:—

"I have discussed the probable origin of domestic pigeons at some, yet quite insufficient, length; because when I first kept pigeons and watched the several kinds, knowing well how true they bred, I felt fully as much difficulty in believing that they could ever have descended from a common parent, as any naturalist could in coming to a similar conclusion in regard to many species of finches, or other large groups of birds, in nature. One circumstance has struck me much; namely, that all the breeders of the various domestic animals and the cultivators of plants, with whom I have ever conversed, or whose treatises I have read, are firmly convinced that the several breeds to which each has attended, are descended from so many aboriginally distinct species. Ask, as I have asked, a celebrated raiser of Hereford cattle, whether his cattle might not have descended from long-horns, and he will laugh you to scorn. I have never met a pigeon, or poultry, or duck, or rabbit fancier, who was not fully convinced that each main breed was descended from a distinct species. Van Mons, in his treatise on pears and apples, shows how utterly he disbelieves that the several sorts, for instance a Ribston-pippin or Codlin-apple, could ever have proceeded from the seeds of the same tree. Innumerable other examples could be given. The explanation, I think, is simple: from long-continued study they are strongly impressed with the differences between the several races; and though they well know that each race varies slightly, for they win their prizes by selecting such slight differences, yet they ignore all general arguments, and refuse to sum up in their minds slight differences accumulated during many successive generations. May not those naturalists who, knowing far less of the laws of inheritance than does the breeder, and knowing no more than he does of the intermediate links in the long lines of descent, yet admit that many of our domestic races have descended from the same parents—may they not learn a lesson of caution, when they deride the idea of species in a state of nature being lineal descendants of other species?"

The actual causes of variation are unknown. Mr. Darwin favors the opinion of the late Mr. Knight, the great philosopher of horticulture, that variability under domestication is somehow connected with excess of food. He also regards the unknown cause as acting chiefly upon the reproductive system of the parents, which system, judging from the effect of confinement or cultivation upon its functions, he concludes to be more susceptible than any other to the action of changed conditions of life. The tendency to vary certainly appears to be much stronger under domestication than in free nature. But we are not sure that the greater variableness of cultivated races is not mainly owing to the far greater opportunities for manifestation and accumulation—a view seemingly all the more favorable to Mr. Darwin's theory. The actual amount of certain changes, such as size or abundance of fruit, size of udder, stands of course in obvious relation to supply of food.

Really, we no more know the reason why the progeny occasionally deviates from the parent than we do why it usually resembles it. Though the laws and conditions governing variation are known to a certain extent, those governing inheritance are apparently inscrutable. "Perhaps," Darwin remarks, "the correct way of viewing the whole subject would be, to look at the inheritance of every character whatever as the rule, and non-inheritance as the anomaly." This, from general and obvious considerations, we have long been accustomed to do. Now, as exceptional instances are expected to be capable of explanation, while ultimate laws are not, it is quite possible that variation may be accounted for, while the great primary law of inheritance remains a mysterious fact.

The common proposition is, that *species reproduce their like*; this is a sort of general inference, only a degree closer to fact than the statement that genera reproduce their like. The true proposition, the fact incapable of further analysis, is, that *individuals reproduce their like*—that characteristics are inheritable. So varieties, or deviations once originated, are perpetuable, like species. Not so likely to be perpetuated, at the outset; for the new form tends to resemble a grand-parent and a long line of similar ancestors, as well as to resemble its immediate progenitors. Two forces which coincide in the ordinary case, where the offspring resembles its parent, act in different directions when it does not and it is uncertain which will prevail. If the remoter, but very potent ancestral influence predominates, the variation disappears with the life of the individual. If that of the immediate parent—feebler no doubt, but closer—the variety survives in the offspring; whose progeny now has a redoubled tendency to produce its own like; whose progeny again is almost sure to produce its like, since it is much the same whether it takes after its mother or its grandmother.

In this way races arise, which under favorable conditions may be as hereditary as species. In following these indications, watching opportunities, and breeding only from those individuals which vary most in a desirable direction, man leads the course of variation as he leads a streamlet,—apparently at will, but never against the force of gravitation,—to a long distance from its source, and makes it more subservient to his use or fancy. He unconsciously strengthens those variations which he prizes when he plants the seed of a favorite fruit, preserves a favorite domestic animal, drowns the uglier kittens of a litter, and allows only the handsomest or the best mousers to propagate. Still more, by methodical selection, in recent times almost marvellous results have been produced in new breeds of cattle, sheep, and poultry, and new varieties of fruit of greater and greater size or excellence.

It is said that all domestic varieties if left to run wild, would revert to their aboriginal stocks. Probably they would wherever various races of one species were left to commingle. At least the abnormal or exaggerated characteristics induced by high feeding, or high cultivation, and prolonged close breeding would promptly disappear; and the surviving stock would soon blend into a homogeneous result (in a way presently explained), which would naturally be taken for the original form; but we could seldom know if it were so. It is by no means certain that the result would be the same if the races ran wild each in a separate region. Dr. Hooker doubts if there is a true reversion in the case of plants. Mr. Darwin's observations rather favor it in the animal kingdom. With mingled races reversion seems well made out in the case of pigeons. The common opinion upon this subject therefore probably has some foundation. But even if we regard varieties as oscillations around a primitive centre or type, still it appears from the readiness with which such varieties originate, that a certain amont of disturbance would carry them beyond the influence of the primordial attraction, where they may become new centres of variation.

Some suppose that races cannot be perpetuated indefinitely even by keeping up the conditions under which they were fixed: but the high antiquity of several, and the actual fixity of many of them, negative this assumption. "To assert that we could not breed our cart and race horses, long and short-horned cattle, and poultry of various breeds, for almost an infinite number of generations would be opposed to all experience."

Why varieties develope so readily and deviate so widely under domestication, while they are apparently so rare or so transient in free nature, may easily be shown. In nature, even with hermaphrodite plants, there is a vast amount of cross fertilization among various individuals of the same species. The inevitable result of this (as was long ago explained in this Journal[7]) is to repress variation, to keep the mass of a species comparatively homogeneous over any area in which it abounds in individuals. Starting from a suggestion of the late Mr. Knight, now so familiar, that close interbreeding diminishes vigor and fertility[8]; and perceiving that bisexuality is ever aimed at in nature,—being attained physiologically in numerous cases where it is not structurally,—Mr. Darwin has worked out the subject in detail, and shown how general is the concurrence, either habitual or occasional, of two hermaphrodite individuals in the reproduction of their kind; and has drawn the philosophical inference that probably no organic being self-fertilizes indefinitely; but that a cross with another individual is occasionally—perhaps at very long intervals—indispensable. We refer the reader to the section on the intercrossing of individuals (p. 96-101), and also to an article in the Gardeners' Chronicle a year and a half ago, for the details of a very interesting contribution to science, irrespective of theory.

In domestication, this intercrossing may be prevented; and in this prevention lies the art of producing varieties. But "the art itself is nature," since the whole art consists in allowing the most universal of all natural tendencies in organic things (inheritance) to operate uncontrolled by other and obviously incidental tendencies. No new power, no artificial force is brought into play either by separating the stock of a desirable variety

---

7   Vol. xvii, [2], 1854, p. 13.
8   We suspect that this is not an ultimate fact, but a natural consequence of inheritance,—the inheritance of disease or of tendency to disease, which close interbreeding perpetuates and accumulates, but wide breeding may neutralize or eliminate.

so as to prevent mixture, or by selecting for breeders those individuals which most largely partake of the peculiarities for which the breed is valued.[9]

We see everywhere around us the remarkable results which nature may be said to have brought about under artificial selection and separation. Could she accomplish similar results when left to herself? Variations might begin, we know they do begin, in a wild state. But would any of them be preserved and carried to an equal degree of deviation? Is there anything in nature which in the long run may answer to artificial selection? Mr. Darwin thinks that there is; and *Natural Selection* is the key-note of his discourse.

As a preliminary, he has a short chapter to show that there is variation in nature, and therefore something for natural selection to act upon. He readily shows that such mere variations as may be directly referred to physical conditions (like the depauperation of plants in a sterile soil, or their dwarfing as they approach an alpine summit, the thicker fur of an animal from far northward, &c.), and also those individual differences which we everywhere recognize but do not pretend to account for, are not separable by any assignable line from more strongly marked varieties; likewise that there is no clear demarcation between the latter and sub-species, or varieties of the highest grade (distinguished from species not by any known inconstancy, but by the supposed lower importance of their characteristics); nor between these and recognized species. "These differences blend into each other in an insensible series, and the series impresses the mind with an idea of an actual passage."

This gradation from species downward is well made out. To carry it one step farther upwards, our author presents in a strong light the differences which prevail among naturalists as to what forms should be admitted to the rank of species. Some genera (and these in some countries) give rise to far more discrepancy than others; and it is concluded that the large or dominant genera are usually the most variable. In a flora so small as the British, 182 plants generally reckoned as varieties, have been ranked by some botanists as species. Selecting the British genera which include the most polymorphous forms, it appears that Babington's Flora gives them 251 species, Bentham's only 112, a difference of 139 doubtful forms. These are nearly the extreme views; but they are the views of two most capable and most experienced judges, in respect to one of the best known floras of the world. The fact is suggestive, that the best-known countries furnish the greatest number of such doubtful cases. Illustrations of this kind may be multiplied to a great extent. They make it plain that,

---

9 The rules and processes of breeders of animals, and their results, are so familiar that they need not be particularized. Less is popularly known about the production of vegetable races. We refer our readers back to this Journal, xxvii, pp. 440-442 (May, 1859), for an abstract of the papers of M. Vilmorin upon this subject.

whether species in nature are aboriginal and definite or not, our practical conclusions about them, as embodied in systematic works, are not *facts* but *judgments*, and largely fallible judgments.

How much of the actual coincidence of authorities is owing to imperfect or restricted observation, and to one naturalist's adopting the conclusions of another without independent observation, this is not the place to consider. It is our impression that species of animals are more definitely marked than those of plants; this may arise from our somewhat extended acquaintance with the latter, and our ignorance of the former. But we are constrained by our experience to admit the strong likelihood, in botany, that varieties on the one hand and what are called closely related species on the other, do not differ except in degree. Whenever the wider difference separating the latter can be spanned by intermediate forms, as it sometimes is, no botanist long resists the inevitable conclusion. Whenever, therefore, this wider difference can be shown to be compatible with community of origin, and explained through natural selection or in any other way, we are ready to adopt the *probable* conclusion; and we see beforehand how strikingly the actual geographical association of related species favors the broader view. Whether we should continue to regard the forms in question as distinct species, depends upon what meaning we shall finally attach to that term; and that depends upon how far the doctrine of derivation can be carried back and how well it can be supported.

In applying his principle of natural selection to the work in hand, Mr. Darwin assumes, as we have seen: 1, some variability of animals and plants in nature; 2, the absence of any definite distinction between slight variations, and varieties of the highest grade; 3, the fact that naturalists do not practically agree, and do not increasingly tend to agree, as to what forms are species and what are strong varieties, thus rendering it probable that there may be no essential and original difference, or no possibility of ascertaining it, at least in many cases; also, 4, that the most flourishing and dominant species of the larger genera on an average vary most (a proposition which can be substantiated only by extensive comparisons, the details of which are not given);—and, 5, that in large genera the species are apt to be closely but unequally allied together, forming little clusters round certain species,—just such clusters as would be formed if we suppose their members once to have been satellites or varieties of a central or parent species, but to have attained at length a wider divergence and a specific character. The fact of such association is undeniable; and the use which Mr. Darwin makes of it seems fair and natural.

The gist of Mr. Darwin's work is to show that such varieties are gradually diverged into species and genera through *natural selection*; that natural selection is the inevitable result of the *struggle for existence* which all living things are engaged in; and that this struggle is an unavoidable consequence of several natural causes, but mainly of the high rate at which all organic beings tend to increase.

Curiously enough, Mr. Darwin's theory is grounded upon the doctrine of Malthus and the doctrine of Hobbes. The elder DeCandolle had conceived the idea of the struggle for existence, and, in a passage which would have delighted the cynical philosopher of Malmesbury, had declared that all nature is at war, one organism with another or with external nature; and Lyell and Herbert had made considerable use of it. But Hobbes in his theory of society and Darwin in his theory of natural history, alone have built their systems upon it. However moralists and political economists may regard these doctrines in their original application to human society and the relation of population to subsistence, their thorough applicability to the great society of the organic world in general is now undeniable. And to Mr. Darwin belongs the credit of making this extended application, and of working out the immensely diversified results with rare sagacity and untiring patience. He has brought to view *real causes* which have been largely operative in the establishment of the actual association and geographical distribution of plants and animals. In this he must be allowed to have made a very important contribution to an interesting department of science, even if his theory fails in the endeavor to explain the origin or diversity of species.

> "Nothing is easier," says our author, "than to admit in words the truth of the universal struggle for life, or more difficult—at least I have found it so—than constantly to bear this conclusion in mind. Yet unless it be thoroughly ingrained in the mind, I am convinced that the whole economy of nature, with every fact on distribution, rarity, abundance, extinction, and variation, will be dimly seen or quite misunderstood. We behold the face of nature bright with gladness, we often see superabundance of food; we do not see, or we forget, that the birds which are idly singing round us mostly live on insects or seeds, and are thus constantly destroying life; or we forget how largely these songsters, or their eggs, or their nestlings, are destroyed by birds and beasts of prey; we do not always bear in mind, that though food may be now superabundant, it is not so at all seasons of each recurring year."—p. 62.
>
> "There is no exception to the rule that every organic being naturally increases at so high a rate, that if not destroyed, the earth would soon be covered by the progeny of a single pair. Even slow-breeding man has doubled in twenty-five years, and at this rate, in a few thousand years, there would literally not be standing-room for his progeny. Linnæus has calculated that

if an annual plant produced only two seeds—and there is no plant so unproductive as this—and their seedlings next year produced two, and so on, then in twenty years there would be a million plants. The elephant is reckoned to be the slowest breeder of all known animals, and I have taken some pains to estimate its probable minimum rate of natural increase: it will be under the mark to assume that it breeds when thirty years old, and goes on breeding till ninety years old, bringing forth three pairs of young in this interval; if this be so, at the end of the fifth century there would be alive fifteen million elephants, descended from the first pair.

"But we have better evidence on this subject than mere theoretical calculations, namely, the numerous recorded cases of the astonishingly rapid increase of various animals in a state of nature, when circumstances have been favorable to them during two or three following seasons. Still more striking is the evidence from our domestic animals of many kinds which have run wild in several parts of the world; if the statements of the rate of increase of slow-breeding cattle and horses in South America, and latterly in Australia, had not been well authenticated, they would have been quite incredible. So it is with plants: cases could be given of introduced plants which have become common throughout whole islands in a period of less than ten years. Several of the plants now most numerous over the wide plains of La Plata, clothing square leagues of surface almost to the exclusion of all other plants, have been introduced from Europe; and there are plants which now range in India, as I hear from Dr. Falconer, from Cape Comorin to the Himalaya, which have been imported from America since its discovery. In such cases, and endless instances could be given, no one supposes that the fertility of these animals or plants has been suddenly and temporarily increased in any sensible degree. The obvious explanation is that the conditions of life have been very favorable, and that there has consequently been less destruction of the old and young, and that nearly all the young have been enabled to breed. In such cases the geometrical ratio of increase, the result of which never fails to be surprising, simply explains the extraordinarily rapid increase and wide diffusion of naturalized productions in their new homes."—pp. 64, 65.

"All plants and animals are tending to increase at a geometrical ratio; all would most rapidly stock any station in which they could anyhow exist; the increase must be checked by destruction at some period of life."—p. 65.

The difference between the most and the least prolific species is of no account.

> "The condor lays a couple of eggs, and the ostrich a score; and yet in the same country the condor may be the more numerous of the two. The Fulmar petrel lays but one egg, yet it is believed to be the most numerous bird in the world."—p. 68.

> "The amount of food gives the extreme limit to which each species can increase; but very frequently it is not the obtaining of food, but the serving as prey to other animals, which determines the average numbers of a species."—p. 68.

> "Climate plays an important part in determining the average numbers of a species, and periodical seasons of extreme cold or drought, I believe to be the most effective of all checks. I estimated that the winter of 1854–55 destroyed four-fifths of the birds in my own grounds; and this is a tremendous destruction, when we remember that ten per cent is an extraordinarily severe mortality from epidemics with man. The action of climate seems at first sight to be quite independent of the struggle for existence; but, in so far as climate chiefly acts in reducing food, it brings on the most severe struggle between the individuals, whether of the same or of distinct species, which subsist on the same kind of food. Even when climate, for instance extreme cold, acts directly, it will be the least vigorous, or those which have got least food through the advancing winter, which will suffer most. When we travel from south to north, or from a damp region to a dry, we invariably see some species gradually getting rarer and rarer, and finally disappearing; and, the change of climate being conspicuous, we are tempted to attribute the whole effect to its direct action. But this is a very false view: we forget that each species, even where it most abounds, is constantly suffering enormous destruction at some period of its life, from enemies or from competitors for the same place and food; and if these enemies or competitors be in the least degree favored by any slight change of climate, they will increase in numbers, and, as each area is already stocked with inhabitants, the other species will decrease. When we travel southward and see a species decreasing in numbers, we may feel sure that the cause lies quite as much in other species being favored, as in this one being hurt. So it is when we travel northward, but in a somewhat lesser degree, for the number of species of

all kinds, and therefore of competitors, decreases northwards; hence in going northward, or in ascending a mountain, we far oftener meet with stunted forms, due to the *directly* injurious action of climate, than we do in proceeding southwards or in descending a mountain. When we reach the Arctic regions, or snow-capped summits, or absolute deserts, the struggle for life is almost exclusively with the elements.

"That climate acts in main part indirectly by favoring other species, we may clearly see in the prodigious number of plants in our gardens which can perfectly well endure our climate, but which never become naturalized, for they cannot compete with our native plants, nor resist destruction by our native animals."—pp. 68, 69.

After an instructive instance in which "cattle absolutely determine the existence of the Scotch Fir," we are referred to cases in which insects determine the existence of cattle.

"Perhaps Paraguay offers the most curious instance of this; for here neither cattle nor horses nor dogs have ever run wild, though they swarm southward and northward in a feral state; and Azara and Rengger have shown that this is caused by the greater number in Paraguay of a certain fly, which lays its eggs in the navels of these animals when first born. The increase of these flies, numerous as they are, must be habitually checked by some means, probably by birds. Hence, if certain insectivorous birds (whose numbers are probably regulated by hawks or beasts of prey) were to increase in Paraguay, the flies would decrease—then cattle and horses would become feral, and this would certainly greatly alter (as indeed I have observed in parts of South America) the vegetation: this again would largely affect the insects; and this, as we have just seen in Staffordshire, the insectivorous birds, and so onwards in ever-increasing circles of complexity. We began this series by insectivorous birds, and we had ended with them. Not that in nature the relations can ever be as simple as this. Battle within battle must ever be recurring with varying success; and yet in the long run the forces are so nicely balanced, that the face of nature remains uniform for long periods of time, though assuredly the merest trifle would often give the victory to one organic being over another. Nevertheless so profound is our ignorance, and so high our presumption, that we marvel when we hear of the extinction of an organic being; and as we do not see the cause, we invoke cataclysms to desolate the world, or invent laws on the duration of the forms of life!"—pp. 72. 73.

"When we look at the plants and bushes clothing an entangled bank, we are tempted to attribute their proportional numbers and kinds to what we call chance. But how false a view is this! Every one has heard that when an American forest is cut down, a very different vegetation springs up; but it has been observed that the trees now growing on the ancient Indian mounds, in the Southern United States, display the same beautiful diversity and proportion of kinds as in the surrounding virgin forests. What a struggle between the several kinds of trees must here have gone on during long centuries, each annually scattering its seeds by the thousand; what war between insect and insect—between insects, snails, and other animals with birds and beasts of prey—all striving to increase, and all feeding on each other or on the trees or their seeds and seedlings, or on the other plants which first clothed the ground and thus checked the growth of the trees! Throw up a handful of feathers, and all must fall to the ground according to definite laws; but how simple is this problem compared to the action and reaction of the innumerable plants and animals which have determined, in the course of centuries, the proportional numbers and kinds of trees now growing on the old Indian ruins!"—pp. 74, 75.

For reasons obvious upon reflection the competition is often, if not generally, most severe between nearly related species when they are in contact, so that one drives the other before it, as the Hanoverian the old English rat, the small Asiatic cockroach in Russia, its greater congener, &c. and this, when duly considered, explains many curious results;—such, for instance, as the considerable number of different genera of plants and animals which are generally found to inhabit any limited area.

"The truth of the principle, that the greatest amount of life can be supported by great diversification of structure, is seen under many natural circumstances. In an extremely small area, especially if freely open to immigration, and where the contest between individual and individual must be severe, we always find great diversity in its inhabitants. For instance, I found that a piece of turf, three feet by four in size, which had been exposed for many years to exactly the same conditions, supported twenty species of plants, and these belonged to eighteen genera and to eight orders, which showed how much these plants differed from each other. So it is with the plants and insects on small and uniform islets; and so in small ponds of fresh water. Farmers find that they can raise most food by a rotation of plants belonging to the most different orders; nature follows what may be called a simultaneous rotation. Most of the animals and plants which live close round any small piece of ground, could live on it (supposing it not to be in any way peculiar in its nature), and may be said to be striving to the utmost to live there; but, it is seen, that where they come into the closest competition with each other, the advantages of diversification of structure, with the accompanying differences of habit and constitution, determine that the inhabitants, which thus jostle each other most closely, shall as a general rule, belong to what we call different genera and orders."—p. 114.

The abundance of some forms, the rarity and final extinction of many others, and the consequent divergence of character or increase of difference among the surviving representatives are other consequences. As favored forms increase, the less favored must diminish in number, for there is not room for all; and the slightest advantage, at first probably inappreciable to human observation, must decide which shall prevail and which must perish, or be driven to another and for it more favorable locality.

We cannot do justice to the interesting chapter upon natural selection by separated extracts. The following must serve to show how the principle is supposed to work.

> "If during the long course of ages and under varying conditions of life, organic beings vary at all in the several parts of their organization, and I think this cannot be disputed; if there be, owing to the high geometrical powers of increase of each species, at some age, season, or year, a severe struggle for life, and this certainly cannot be disputed; then, considering the infinite complexity of the relations of all organic beings to each other and to their conditions of existence, causing an infinite diversity in structure, constitution, and habits, to be advantageous to them, I think it would be a most extraordinary fact if no variation ever had occurred useful to each being's own welfare, in the same way as so many variations have occurred useful to man. But if variations useful to any organic being do occur, assuredly individuals thus characterized will have the best chance of being preserved in the struggle for life; and from the strong principle of inheritance they will tend to produce offspring similarly characterized. This principle

of preservation I have called, for the sake of brevity, Natural Selection." pp. 126, 127.

"In order to make it clear how, as I believe, natural selection acts, I must beg permission to give one or two imaginary illustrations. Let us take the case of a wolf, which preys on various animals, securing some by craft, some by strength, and some by fleetness; and let us suppose that the fleetest prey, a deer for instance, had from any change in the country increased in numbers, or that other prey had decreased in numbers, during that season of the year when the wolf is hardest pressed for food. I can under such circumstances see no reason to doubt that the swiftest and slimmest wolves would have the best chance of surviving, and so be preserved or selected,—provided always that they retained strength to master their prey at this or at some other period of the year, when they might be compelled to prey on other animals. I can see no more reason to doubt this, than that man can improve the fleetness of his greyhounds by careful and methodical selection, or by that unconscious selection which results from each man trying to keep the best dogs without any thought of modifying the breed.

"Even without any change in the proportional numbers of the animals on which our wolf preyed, a cub might be born with an innate tendency to pursue certain kinds of prey. Nor can this be thought very improbable; for we often observe great differences in the natural tendencies of our domestic animals; one cat, for instance, taking to catch rats, another mice; one cat, according to Mr. St. John, bringing home winged game, another hares or rabbits, and another hunting on marshy ground and almost nightly catching woodcocks or snipes. The tendency to catch rats rather than mice is known to be inherited. Now, if any slight innate change of habit or of structure benefited an individual wolf, it would have the best chance of surviving and of leaving offspring. Some of its young would probably inherit the same habits or structure, and by the repetition of this process, a new variety might be formed which would either supplant or coexist with the parent-form of wolf. Or, again, the wolves inhabiting a mountainous district, and those frequenting the lowlands, would naturally be forced to hunt different prey; and from the continued preservation of the individuals best fitted for the two sites, two varieties might slowly be formed. These varieties would cross and blend where they met; but to this subject of intercrossing we shall soon have to return. I may add, that, according to Mr. Pierce, there are two varieties of the wolf inhabiting the Catskill Mountains in the United States, one with a light greyhound-like form, which pursues deer, and the other more bulky, with shorter legs, which more frequently attacks the shepherd's flocks."—pp. 90, 91.

We eke out the illustration here with a counterpart instance, viz., the remark of Dr. Bachman that "The deer that reside permanently in the swamps of Carolina are taller and longer-legged than those in the higher grounds."[10]

The limits allotted to this article are nearly reached, yet only four of the fourteen chapters of the volume have been touched. These, however, contain the fundamental principles of the theory and most of those applications of it which are capable of something like verification, relating as they do to the phenomena now occurring. Some of our extracts also show how these principles are thought to have operated through the long lapse of the ages. The chapters from the sixth to the ninth inclusive are designed to obviate difficulties and objections, "some of them so grave that to this day," the author frankly says, he "can never reflect on them without being staggered." We do not wonder at it. After drawing what comfort he can from "the imperfection of the geological record" (chap. 9), which we suspect is scarcely exaggerated, the author considers the geological succession of organic beings (chap. 10), to see whether they better accord with the common view of the immutability of species, or with that of their slow and gradual modification. Geologists must settle that question. Then follow two most interesting and able chapters on the geographical distribution of plants and animals, the summary of which we should be glad to cite; then a fitting chapter upon classification, morphology, embryology, &c., as viewed in the light of this theory, closes the argument; the fourteenth chapter being a recapitulation.

The interest for the general reader heightens as the author advances on his perilous way and grapples manfully with the most formidable difficulties.

To account, upon these principles, for the gradual elimination and segregation of nearly allied forms,—such as varieties, sub-species, and closely-related or representative species,—also in a general way for their geographical association and present range, is comparatively easy, is apparently within the bounds of possibility, and even of probability. Could we stop here we should be fairly contented. But, to complete the system, to carry out the principles to their ultimate conclusion, and to explain by them many facts in geographical distribution which would still remain anomalous, Mr. Darwin is equally bound to account for the formation of genera, families, orders, and even classes, by natural selection. He

---

10   Quadrupeds of America, ii, p. 239.

does "not doubt that the theory of descent with modification embraces all the members of the same class," and he concedes that analogy would press the conclusion still farther; while he admits that "the more distinct the forms are, the more the arguments fall away in force." To command assent we naturally require decreasing probability to be overbalanced by an increased weight of evidence. An opponent might plausibly, and perhaps quite fairly, urge that the links in the chain of argument are weakest just where the greatest stress falls upon them.

To which Mr. Darwin's answer is, that the best parts of the testimony have been lost. He is confident that intermediate forms must have existed; that in the olden times when the genera, the families and the orders diverged from their parent stocks, gradations existed as fine as those which now connect closely related species with varieties. But they have passed and left no sign. The geological record, even if all displayed to view, is a book from which not only many pages, but even whole alternate chapters have been lost out, or rather which were never printed from the autographs of nature. The record was actually made in fossil lithography only at certain times and under certain conditions (i.e., at periods of slow subsidence and places of abundant sediment); and of these records all but the last volume is out of print; and of its pages only local glimpses have been obtained. Geologists, except Lyell, will object to this,—some of them moderately, others with vehemence. Mr. Darwin himself admits, with a candor rarely displayed on such occasions, that he should have expected more geological evidence of transition than he finds, and that all the most eminent palæontologists maintain the immutability of species.

The general fact, however, that the fossil fauna of each period as a whole is nearly intermediate in character between the preceding and the succeeding faunas, is much relied on. We are brought one step nearer to the desired inference by the similar "fact, insisted on by all palæontologists, that fossils from two consecutive formations are far more closely related to each other, than are the fossils of two remote formations. Pictet gives a well-known instance,—the general resemblance of the organic remains from the several stages of the chalk formation, though the species are distinct at each stage. This fact alone, from its generality seems to have shaken Prof. Pictet in his firm belief in the immutability of species." (p. 335). What Mr. Darwin now particularly wants to complete his inferential evidence is a proof that the same gradation may be traced in later periods, say in the tertiary, and between that period and the present; also that the later gradations are finer, so as to leave it doubtful whether the succession is one of species,—believed on the one theory to be independent, on the other, derivative,—or of varieties, which are confessedly derivative. The proof of the finer gradation appears to be forthcoming. Des Hayes and Lyell have concluded that many of the middle tertiary and a large proportion of the later tertiary mollusca are specifically identical with living species; and this is still the almost universally prevalent view. But Mr. Agassiz states that, "in every instance where he had sufficient materials, he had found that the species of the two epochs supposed to be identical by Des Hayes and Lyell were in reality distinct, although closely allied species."[11] Moreover he is now satisfied, as we understand, that the same gradation is traceable not merely in each great division of the tertiary, but in particular deposits or successive beds, each answering to a great number of years; where what have passed unquestioned as members of one species, upon closer examination of numerous specimens exhibit differences which in his opinion entitle them to be distinguished into two, three, or more species. It is plain, therefore, that whatever conclusions can be fairly drawn from the present animal and vegetable kingdoms in favor of a gradation of varieties into species, or into what may be regarded as such, the same may be extended to the tertiary period. In both cases, what some call species others call varieties; and in the later tertiary shells this difference in judgment affects almost half of the species!

We pass to a second difficulty in the way of Mr. Darwin's theory; to a case where we are perhaps entitled to demand of him evidence of gradation like that which connects the present with the tertiary mollusca. Wide, very wide is the gap, anatomically and physiologically (we do not speak of the intellectual) between the highest quadrumana and man; and comparatively recent, if ever, must the line have bifurcated. But where is there the slightest evidence of a common progenitor? Perhaps Mr. Darwin would reply by another question: where are the fossil remains of the men who made the flint knives and arrow-heads of the Somme Valley?

We have a third objection, one, fortunately, which has nothing to do with geology. We can only state it here, in brief terms. The chapter on hybridism is most ingenious, able, and instructive. If sterility of crosses is a special, original arrangement to prevent the confusion of species by mingling, as is generally assumed, then, since varieties cross readily and their offspring is fertile *inter se*, there is a fundamental distinction between varieties and species. Mr. Darwin therefore labors to show that it is not a special endowment, but an incidental acquirement. He does show that the sterility of crosses is of all degrees;—upon which we have only to say, *Natura non facit saltum*, here any more than elsewhere. But, upon his theory he is bound to show how sterility might be acquired, through natural selection or through something else. And the difficulty is, that, whereas individuals of the very same blood tend to be sterile, and somewhat remoter unions diminish this tendency, and when they have diverged into two varieties the cross-breeds between the two are more fertile than either pure stock,—yet when they have diverged only one

---

11   Proceedings of the American Academy of Arts and Sciences, iv, p. 178.

degree more the whole tendency is reversed, and the mongrel is sterile, either absolutely or relatively. He who explains the genesis of species through purely natural agencies should assign a natural cause for this remarkable result; and this Mr. Darwin has not done. Whether original or derived, however, this arrangement to keep apart those forms which have, or have acquired (as the case may be) a certain moderate amount of difference, looks to us as much designed for the purpose, as does a rachet to prevent reverse motion in a wheel. If species have originated by divergence, this keeps them apart.

Here let us suggest a possibly attainable test of the theory of derivation, a kind of instance which Mr. Darwin may be fairly asked to produce,—viz., an instance of two varieties, or what may be assumed as such, which have diverged enough to reverse the movement, to bring out some sterility in the crosses. The best marked human races might offer the most likely case. If mulattoes are sterile or tend to sterility, as some naturalists confidently assert, they afford Mr. Darwin a case in point. If, as others think, no such tendency is made out, the required evidence is wanting.

A fourth and the most formidable difficulty is that of the production and specialization of organs.

It is well said that all organic beings have been formed on two great laws; Unity of type, and Adaptation to the conditions of existence.[12] The special teleologists, such as Paley, occupy themselves with the latter only; they refer particular facts to special design, but leave an overwhelming array of the widest facts inexplicable. The morphologists build on unity of type, or that fundamental agreement in the structure of each great class of beings, which is quite independent of their habits or conditions of life; which requires each individual "to go through a certain formality," and to accept, at least for a time, certain organs, whether they are of any use to him or not. Philosophical minds form various conceptions for harmonizing the two views theoretically. Mr. Darwin harmonizes and explains them naturally. Adaptation to the conditions of existence is the result of Natural Selection; Unity of type, of unity of descent. Accordingly, as he puts his theory, he is bound to account for the origination of new organs, and for their diversity in each great type, for their specialization, and every adaptation of organ to function and of structure to condition, through natural agencies. Whenever he attempts this he reminds us of Lamarck, and shows us how little light the science of a century devoted to structural investigation has thrown upon the mystery of organization. Here purely natural explanations fail. The organs being given, natural selection may account for some improvement; if given of a variety of

---

12   Owen adds a third, viz:—Vegetative Repetition; but this, in the vegetable kingdom is simply Unity of Type.

sorts or grades, natural selection might determine which should survive and where it should prevail.

On all this ground the only line for the theory to take is to make the most of gradation and adherence to type as suggestive of derivation, and unaccountable upon any other scientific view,—deferring all attempts to explain *how* such a metamorphosis was effected, until naturalists have explained *how* the tadpole is metamorphosed into a frog, or one sort of polyp into another. As to *why* it is so, the philosophy of efficient cause, and even the whole argument from design, would stand, upon the admission of such a theory of derivation, precisely where they stand without it. At least there is, or need be, no ground of difference here between Darwin and Agassiz. The latter will admit, with Owen and every morphologist, that hopeless is the attempt to explain the similarity of pattern in members of the same class by utility or the doctrine of final causes. "On the ordinary view of the independent creation of each being, we can only say that so it is, that it has so pleased the Creator to construct each animal and plant." Mr. Darwin, in proposing a theory which suggests a *how* that harmonizes these facts into a system, we trust implies that all was done wisely, in the largest sense designedly, and by an Intelligent First Cause. The contemplation of the subject on the intellectual side, the amplest exposition of the Unity of Plan in Creation, considered irrespective of natural agencies, leads to no other conclusion.

We are thus, at last, brought to the question; what would happen if the derivation of species were to be substantiated, either as a true physical theory, or as a sufficient hypothesis? What would come of it? The enquiry is a pertinent one, just now. For, of those who agree with us in thinking that Darwin has not established his theory of derivation, many will admit with us that he has rendered a theory of derivation much less improbable than before; that such a theory chimes in with the established doctrines of physical science, and is not unlikely to be largely accepted long before it can be proved. Moreover, the various notions that prevail,—equally among the most and the least religious,—as to the relations between natural agencies or phenomena and Efficient Cause, are seemingly more crude, obscure, and discordant than they need be.

It is not surprising that the doctrine of the book should be denounced as atheistical. What does surprise and concern us is, that it should be so denounced by a scientific man, on the broad assumption that a material connection between the members of a series of organized beings is inconsistent with the idea of their being intellectually connected with one another through the Deity, i.e., as products of one mind, as indicating and realizing a preconceived plan. An assumption the rebound of which is somewhat fearful to contemplate, but fortunately one which every natural birth protests against.

It would be more correct to say, that the theory in itself is perfectly compatible with an atheistic view of the universe. That is true; but it is equally true of physical theories generally. Indeed, it is more true of the theory of gravitation, and of the nebular hypothesis, than of the hypothesis in question. The latter merely takes up a *particular, proximate cause,* or set of such causes, from which, it is argued, the present diversity of species has or may have *contingently* resulted. The author does not say *necessarily* resulted; that the actual results in mode and measure, and none other must have taken place. On the other hand the theory of gravitation, and its extension in the nebular hypothesis, assume a *universal and ultimate* physical cause, from which the effects in nature must *necessarily* have resulted. Now it is not thought, at least at the present day, that the establishment of the Newtonian theory was a step towards atheism or pantheism. Yet the great achievement of Newton consisted in proving that certain forces, (blind forces, so far as the theory is concerned,) acting upon matter in certain directions, must *necessarily* produce planetary orbits of the exact measure and form in which observation shows them to exist;—a view which is just as consistent with eternal necessity, either in the atheistic or the pantheistic form, as it is with theism.

Nor is the theory of derivation particularly exposed to the charge of the atheism of fortuity; since it undertakes to assign real causes for harmonious and systematic results. But of this, a word at the close.

The value of such objections to the theory of derivation may be tested by one or two analogous cases. The common scientific as well as popular belief is that of the original, independent creation of oxygen and hydrogen, iron, gold, and the like. Is the speculative opinion, now increasingly held, that some or all of the supposed elementary bodies are derivative or compound, developed from some preceding forms of matter, irreligious? Were the old alchemists atheists as well as dreamers in their attempts to transmute earth into gold? Or, to take an instance from force (power),—which stands one step nearer to efficient cause than form—was the attempt to prove that heat, light, electricity, magnetism, and even mechanical power are variations or transmutations of one force, atheistical in its tendency? The supposed establishment of this view is reckoned as one of the greatest scientific triumphs of this century.

Perhaps, however, the objection is brought, not so much against the speculation itself, as against the attempt to show how derivation might have been brought about. Then the same objection applies to a recent ingenious hypothesis made to account for the genesis of the chemical elements out of the etherial medium, and to explain their several atomic weights and some other characteristics by their successive complexity,— hydrogen consisting of so many atoms of etherial substance united in a particular order, and so on. The speculation interested the philosophers of the British Association, and was thought innocent, but unsupported by facts. Surely Mr. Darwin's theory is none the worse, morally, for having some foundation in fact.

In our opinion, then, it is far easier to vindicate a theistic character for the derivative theory, than to establish the theory itself upon adequate scientific evidence. Perhaps scarcely any philosophical objection can be urged against the former to which the nebular hypothesis is not equally exposed. Yet the nebular hypothesis finds general scientific acceptance, and is adopted as the basis of an extended and recondite illustration in Mr. Agassiz's great work.[13]

How the author of this book harmonizes his scientific theory with his philosophy and theology, he has not informed us. Paley, in his celebrated analogy with the watch, insists that if the time-piece were so constructed as to produce other similar watches, after a manner of generation in animals, the argument from design would be all the stronger. What is to hinder Mr. Darwin from giving Paley's argument a further *a-fortiori* extension to the supposed case of a watch which sometimes produces better watches, and contrivances adapted to successive conditions, and so at length turns out a chronometer, a town-clock, or a series of organisms of the same type? From certain incidental expressions at the close of the volume, taken in connection with the motto adopted from Whewell, we judge it probable that our author regards the whole system of nature as one which had received at its first formation the impress of the will of its Author, foreseeing the varied yet necessary laws of its action throughout the whole of its existence, ordaining when and how each particular of the stupendous plan should be realized in effect, and—with Him to whom to will is to do—in ordaining doing it. Whether profoundly philosophical or not, a view maintained by eminent philosophical physicists and theologians, such as Babbage on the one hand and Jowett on the other, will hardly be denounced as atheism. Perhaps Mr. Darwin would prefer to express his idea in a more general way, by adopting the thoughtful words of one of the most eminent naturalists of this or any age, substituting the word *action* for 'thought,' since it is the former (from which alone the latter can be inferred) that he has been considering. "Taking nature as exhibiting thought for my guide, it appears to me that while human thought is consecutive, Divine thought is simultaneous, embracing at the same time and forever, in the past, the present and the future, the most diversified relations among hundreds of thousands of organized beings, each of which may present complications again, which, to study and understand even imperfectly,—as for instance man himself—mankind has already spent thousands of years."[14] In thus conceiving of the Divine Power in act as cöetaneous with Divine Thought, and of both as far as

---

13   Contrib. Nat. Hist. Amer., i, p. 127-131.
14   Op. cit., p. 130.

may be apart from the human element of time, our author may regard the intervention of the Creator either as, humanly speaking, *done from all time*, or else as *doing through all time*. In the ultimate analysis we suppose that every philosophical theist must adopt one or the other conception.

A perversion of the first view leads towards atheism, the notion of an eternal sequence of cause and effect, for which there is no first cause,—a view which few sane persons can long rest in. The danger which may threaten the second view is pantheism. We feel safe from either error, in our profound conviction that there is order in the universe; that order presupposes mind; design, will; and mind or will, personality. Thus guarded, we much prefer the second of the two conceptions of causation, as the more philosophical as well as Christian view,—a view which leaves us with the same difficulties and the same mysteries in nature as in Providence, and no other. Natural law, upon this view, is the human conception of continued and orderly Divine action.

We do not suppose that less power, or other power, is required to sustain the universe and carry on its operations, than to bring it into being. So, while conceiving no improbability of "interventions of Creative mind in nature," if by such is meant the bringing to pass of new and fitting events at fitting times, we leave it for profounder minds to establish, if they can, a rational distinction in kind between His working in nature carrying on operations, and in initiating those operations.

We wished under the light of such views, to examine more critically the doctrine of this book, especially of some questionable parts;—for instance, its explanation of the natural development of organs, and its implication of a "necessary acquirement of mental power" in the ascending scale of gradation. But there is room only for the general declaration that we cannot think the Cosmos a series which began with chaos and ends with mind, or of which mind is a result: that if by the successive origination of species and organs through natural agencies, the author means a series of events which succeed each other irrespective of a continued directing intelligence,—events which mind does not order and shape to destined ends,—then he has not established that doctrine, nor advanced towards its establishment, but has accumulated improbabilities beyond all belief. Take the formation and the origination of the successive degrees of complexity of eyes as a specimen. The treatment of this subject (pp. 188, 189), upon one interpretation is open to all the objections referred to; but if, on the other hand, we may rightly compare the eye "to a telescope, perfected by the long continued efforts of the highest human intellects," we could carry out the analogy, and draw satisfactory illustrations and inferences from it. The essential, the directly intellectual thing is the making of the improvements in the telescope or the steam-engine. Whether the successive improvements, being small at each step, and consistent with the general type of the instrument, are applied to some of the individual machines, or entire new machines are constructed for each, is a minor matter. Though if machines could engender, the adaptive method would be most economical; and economy is said to be a paramount law in nature. The origination of the improvements, and the successive adaptations to meet new conditions or subserve other ends, are what answer to the supernatural, and therefore remain inexplicable. As to bringing them into use, though wisdom foresees the result, the circumstances and the natural competition will take care of that, in the long run. The old ones will go out of use fast enough, except where an old and simple machine remains still best adapted to a particular purpose or condition,—as, for instance, the old Newcomen engine for pumping out coal-pits. If there's a Divinity that shapes these ends, the whole is intelligible and reasonable; otherwise, not.

We regret that the necessity of discussing philosophical questions has prevented a fuller examination of the theory itself, and of the interesting scientific points which are brought to bear in its favor. One of its neatest points, certainly a very strong one for the local origination of species, and their gradual diffusion under natural agencies, we must reserve for some other convenient opportunity.

The work is a scientific one, rigidly restricted to its direct object; and by its science it must stand or fall. Its aim is, probably not to deny creative intervention in nature,—for the admission of the independent origination of certain types does away with all antecedent improbability of as much intervention as may be required,—but to maintain that Natural Selection, in explaining the facts, explains also many classes of facts which thousand-fold repeated independent acts of creation do not explain, but leave more mysterious than ever. How far the author has succeeded, the scientific world will in due time be able to pronounce.

As these sheets are passing through the press a copy of the second edition has reached us. We notice with pleasure the insertion of an additional motto on the reverse of the title-page, directly claiming the theistic view which we have vindicated for the doctrine. Indeed these pertinent words of the eminently wise Bishop Butler, comprise, in their simplest expression, the whole substance of our latter pages:—

> "The only distinct meaning of the word 'natural' is *stated, fixed,* or *settled*; since what is natural as much requires and presupposes an intelligent mind to render it so, i.e., to effect it continually or at stated times, as what is supernatural or miraculous does to effect it for once."

6. Fleeming Jenkin

(1833–1885)

Jenkin, F. 1867. The origin of species. *The North British Review* 46:277-318. Our extract is from the section on "Variability", pp. 279-286.

Variability.—Darwin's theory requires that there shall be no limit to the possible difference between descendants and their progenitors, or, at least, that if there be limits, they shall be at so great a distance as to comprehend the utmost differences between any known forms of life. The variability required, if not infinite, is indefinite. Experience with domestic animals and cultivated plants shows that great variability exists. Darwin calls special attention to the differences between the various fancy pigeons, which, he says, are descended from one stock; between various breeds of cattle and horses, and some other domestic animals. He states that these differences are greater than those which induce some naturalists to class many specimens as distinct species. These differences are infinitely small as compared with the range required by his theory, but he assumes that by accumulation of successive differences any degree of variation may be produced; he says little in proof of the possibility of such an accumulation, seeming rather to take for granted that if Sir John Sebright could with pigeons produce in six years a certain head and beak of say half the bulk possessed by the original stock, then in twelve years this bulk could be reduced to a quarter, in twenty-four to an eighth, and so farther. Darwin probably never believed or intended to teach so extravagant a proposition, yet by substituting a few myriads of years for that poor period of six years, we obtain a proposition fundamental in his theory. That theory rests on the assumption that natural selection can do slowly what man's selection does quickly; it is by showing how much man can do, that Darwin hopes to prove how much can be done without him. But if man's selection cannot double, treble, quadruple, centuple, any special divergence from a parent stock, why should we imagine that natural selection should have that power? When we have granted that the 'struggle for life' might produce the pouter or the fantail, or any divergence man can produce, we need not feel one whit the more disposed to grant that it can produce divergences beyond man's power. The difference between six years and six myriads, blinding by a confused sense of immensity, leads men to say hastily that if six or sixty years can make a pouter out of a common pigeon, six myriads may change a pigeon to something like a thrush; but this seems no more accurate than to conclude that because we observe that a cannon-ball has traversed a mile in a minute, therefore in an hour it will be sixty miles off, and in the course of ages that it will reach the fixed stars. This really might be the conclusion drawn by a savage seeing a cannon-ball shot off by a power the nature of which was wholly unknown to him, and traversing a vast distance with a velocity confusing his brain, and removing the case from the category of stones and arrows, which he well knows will not go far, though they start fast. Even so do the myriads of years confuse our speculations, and seem to remove natural selection from man's selection; yet, Darwin would be the first to allow, that the same laws probably or possibly govern the variation, whether the selection be slow or rapid. If the intelligent savage were told, that though the cannon-ball started very fast, it went slower and slower every instant, he would probably conclude that it would not reach the stars, but presently come to rest like his stone and arrow. Let us examine whether there be not a true analogy between this case and the variation of domestic animals.

We all believe that a breeder, starting business with a considerable stock of average horses, could, by selection, in a very few generations, obtain horses able to run much faster than any of their sires or dams; in time perhaps he would obtain descendants running twice as fast as their ancestors, and possibly equal to our race-horses. But would not the difference in speed between each successive generation be less and less? Hundreds of skilful men are yearly breeding thousands of racers. Wealth and honour await the man who can breed one horse to run one part in five thousand faster than his fellows. As a matter of experience, have our racers improved in speed by one part in a thousand during the last twenty generations? Could we not double the speed of a cart-horse in twenty generations? Here is the analogy with our cannon-ball; the rate of variation in a given direction is not constant, is not erratic; it is a constantly diminishing rate, tending therefore to a limit.

It may be urged that the limit in the above case is not fixed by the laws of variation but by the laws of matter; that bone and sinew cannot make a beast of the racer size and build go faster. This would be an objection rather to the form than to the essence of the argument. The existence of a limit, as proved by the gradual cessation of improvement, is the point which we aim at establishing. Possibly in every case the limit depends on some physical difficulty, sometimes apparent, more often concealed; moreover, no one can *a priori* calculate what bone and sinew may be capable of doing, or how far they can be improved; but it is unnecessary further to combat this objection, for whatever be the peculiarity aimed at by fancy-breeders, the same fact recurs. Small terriers are valuable, and the limit below which a terrier of good shape would be worth its weight in silver, perhaps in gold, is nearly as well fixed as the possible speed of a race-horse. The points of all prize cattle, of all prize flowers, indicate limits. A rose called 'Senateur Vaisse' weighs 300 grains, a wild rose weighs 30 grains. A gardener, with a good stock of wild roses, would soon raise seedlings with flowers of double, treble, the weight of his first briar flowers. He or his grandson would very slowly approach the 'Cloth of Gold' or Senateur Vaisse,' [sic] and if the gradual rate of increase in weight were systematically noted, it would point with mathematical accuracy to the weight which could not be surpassed.

We are thus led to believe that whatever new point in the variable beast, bird, or flower, be chosen as desirable by a fancier, this point can be rapidly approached at first, but that the rate of approach quickly diminishes, tending to a limit never to be attained. Darwin says that our oldest cultivated plants still yield new varieties. Granted; but the new variations are not successive variations in one direction. Horses could be produced with very long or with very short ears, very long or short hair, with large or small hooves, with peculiar colour, eyes, teeth, perhaps. In short, whatever variation we perceive of ordinary occurrence might by selection be carried to an extravagant excess. If a large annual prize were offered for any of these novel peculiarities, probably the variation in the first few years would be remarkable, but in twenty years' time the judges would be much puzzled to which breeder the prize should fall, and the maximum excellence would be known and expressed in figures, so that an eighth of an inch more or less would determine success or failure.

A given animal or plant appears to be contained, as it were, within a sphere of variation; one individual lies near one portion of the surface, another individual, of the same species, near another part of the surface; the average animal at the centre. Any individual may produce descendants varying in any direction, but is more likely to produce descendants varying towards the centre of the sphere, and the variations in that direction will be greater in amount than the variations towards the surface. Thus, a set of racers of equal merit indiscriminately breeding will produce more colts and foals of inferior than of superior speed, and the falling off of the degenerate will be greater than the improvement of the select. A set of Clydesdale prize horses would produce more colts and foals of inferior than superior strength. More seedlings of 'Senateur Vaisse' will be inferior to him in size and colour than superior. The tendency to revert, admitted by Darwin, is generalized in the simile of the sphere here suggested. On the other hand, Darwin insists very sufficiently on the rapidity with which new peculiarities are produced; and this rapidity is quite as essential to the argument now urged as subsequent slowness.

We hope this argument is now plain. However slow the rate of variation might be, even though it were only one part in a thousand per twenty or two thousand generations, yet if it were constant or erratic we might believe that, in untold time, it would lead to untold distance; but if in every case we find that deviation from an average individual can be rapidly effected at first, and that the rate of deviation steadily diminishes till it reaches an almost imperceptible amount, then we are as much entitled to assume a limit to the possible deviation as we are to the progress of a cannon-ball from a knowledge of the law of diminution in its speed. This limit to the variation of species seems to be established for all cases of man's selection. What argument does Darwin offer showing that the law of variation will be different when the variation occurs slowly, not rapidly? The law may be different, but is there any experimental ground for believing that it *is* different? Darwin says (p. 153), 'The struggle between natural selection, on the one hand, and the tendency to reversion and variability on the other hand, will in the course of time cease, and that the most abnormally developed organs may be made constant, I can see no reason to doubt.' But what reason have we to believe this? Darwin says the variability will disappear by the continued rejection of the individuals tending to revert to a former condition; but is there any experimental ground for believing that the variability *will* disappear; and, secondly, if the variety can become fixed, that it will in time become ready to vary still more in the original direction, passing that limit which we think has just been shown to exist in the case of man's selection? It is peculiarly difficult to see how natural selection could reject individuals having a tendency to produce offspring reverting to an original stock. The tendency to produce offspring more like their superior parents than their inferior grandfathers can surely be of no advantage to any individual in the struggle for life. On the contrary, most individuals would be benefited by producing imperfect offspring, competing with them at a disadvantage; thus it would appear that natural selection, if it select anything, must select the most perfect individuals, having a tendency to produce the fewest and least perfect competitors; but it may be urged that though the tendency to produce good offspring is injurious to the parents, the improved offspring would live and receive by inheritance the fatal tendency of producing in their turn parricidal descendants. Yet this is contending that in the struggle for life natural selection can gradually endow a race with a quality injurious to every individual which possesses it. It really seems certain that natural selection cannot tend to obliterate the tendency to revert; but the theory advanced appears rather to be that, if owing to some other qualities a race is maintained for a very long time different from the average or original race (near the surface of our sphere), then it will in time spontaneously lose the tendency to relapse, and acquire a tendency to vary outside the sphere. What is to produce this change? Time simply, apparently. The race is to be kept constant, to all appearance, for a very long while, but some subtle change due to time is to take place; so that, of two individuals just alike in every feature, but one born a few thousand years after the other, the first shall tend to produce relapsing offspring, the second shall not. This seems rather like the idea that keeping a bar of iron hot or cold for a very long time would leave it permanently hot or cold at the end of the period when the heating or cooling agent was withdrawn. This strikes us as absurd now, but Bacon believed it possibly true. So many things may happen in a very long time, that time comes to be looked on as an agent capable of doing great and unknown things. Natural selection, as we contend, could hardly select an individual because it bred true. Man does. He chooses for sires those horses which he sees not only run fast themselves, but produce fine foals. He never gets rid of the tendency to revert. Darwin says species of pigeons have bred true for centuries. Does he believe that it would not be easier by selection to diminish the peculiarities of the pouter pigeon than to increase them? and what does this mean, but that the tendency to revert exists? It is possible that by man's selection this tendency may be diminished as any other quality may be somewhat increased or diminished, but, like all other qualities, this seems rapidly to approach a limit which there is no obvious reason to suppose 'time' will alter.

But not only do we require for Darwin's theory that time shall first permanently fix the variety near the outside of the assumed sphere of variation, we require that it shall give the power of varying beyond that sphere. It may be urged that man's rapid selection does away with this power; that if each little improvement were allowed to take root during a few hundred generations, there would be no symptom of a decrease of the rate of variation, no symptom that a limit was approached. If this be so, breeders of race-horses and prize flowers had better change their tactics; instead of selecting the fastest colts and finest flowers to start with, they ought to begin with very ordinary beasts and species. They should select the descendants which might be rather better in the first generation, and then should carefully abstain from all attempts at improvement for twenty, thirty, or one hundred generations. Then they might take a little step forward, and in this way, in time, they or their children's children would obtain breeds far surpassing those produced by their over-hasty competitors, who would be brought to a stand by limits which would never be felt or perceived by the followers of the maxim, *Festina lente*. If we are told that the time during which a breeder or his descendants could afford to wait bears no proportion to the time used by natural selection, we may answer that we do not expect the enormous variability supposed to be given by natural selection, but that we do expect to observe some step in that direction, to find that by carefully approaching our limit by slow degrees, that limit would be removed a little further off. Does any one think this would be the case?

There is indeed one view upon which it would seem natural to believe that the tendency to revert may diminish. If the peculiarities of an animal's structure are simply determined by inheritance, and not by any law of growth, and if the child is more likely to resemble its father than its grandfather, its grandfather than its great-grandfather, etc., then the chances that an animal will revert to the likeness of an ancestor a thousand generations back will be slender. This is perhaps Darwin's view. It depends on the assumption that there is no typical or average animal, no sphere of variation, with centre and limits, and cannot be made use of to prove that assumption. The opposing view is that of a race maintained by a continual force in an abnormal condition, and returning to that condition so soon as the force is removed; returning not suddenly, but by similar steps with those by which it first left the average state, restrained by the tendency to resemble its immediate progenitors. *A priori*, perhaps, one view is as probable as the other; or in other words, as we are ignorant of the reasons why atoms fashion themselves into bears and squirrels, one fancy is as likely to meet with approval as another. Experiments conducted in a limited time, point as already said to a limit, with a tendency to revert. And while admitting that the tendency to revert may be diminished though not extinguished, we are unaware of any reason for supposing that pouters, after a thousand generations of true breeding, have acquired a fresh power of doubling their crops, or that the oldest breed of Arabs are likely to produce 'sports' vastly surpassing their ancestors in speed. Experiments conducted during the longest time at our disposal show no probability of surpassing the limits of the sphere of variation, and why should we concede that a simple extension of time will reverse the rule?

The argument may be thus resumed.

Although many domestic animals and plants are highly variable, there appears to be a limit to their variation in any one direction. This limit is shown by the fact that new points are at first rapidly gained, but afterwards more slowly, while finally no further perceptible change can be effected. Great, therefore, as the variability is, we are not free to assume that successive variations of the same kind can be accumulated. There is no experimental reason for believing that the limit would be removed to a greater distance, or passed, simply because it was approached by very slow degrees, instead of by more rapid steps. There is no reason to believe that a fresh variability is acquired by long selection of one form; on the contrary, we know that with the oldest breeds it is easier to bring about a diminution than an increase in the points of excellence. The sphere of variation is a simile embodying this view;—each point of the sphere corresponding to a different individual of the same race, the centre to the average animal, the surface to the limit in various directions. The individual near the centre may have offspring varying in all directions with nearly equal rapidity. A variety near the surface may be made to approach it still nearer, but has a greater tendency to vary in every other direction. The sphere may be conceived as large for some species and small for others.

7. St. George Jackson Mivart

(1827–1900)

Mivart, St. G.J. 1871. *On the Genesis of Species*. D. Appleton and Company, New York. Our extract is from Chapter 11: Specific Genesis, pp. 235-258.

Having now severally reviewed the principal biological facts which bear upon specific manifestation, it remains to sum up the results, and to endeavor to ascertain what, if any thing, can be said *positively*, as well as negatively, on this deeply interesting question.

In the preceding chapters it has been contended, in the first place, that no mere survival of the fittest accidental and minute variations can account for the incipient stages of useful structures, such as, e.g., the heads of flat-fishes, the baleen of whales, vertebrate limbs, the laryngeal structures of the new-born kangaroo, the pedicellariæ of Echinoderms, or for many of the facts of mimicry, and especially those last touches of mimetic perfection, where an insect not only mimics a leaf, but one worm-eaten and attacked by fungi.

Also, that structures like the hood of the cobra and the rattle of the rattlesnake seem to require another explanation.

Again, it has been contended that instances of color, as in some apes; of beauty, as in some shell-fish; and of utility, as in many orchids, are examples of conditions which are quite beyond the power of Natural Selection to originate and develop.

Next, the peculiar mode of origin of the eye (by the simultaneous and concurrent modification of distinct parts), with the wonderful refinement of the human ear and voice, has been insisted on; as also, that the importance of all these facts is intensified through the necessity (admitted by Mr. Darwin) that many individuals should be similarly and simultaneously modified in order that slightly favorable variations may hold their own in the struggle for life, against the overwhelming force and influence of mere number.

Again, we have considered, in the third chapter, the great improbability that from minute variations in all directions alone and unaided, save by the survival of the fittest, closely-similar structures should independently arise; though, on a non-Darwinian evolutionary hypothesis, their development might be expected *a priori*. We have seen, however, that there are many instances of wonderfully close similarity which are not due to genetic affinity; the most notable instance, perhaps, being that brought forward by Mr. Murphy, namely, the appearance of the same eye-structure in the vertebrate and molluscous sub-kingdoms. A curious resemblance, though less in degree, has also been seen to exist between the auditory organs of fishes and of Cephalopods. Remarkable similarities between certain placental and implacental mammals, between the bird's-head processes of Polyzoa and the pedicellariæ of Echinoderms, between Ichthyosauria and Cetacea, with very many other similar coincidences, have also been pointed out.

Evidence has also been brought forward to show that similarity is sometimes directly induced by very obscure conditions, at present quite inexplicable, e.g., by causes immediately connected with geographical distribution; as in the loss of the tail in certain forms of Lepidoptera and in simultaneous modifications of color in others, and in the direct modification of young English oysters, when transported to the shore of the Mediterranean.

Again, it has been asserted that certain groups of organic forms seem to have an innate tendency to remarkable developments of some particular kind, as beauty and singularity of plumage in the group of birds of paradise.

It has also been contended that there is something to be said in favor of sudden, as opposed to exceedingly minute and gradual modifications, even if the latter are not fortuitous. Cases were brought forward in Chapter IV., such as the bivalve just mentioned, twenty-seven kinds of American trees simultaneously and similarly modified, also the independent production of pony breeds, and the case of the English greyhounds in Mexico, the offspring of which produced directly acclimated progeny. Besides these, the case of the Normandy pigs, of *Datura tatula*, and also of the black-shouldered peacock, have been spoken of. The teeth of the labyrinthodon, the hand of the potto, the whalebone of whales, the wings of birds, the climbing tendrils of some plants, etc., have also been adduced as instances of structures, the origin and production of which are probably due rather to considerable modifications than to minute increments.

It has also been shown that certain forms which were once supposed to be especially transitional and intermediate (as, e.g., the aye-aye) are really by no means so; while the general rule, that the progress of forms has been "from the more general to the more special," has been shown to present remarkable exceptions, as, e.g., Macrauchenia, the Glyptodon, and the sabre-toothed tiger (Machairodus).

Next, as to specific stability, it has been seen that there may be a certain limit to normal variability, and that if changes take place they may be expected *a priori* to be marked and considerable ones, from the facts of the inorganic world, and perhaps also of the lowest forms of the organic world. It has also been seen that with regard to minute spontaneous variations in races, there is a rapidly-increasing difficulty in intensifying them, in any one direction, by ever such careful breeding. Moreover, it has appeared that different species show a tendency to variability in special directions, and probably in different degrees, and that at any rate Mr. Darwin himself concedes the existence of an internal barrier to change when he credits the goose with "a singularly inflexible organization;" also, that he admits the presence of an *internal* proclivity to change when he speaks of "a whole organization seeming to have become plastic, and tending to depart from the parental type."

We have seen also that a marked tendency to reversion does exist, inasmuch as it sometimes takes place in a striking manner, as exemplified in the white silk fowl in England, *in spite of* careful selection in breeding.

Again, we have seen that a tendency exists in nature to eliminate hybrid races, by whatever means that elimination is effected, while no similar tendency bars the way to an indefinite blending of varieties. This has also been enforced by statements as to the prepotency of certain pollen of identical species, but of distinct races.

To all the preceding considerations have been added others derived from the relations of species to past time. It has been contended that we have as yet no evidence of minutely intermediate forms connecting uninterruptedly together undoubtedly distinct species. That while even "horse ancestry" fails to supply such a desideratum, in very strongly-marked and exceptional kinds (such as the Ichthyosauria, Chelonia, and Anoura), the absence of links is very important and significant. For if every species, without exception, has arisen by minute modifications, it seems incredible that a small percentage of such transitional forms should not have been preserved. This, of course, is especially the case as regards the marine Ichthyosauria and Plesiosauria, of which such numbers of remains have been discovered.

Sir William Thomson's great authority has been seen to oppose itself to "Natural Selection," by limiting, on astronomical and physical grounds, the duration of life on this planet to about one hundred million years. This period, it has been contended, is not nearly enough, on the one hand, for the evolution of all organic forms by the exclusive action of mere minute, fortuitous variations; on the other hand, for the deposition of all the strata which must have been deposited, if minute fortuitous variation was the manner of successive specific manifestation.

Again, the geographical distribution of existing animals has been seen to present difficulties which, though not themselves insurmountable, yet have a certain weight when taken in conjunction with all the other objections.

The facts of homology, serial, bilateral, and vertical, have also been passed in review. Such facts, it has been contended, are not explicable without admitting the action of what may most conveniently be spoken of as an *internal* power, the existence of which is supported by facts not only of comparative anatomy but of teratology and pathology also. "Natural Selection" also has been shown to be impotent to explain these phenomena, while the existence of such an internal power of homologous evolution diminishes the *a priori* improbability of an analogous law of specific origination.

All these various considerations have been supplemented by an endeavor to show the utter inadequacy of Mr. Darwin's theory with regard to the higher psychical phenomena of man (especially the evolution of moral conceptions), and with regard to the evolution of individual organisms by the action of Pangenesis. And it was implied that if Mr. Darwin's latter hypothesis can be shown to be untenable, an antecedent doubt is thus thrown upon his other conception, namely, the theory of "Natural Selection."

A cumulative argument thus arises against the prevalent action of "Natural Selection," which, to the mind of the author, is conclusive. As before observed, he was not originally disposed to reject Mr. Darwin's fascinating theory. Reiterated endeavors to solve its difficulties have, however, had the effect of convincing him that that theory as the one or as the leading explanation of the successive evolution and manifestation of specific forms is untenable. At the same time he admits fully that "Natural Selection" acts and must act, and that it plays in the organic world a certain though a secondary and subordinate part.

The one *modus operandi* yet suggested having been found insufficient, the question arises, Can another be substituted in its place? If not, can any thing that is positive, and if any thing, what, be said as to the question of specific origination?

Now, in the first place, it is of course axiomatic that the laws which conditioned the evolution of extinct and of existing species are of as much efficacy at this moment as at any preceding period, that they *tend* to the manifestation of new forms as much now as ever before. It by no means necessarily follows, however, that this tendency is actually being carried into effect, and that new species of the higher animals and plants are actually now produced. They may be so or they may not, according as existing circumstances favor, or conflict with, the action of those laws. It is possible that lowly-organized creatures may be continually evolved at the present day, the requisite conditions being more or less easily supplied. There is, however, no similar evidence at present as to higher forms; while, as we have seen in Chapter VII., there are *a priori* considerations which militate against their being similarly evolved.

The presence of wild varieties and the difficulty which often exists in the determination of species are sometimes adduced as arguments that high forms are now in process of evolution. These facts, however, do not necessarily prove more than that some species possess a greater variability than others, and (what is indeed unquestionable) that species have often been unduly multiplied by geologists and botanists. It may be, for example, that Wagner was right, and that all the American monkeys of the genus Cebus may be reduced to a single species or to two.

With regard to the lower organisms, and supposing views recently advanced to become fully established, there is no reason to think that the forms said to be evolved were new species, but rather reappearances of definite kinds which had appeared before and will appear again under the same conditions. In the same way, with higher forms similar conditions must educe similar results, but here practically similar conditions can rarely obtain because of the large part which "descent" and "inheritance" always play in such highly-organized forms.

Still it is conceivable that different combinations at different times may have occasionally the same outcome, just as the multiplications of different numbers may have severally the same result.

There are reasons, however, for thinking it possible that the human race is a witness of an exceptionally unchanging and stable condition of things, if the calculations of Mr. Croll are valid as to how far variations in the eccentricity in the earth's orbit together with the precession of the equinoxes have produced changes in climate. Mr. Wallace has pointed out[1] that the last 60,000 years having been exceptionally unchanging as regards these conditions, specific evolution may have been exceptionally rare. It becomes, then, possible to suppose that for a similar period stimuli to change in the manifestation of animal forms may have been exceptionally few and feeble—that is, if the conditions of the earth's orbit have been as exceptional as stated. However, even if new species are actually now being evolved as actively as ever, or if they have been so quite recently, no conflict thence necessarily arises with the view here advocated. For it by no means follows that if some examples of new species have recently been suddenly produced from individuals of antecedent species, we ought to be able to put our fingers on such cases; as Mr. Murphy well observes[2] in a passage before quoted, "If a species were to come suddenly into being in the wild state, as the Ancon sheep did under domestication, how could we ascertain the fact? If the first of a newly-born species were found, the fact of its discovery would tell nothing about its origin. Naturalists would register it as a very rare

---

1   See Nature, March 3, 1870, p. 454. Mr. Wallace says (referring to Mr. Croll's paper in the *Phil. Mag.*), "As we are now, and have been for 60,000 years, in a period of low eccentricity, *the rate of change of species during that time may be no measure of the rate that has generally obtained in past geological epochs.*"
2   "Habit and Intelligence," vol. i., p. 344.

species, having been only once met with, but they would have no means of knowing whether it were the first or last of its race."

But are there any grounds for thinking that in the genesis of species an *internal* force or tendency interferes, cooperates with, and controls the action of external conditions?

It is here contended that there are such grounds, and that though inheritance, reversion, atavism, Natural Selection, etc., play a part not unimportant, yet that such an internal power is a great, perhaps the main, determining agent.

It will, however, be replied that such an entity is no *vera causa*; that if the conception is accepted, it is no real explanation; and that it is merely a roundabout way of saying that the facts are as they are, while the cause remains unknown. To this it may be rejoined that for all who believe in the existence of the abstraction "force" at all, other than will, this conception of an internal force must be accepted and located somewhere—cannot be eliminated altogether; and that therefore it may as reasonably be accepted in this mode as in any other.

It was urged at the end of the third chapter that it is congruous to credit mineral species with an internal power or force. By such a power it may be conceived that crystals not only assume their external symmetry, but even repair it when injured. Ultimate chemical elements must also be conceived as possessing an innate tendency to form certain unions, and to cohere in stable aggregations. This was considered toward the end of Chapter VIII.

Turning to the organic world, even on the hypothesis of Mr. Herbert Spencer or that of Mr. Darwin, it is impossible to escape the conception of innate internal forces. With regard to the physiological units of the former, Mr. Spencer himself, as we have seen, distinctly attributes to them "an *innate* tendency" to evolve the parent-form from which they sprang. With regard to the gemmules of Mr. Darwin, we have seen, in Chapter X., with how many innate powers, tendencies, and capabilities, they must each be severally endowed, to reproduce their kind, to evolve complex organisms or cells, to exercise germinative affinity, etc.

If then (as was before said at the end of Chapter VIII.) such innate powers must be attributed to chemical atoms, to mineral species, to gemmules, and to physiological units, it is only reasonable to attribute such to each individual organism.

The conception of such internal and latent capabilities is somewhat like that of Mr. Galton, before mentioned, according to which the organic world consists of entities, each of which is, as it were, a spheroid with many facets on its surface, upon one of which it reposes in stable equilibrium. When by the accumulated action of incident forces this equilibrium is disturbed, the spheroid is supposed to turn over until it settles on an adjacent facet once more in stable equilibrium.

The internal tendency of an organism to certain considerable and definite changes would correspond to the facets on the surface of the spheroid.

It may be objected that we have no knowledge as to how terrestrial, cosmical, and other forces, can affect organisms so as to stimulate and evolve these latent, merely potential forms. But we have had evidence that such mysterious agencies *do* affect organisms in ways as yet inexplicable, in the very remarkable effects of geographical conditions which were detailed in the third chapter.

It is quite conceivable that the material organic world may be so constituted that the simultaneous action upon it of all known forces, mechanical, physical, chemical, magnetic, terrestrial, and cosmical, together with other as yet unknown forces which probably exist, may result in changes which are harmonious and symmetrical, just as the internal nature of vibrating plates causes particles of sand scattered over them to assume definite and symmetrical figures when made to oscillate in different ways by the bow of a violin being drawn along their edges. The results of these combined internal powers and external influences might be represented under the symbol of complex series of vibrations (analogous to those of sound or light) forming a most complex harmony or a display of most varied colors. In such a way the reparation of local injuries might be symbolized as a filling up and completion of an interrupted rhythm. Thus also monstrous aberrations from typical structure might correspond to a discord, and sterility from crossing be compared with the darkness resulting from the interference of waves of light.

Such symbolism will harmonize with the peculiar reproduction, before mentioned, of heads in the body of certain annelids, with the facts of serial homology, as well as those of bilateral and vertical symmetry. Also, as the atoms of a resonant body may be made to give out sound by the juxtaposition of a vibrating tuning-fork, so it is conceivable that the physiological units of a living organism may be so influenced by surrounding conditions (organic and other) that the accumulation of these conditions may upset the previous rhythm of such units, producing modifications in them—a fresh chord in the harmony of Nature—a new species!

But it may be again objected that to say that species arise by the help of an innate power possessed by organisms is no explanation, but is a reproduction of the absurdity, *l'opium endormit parcequ'il a une vertu soporifique*. It is contended, however, that this objection does not apply, even if it be conceded that there is that force in Molière's ridicule which is generally attributed to it.[3] Much, however, might be said in opposition to more than one of that brilliant dramatist's smart philosophical epigrams, just as to the theological ones of Voltaire, or to the biological one of that other Frenchman who for a time discredited a cranial skeletal theory by the phrase "Vertèbre pensante."[4]

In fact, however, it is a real explanation of how a man lives to say that he lives independently, on his own income, instead of being supported by his relatives and friends. In the same way, there is fully as real a distinction between the production of new specific manifestations entirely *ab externo*, and by the production of the same through an innate force and tendency, the determination of which into action is occasioned by external circumstances.

To say that organisms possess this innate power, and that by it new species are from time to time produced, is by no means a mere assertion that they *are* produced, and in an unknown mode. It is the negation of that view which deems external forces alone sufficient, and at the same time the assertion of something positive, to be arrived at by the process of *reductio ad absurdum*.

All physical explanations result ultimately in such conceptions of innate power, or else in that of will-force. The far-famed explanation of the celestial motions ends in the conception that every particle of matter has the innate power of attracting every other particle directly as the mass, and inversely as the square of the distance.

We are logically driven to this positive conception if we do not accept the view that there is no force but volition, and that all phenomena whatever are the immediate results of the action of intelligent and self-conscious will.

We have seen that the notion of sudden changes—saltatory actions in Nature—has received countenance from Prof. Huxley.[5] We must conceive that these jumps are orderly, and according to law, inasmuch as the whole cosmos is such. Such orderly evolution harmonizes with a teleology derived, not indeed from external Nature directly, but from the mind of man. On this point, however, more will be said in the next chapter. But, once more, if new species are not manifested by the action of external conditions upon minute indefinite individual differences, in what precise way may we conceive that manifestation to have taken place?

---

[3] If any one were to contend that beside the opium there existed a real distinct objective entity, "its soporific virtue," he would be open to ridicule indeed. But the constitution of our minds is such that we cannot but distinguish ideally a thing from its even essential attributes and qualities. The joke is sufficiently amusing, however, regarded as the solemn enunciation of a mere truism.

[4] Noticed by Prof. Owen in his "Archetype," p. 76. Recently it has been attempted to discredit Darwinism in France by speaking of it as *"de la science mousseuse!"*

[5] "Lay Sermons," p. 342.

Are new species now evolving, as they have been from time to time evolved? If so, in what way and by what conceivable means?

In the first place, they must be produced by natural action in preëxisting material, or by supernatural action.

For reasons to be given in the next chapter, the second hypothesis need not be considered.

If, then, new species are and have been evolved from preëxisting material, must that material have been organic or inorganic?

As before said, additional arguments have lately been brought forward to show that individual organisms *do* arise from a basis of *inorganic* material only. As, however, this at the most appears to be the case, if at all, only with the lowest and most minute organisms exclusively, the process cannot be observed, though it may perhaps be fairly inferred.

We may therefore, if for no other reason, dismiss the notion that highly-organized animals and plants can be suddenly or gradually built up by any combination of physical forces and natural powers acting externally and internally upon and in merely inorganic material as a base.

But the question is, How have the highest kinds of animals and plants arisen? It seems impossible that they can have appeared otherwise than by the agency of antecedent organisms not greatly different from them.

A multitude of facts, ever increasing in number and importance, all point to such a mode of specific manifestation.

One very good example has been adduced by Prof. Flower in the introductory lecture of his first Hunterian Course.[6] It is the reduction in size, to a greater or less degree, of the second and third digits of the foot in Australian marsupials, and this, in spite of the very different form and function of the foot in different groups of those animals.

A similarly significant evidence of relationship is afforded by processes of the zygomatic region of the skull in certain edentates existing and extinct.

Again, the relation between existing and recent faunas of the different regions of the world, and the predominating (though by no means exclusive) march of organization, from the more general to the more special point in the same direction.

Almost all the facts brought forward by the patient industry of Mr. Darwin in support of his theory of "Natural Selection," are of course available as evidence in favor of the agency of preëxisting and similar animals in specific evolution.

Now the new forms must be produced by changes taking place in organisms in, after, or before their birth, either in their embryonic, or toward or in their adult, condition.

---

6   Introductory Lecture of February 14, 1870, pp. 24-30, Figs.1-4. (Churchill & Sons.)

Examples of strange births are sufficiently common, and they may arise either from direct embryonic modifications or apparently from some obscure change in the parental action. To the former category belong the hosts of instances of malformation through arrest of development, and perhaps generally monstrosities of some sort are the result of such affections of the embryo. To the second category belong all cases of hybridism, of cross-breed, and in all probability the new varieties and forms, such as the memorable one of the black-shouldered peacock. In all these cases we do not have abortions or monstrosities, but more or less harmonious forms, often of great functional activity, endowed with marked viability and generative prepotency, except in the case of hybrids, when we often find even a more marked generative impotency.

It seems probable therefore that new species may arise from some constitutional affection of parental forms—an affection mainly, if not exclusively, of their generative system. Mr. Darwin has carefully collected[7] numerous instances to show how excessively sensitive to various influences this system is. He says:[8] "Sterility is independent of general health, and is often accompanied by excess of size, or great luxuriance," and, "No one can tell, till he tries, whether any particular animal will breed under confinement, or any exotic plant seed freely under culture." Again, "When a new character arises, whatever its nature may be, it generally tends to be inherited, at least in a temporary, and sometimes in a most persistent manner."[9] Yet the obscure action of conditions will alter characters long inherited, as the grandchildren of Aylesbury ducks removed to a distant part of England, completely lost their early habit of incubation, and hatched their eggs at the same time with the common ducks of the same place."[10]

Mr. Darwin quotes Mr. Bartlett as saying: "It is remarkable that lions breed more freely in travelling collections than in the zoological gardens; probably the constant excitement and irritation produced by moving from place to place, or change of air, may have considerable influence in the matter."[11]

Mr. Darwin also says: "There is reason to believe that insects are affected by confinement like the higher animals," and he gives examples.[12]

Again, he gives examples of change of plumage in the linnet, bunting, oriole, and other birds, and of the temporary modification of the horns of a male deer during a voyage.[13]

---

7 "'See especially "Animals and Plants under Domestication," vol. ii., chap. xviii.
8 "Origin of Species," 5th edit., pp. 323, 324.
9 "Animals and Plants under Domestication," vol. ii., p. 2.
10 Ibid., p. 25.
11 Ibid., p. 151.
12 "Animals and Plants under Domestication," vol. ii., p. 157.
13 Ibid., p. 158.

Finally, he adds that these changes cannot be attributed to loss of health or vigor, "when we reflect how healthy, long-lived, and vigorous many animals are under captivity, such as parrots, and hawks when used for hawking, chetahs when used for hunting, and elephants. The reproductive organs themselves are not diseased; and the diseases from which animals in menageries usually perish, are not those which in any way affect their fertility. No domestic animal is more subject to disease than the sheep, yet it is remarkably prolific...It would appear that any change in the habits of life, whatever these habits may be, if great enough, tends to affect in an inexplicable manner the powers of reproduction."

Such, then, is the singular sensitiveness of the generative system.

As to the means by which that system is affected, we see that a variety of conditions affect it; but as to the modes in which they act upon it, we have as yet little if any clew.

We have also seen the singular effects (in tailed Lepidoptera, etc.) of causes connected with geographical distribution, the mode of action of which is as yet quite inexplicable; and we have also seen the innate tendency which there appears to be in certain groups (birds of paradise, etc.) to develop peculiarities of a special kind.

It is, to say the least, probable that other influences exist, terrestrial and cosmical, as yet unnoted. The gradually accumulating or diversely combining actions of all these on highly-sensitive structures, which are themselves possessed of internal responsive powers and tendencies, may well result in occasional repeated productions of forms harmonious and vigorous, and differing from the parental forms in proportion to the result of the combining or conflicting action of all external and internal influences.

If, in the past history of this planet, more causes ever intervened, or intervened more energetically than at present, we might *a priori* expect a richer and more various evolution of forms more radically differing than any which could be produced under conditions of more perfect equilibrium. At the same time, if it be true that the last few thousand years have been a period of remarkable and exceptional uniformity as regards this planet's astronomical relations, there are then some grounds for thinking that organic evolution may have been exceptionally depressed during the same epoch.

Now, as to the fact that sudden changes and sudden developments have occurred, and as to the probability that such changes are likely to occur, evidence was given in Chapter IV.

In Chapter V. we also saw that minerals become modified suddenly and considerably by the action of incident forces—as, e.g., the production of hexagonal tabular crystals of carbonate of copper by sulphuric acid, and of long rectangular prisms by ammonia, etc.

We have thus a certain antecedent probability that if changes are produced in specific manifestation through incident forces, these changes will be sensible and considerable, not minute and infinitesimal.

Consequently, it is probable that new species have appeared from time to time with comparative suddenness, and that they still continue so to arise if all the conditions necessary for specific evolution now obtain.

This probability will be increased if the observations of Dr. Bastian are confirmed by future investigation. According to his report, when the requisite conditions were supplied, the transformations which appeared to take place (from very low to higher organisms) were sudden, definite, and complete.

Therefore, if this is so, there must probably exist in higher forms a similar tendency to such change. That tendency may indeed be long suppressed, and ultimately modified by the action of heredity—an action which would increase in force with the increase in the perfection and complexity of the organism affected. Still we might expect that such changes as do take place would be also sudden, definite, and complete.

Moreover, as the same causes produce the same effects, several individual parent-forms must often have been similarly and simultaneously affected. That they should be so affected—at least that several similarly-modified individuals should simultaneously arise—has been seen to be a generally necessary circumstance for the permanent duration of such new modifications.

It is also conceivable that such new forms may be endowed with excessive constitutional strength and viability, and with generative prepotency, as was the case with the black-shouldered peacock in Sir J. Trevelyan's flock. This flock was entirely composed of the common kind, and yet the new form rapidly developed itself, "*to the extinction of the previously-existing breed.*"[14]

Indeed, the notion accepted by both Mr. Darwin and Mr. Herbert Spencer, and which is plainly the fact (namely, that changes of conditions and incident forces, within limits, augment the viability and fertility of individuals), harmonizes well with the suggested possibility as to an augmented viability and prepotency in new organic forms evolved by peculiar consentaneous actions of conditions and forces, both external and internal.

The remarkable series of changes noted by Dr. Bastian were certainly not produced by external incident forces *only*, but by these acting on a peculiar *materia*, having special properties and powers. Therefore, the changes were induced by the consentaneous action of internal and external forces.[15] In the same way, then, we may expect

---

14 "Animals and Plants under Domestication," vol. i. p. 291.
15 Though hardly necessary, it may be well to remark that the views here advocated in no way depend upon the truth of the doctrine of Spontaneous Generation.

changes in higher forms to be evolved by similar united action of internal and external forces.

One other point may here be alluded to. When the remarkable way in which structure and function simultaneously change, is borne in mind; when those numerous instances in which Nature has supplied similar wants by similar means, as detailed in Chapter III., are remembered; when also all the wonderful contrivances of orchids, of mimicry, and the strange complexity of certain instinctive actions are considered—then the conviction forces itself on many minds that the organic world is the expression of an intelligence of some kind. This view has been well advocated by Mr. Joseph John Murphy, in his recent work so often here referred to.

This intelligence, however, is evidently not altogether such as ours, or else has other ends in view than those most obvious to us. For the end is often attained in singularly roundabout ways, or with a prodigality of means which seems out of all proportion with the result: not with the simple action directed to one end which generally marks human activity.

Organic Nature then speaks clearly to many minds of the action of an intelligence resulting, on the whole and in the main, in order, harmony, and beauty, yet of an intelligence the ways of which are not such as ours.

This view of evolution harmonizes well with theistic conceptions; not, of course, that this harmony is brought forward as an argument in its favor generally, but it will have weight with those who are convinced that Theism reposes upon solid grounds of reason as *the* rational view of the universe. To such it may be observed that, thus conceived, the Divine action has that slight amount of resemblance to, and that wide amount of divergence from, what human action would be, which might be expected *a priori*—might be expected, that is, from a Being whose nature and aims are utterly beyond our power to imagine, however faintly, but whose truth and goodness are the fountain and source of our own perceptions of such qualities.

The view of evolution maintained in this work, though arrived at in complete independence, yet seems to agree in many respects with the views advocated by Prof. Owen in the last volume of his "Anatomy of Vertebrates," under the term "derivation." He says:[16] "Derivation holds that every species changes in time, by virtue of inherent tendencies thereto. 'Natural Selection' holds that no such change can take place without the influence of altered external circumstances.[17] 'Derivation' sees among the effects of the innate tendency to change irrespective of

---
16 Vol. iii., p. 808.
17 This is hardly an exact representation of Mr. Darwin's view. On his theory, if a favorable variation happens to arise (the external circumstances remaining the same), it will yet be preserved.

altered circumstances, a manifestation of creative power in the variety and beauty of the results; and, in the ultimate forthcoming of a being susceptible of appreciating such beauty, evidence of the preordaining of such relation of power to the appreciation. 'Natural Selection' acknowledges that if ornament or beauty, in itself, should be a purpose in creation, it would be absolutely fatal to it as a hypothesis."

"'Natural Selection' sees grandeur in the view of life, with its several powers, having been originally breathed by the Creator into a few forms or into one. 'Derivation' sees therein a narrow invocation of a special miracle and an unworthy limitation of creative power, the grandeur of which is manifested daily, hourly, in calling into life many forms, by conversion of physical and chemical into vital modes of force, under as many diversified conditions of the requisite elements to be so combined."

The view propounded in this work allows, however, a greater and more important part to the share of external influences, it being believed by the author, however, that these external influences equally with the internal ones are the results of one harmonious action underlying the whole of Nature, organic and inorganic, cosmical, physical, chemical, terrestrial, vital, and social.

According to this view, an internal law presides over the actions of every part of every individual, and of every organism as a unit, and of the entire organic world as a whole. It is believed that this conception of an internal innate force will ever remain necessary, however much its subordinate processes and actions may become explicable:

That by such a force, from time to time, new species are manifested by ordinary generation just as *Pavo nigripennis* appeared suddenly, these new forms not being monstrosities but harmonious self-consistent wholes. That thus, as specific distinctness is manifested by obscure sexual conditions, so in obscure sexual modifications specific distinctions arise.

That these "jumps" are considerable in comparison with the minute variations of "Natural Selection"—are in fact sensible steps, such as discriminate species from species.

That the latent tendency which exists to these sudden evolutions is determined to action by the stimulus of external conditions.

That "Natural Selection" rigorously destroys monstrosities, and abortive and feeble attempts at the performance of the evolutionary process.

That "Natural Selection" removes the antecedent species rapidly when the new one evolved is more in harmony with surrounding conditions.

That "Natural Selection" favors and develops useful variations, though it is impotent to originate them or to erect the physiological barrier which seems to exist between species.

By some such conception as this, the difficulties here enumerated, which beset the theory of "Natural Selection" pure and simple, are to be got over.

Thus, for example, the difficulties discussed in the first chapter—namely, those as to the origins and first beginnings of certain structures—are completely evaded.

Again, as to the independent origin of closely-similar structures, such as the eyes of the Vertebrata and cuttlefishes, the difficulty is removed if we may adopt the conception of an innate force similarly directed in each case, and assisted by favorable external conditions.

Specific stability, limitation to variability, and the facts of reversion, all harmonize with the view here put forward. The same may be said with regard to the significant facts of homology, and of organic symmetry; and our consideration of the hypothesis of Pangenesis in Chapter X., has seemed to result in a view as to innate powers which accords well with what is here advocated.

The evolutionary hypothesis here advocated also serves to explain all those remarkable facts which were stated in the first chapter to be explicable by the theory of Natural Selection, namely, the relation of existing to recent faunas and floras; the phenomena of homology and of rudimentary structures; also the processes gone through in development; and lastly, the wonderful facts of mimicry.

Finally, the view adopted is the synthesis of many distinct and, at first sight, conflicting conceptions, each of which contains elements of truth, and all of which it appears to be able more or less to harmonize.

Thus it has been seen that "Natural Selection" is accepted. It acts and must act, though alone it does not appear capable of fulfilling the task assigned to it by Mr. Darwin.

Pangenesis has probably also much truth in it, and has certainly afforded valuable and pregnant suggestions, but unaided and alone it seems inadequate to explain the evolution of the individual organism.

Those three conceptions of the organic world which may be spoken of as the teleological, the typical, and the transmutationist, have often been regarded as mutually antagonistic and conflicting.

The genesis of species as here conceived, however, accepts, locates, and harmonizes all the three.

Teleology concerns the ends for which organisms were designed. The recognition, therefore, that their formation took place by an evolution not fortuitous, in no way invalidates the acknowledgment of their final causes if on other grounds there are reasons for believing that such final causes exist.

Conformity to type, or the creation of species according to certain "divine ideas," is in no way interfered with by such a process of evolution as is here advocated. Such "divine ideas" must be accepted or declined upon quite other grounds than the mode of their realization, and of their manifestation in the world of sensible phenomena.

Transmutationism (an old name for the evolutionary hypothesis), which was conceived at one time to be the very antithesis to the two preceding conceptions, harmonizes well with them if the evolution be conceived to be orderly and designed. It will in the next chapter be shown to be completely in harmony with conceptions, upon the acceptance of which " final causes" and "divine ideal archetypes" alike depend.

Thus then, if the cumulative argument put forward in this book is valid, we must admit the insufficiency of " Natural Selection" both on account of the residuary phenomena it fails to explain, and on account of certain other phenomena which seem actually to conflict with that theory. We have seen that though the laws of Nature are constant, yet some of the conditions which determine specific change may be exceptionally absent at the present epoch of the world's history; also that it is not only possible, but highly probable, that an internal power or tendency is an important if not the main agent in evoking the manifestation of new species on the scene of realized existence, and that in any case, from the facts of homology, innate internal powers to the full as mysterious must anyhow be accepted, whether they act in specific origination or not. Besides all this, we have seen that it is probable that the action of this innate power is stimulated, evoked, and determined by external conditions, and also that the same external conditions, in the shape of "Natural Selection," play an important part in the evolutionary process: and finally, it has been affirmed that the view here advocated, while it is supported by the facts on which Darwinism rests, is not open to the objections and difficulties which oppose themselves to the reception of "Natural Selection," as the exclusive or even as the main agent in the successive and orderly evolution of organic forms in the *genesis of species*.

8. Erich Wasmann

(1859–1931)

> Wasmann, E. 1910. *Modern Biology and the Theory of Evolution.* Third edition. B. Herder, St. Louis, Missouri. Our extract is from Chapter IX: Thoughts on Evolution, section 6 "Systematic and Natural Species", pp. 296-302.

Linnæus, who is to be regarded as the originator of our present conception of systematic species, and who, therefore, has been called the father of the theory of permanence, enunciated the following dictum: *Tot species numeramus, quot diversae formae in principio sunt creatae—* we reckon so many (systematic) species as there were different forms created in the beginning.

How must this dictum be worded to make it agree with the theory of evolution? According to it, the systematic species of the present time do not represent the originally created forms, but are the result of a process of evolution, uniting the species of the present and the past in natural series of forms, the members of which are related to one another, and each of which points back to an original primitive form, whence it is derived. If we designate each of these independent series of forms, not related to other series or families, as a natural species,[1] we can still assent to Linnæus's dictum: *Tot species numeramus, quot diversae formae in principio sunt creatae.* We reckon so many natural species as there were

---

1 A similar view regarding natural species has already been expressed by Father T. Pesch in his *Philosophia naturalis*, II, p. 334, in order to explain the facts supporting the theory of evolution. He quotes a number of passages from St. Thomas Aquinas and from Suarez in favour of his view. Of course we are here speaking of the *species physicae* of natural philosophy, not of the *species metaphysicae* of logic. Almost inconceivable mistakes as to my definition of natural species have been made by many reviewers of the first edition of this work, some of them being experienced zoologists. Escherich in the Supplement to the *Allgemeine Zeitung* for February 10, and 11, 1905, gave it far too narrow an interpretation, and Haeckel, Forel and others simply followed him and made the same mistake, without examining the matter for themselves. Another mistake was made by Friese (*Wiener Entomologische Zeitung*, 1904, No. 10) and Schroeder (*Zeitschrift für wissenschaftl. Insektenbiologie*, 1905, Part 4), who believe my distinction between systematic and natural species to be identical with that between biological and morphological species; the biological and the morphological species are but two different aspects of the systematic species, whilst the natural species comprises all the members of the same line of ancestry or pedigree, and therefore is much wider from the point of view of natural science. I trust that these remarks will prevent further misunderstandings.

different primitive forms created in the beginning.[2] Each of these natural species has in the course of evolution differentiated itself into more or less systematic species. How many systematic species, genera, and families belong to a natural species, cannot yet be stated with certainty in most cases. Still less are we able to say how many natural species there are, i.e. how many lines of ancestry independent of one another. We must leave the decision to the phylogenetic research of future ages, if indeed it ever succeeds in arriving at one.

The varying degrees of capacity for evolution possessed by the primitive forms of the different natural species depend primarily upon the interior laws of evolution impressed upon their organic constitution; we are probably justified in regarding the chromatin substance of the germ-cells as the material designed to transmit these laws.[3] The interaction of these interior factors in evolution and of the surrounding exterior influences, through which many kinds of adaptation came about, have produced the ramifications from the parent stock of the natural species, and they have been affected also by cross-breeding (amphimixis) and natural selection.

But, it may be asked, what is the practical advantage of distinguishing thus natural and systematic species, if we are still unable to determine which forms actually constitute a natural species, and how many such natural species there are? To this question we may answer: *Firstly*, in many cases we are able at the present day to decide in some degree the group of forms which belong to a natural species, *although we may not yet know with certainty its full extent.*[4] For instance we may reckon, as belonging to one natural species, all the varieties of beetle of the *Paussidae* family, from the Tertiary period to the present time;[5] but as the *Paussidae*, even if they are the outcome, not of a monophyletic, but of a diphyletic evolution (cf. Chapter X, §9), are related phylogenetically to the *Carabidae*, and these again to other families of beetles, the real extent of the natural species in question is probably much greater. With still greater certainty may all the varieties of *Staphylinidae* belonging to the group *Lomechusa* be regarded as forming a natural species. We may therefore rightly say: All the *Lomechusini* form *one* natural species and not more than one. But we do not mean to limit the extent of this natural

---

2   For readers who have studied philosophy, it is perhaps needless to remark again (as I do for the benefit of some of my critics), that the creation of the first organisms is not to be understood as a *creatio e nihilo*, but as a production of organisms out of matter. On this subject see the sections on Spontaneous Generation (p. 193), and on the Philosophical Limitations of the Theory of Evolution (p. 279).

3   See Chapter VI, p. 169 and p. 177, &c.

4   I have italicised these words because they were overlooked by Escherich and other reviewers in the former edition.

5   Cf. *Stimmen aus Maria-Laach*, LIII, 1897, pp. 400 and 520, &c., 'Die Familie der Paussiden'; also 'Neue Beiträge zur Kenntnis der Paussiden mit biologischen und phylogenetischen Bemerkungen' (*Notes from the Leyden Museum*, XXV, 1904).

species to the *Lomechusini*, for this group of *Staphylinidae* is connected phylogenetically with other groups of the same family, and the whole family of *Staphylinidae* with other families of beetles, &c.

If we consider the numerous genera and species of ants from the earliest Jurassic period to the present day, we can hardly doubt that they are offshoots of one single natural species, and are not several natural species. The same remark applies to the family of termites, with its great variety of fossil and still existent genera and species.[6] If we trace back the history of the primitive varieties of the Palæozoic age, which even then formed several distinct classes, whence our present orders of insects branched off probably in the Mesozoic age,[7] we may succeed perhaps, in course of time, in proving these varieties of primitive insects to be offshoots of some original stock, which possibly is connected with the earliest marine Arthropoda, so that eventually many hundreds of thousands of systematic species may unite to form one single line, one single natural species.

This is at present all a matter of pure hypothesis; but these examples serve to show plainly that the limits to be assigned to the natural species become more and more uncertain the higher the division of the animal system and the more remote the historical period of animal life under consideration. It will therefore be best for practical purposes to describe as natural species only those groups of forms which investigation has shown with sufficient probability to be uniform genealogical series.

Thus, for instance, we may class as one natural species all the present varieties of horse (*Equidae*) and their fossil ancestors, comprising various systematic genera, although we do not yet know how far the limits of this natural species may be extended into the past of which palæontology takes account.[8] Among Molluscs, the Ammonites may be mentioned as a group of forms very rich in systematic families, genera, and species; they can be traced from the Devonian to the Cretaceous period through a long series of geological strata, as a uniform, close line of forms, that we must reckon as all belonging to one natural species, not to many. I might add many other instances, but those already given will suffice to show that the distinction between systematic and natural species is by no means devoid of actual foundation. It is in fact practically necessary, if we are to have a scientific knowledge of comparative morphology and biology.[9]

Secondly: The distinction is of far greater importance from the point of view of philosophy. It supplies us with a firm philosophical basis, upon

---

6 See p. 276.
7 Cf. A. Handlirsch, *Die fossilen Insekten*, Leipzig, 1906.
8 Fleischmann's criticism of 'the stock instance of the theory of descent' (*Die Deszendenztheorie*, chapter v) seems only to confirm the above statement, and not to prove much against the relationship of the *Equidae* to one another.
9 Further information on this subject, derived from my own investigations, will be found in the next chapter.

which the theories of creation and descent can easily be reconciled with one another. It is obvious that the possession of such a basis is of the utmost importance to those concerned with the defence of Christianity. Our monistic opponents are fond of adopting the device of directing their attacks against the theory of permanence, when they are really aiming them at the theory of creation. They declare the two theories to be identical, and hope, by overthrowing the one, to secure the downfall of the other. But their hopes are doomed to disappointment, if we resolutely maintain the distinction just laid down. *If we believe that only the natural species in their primitive forms were created, but that it is left to natural science to determine the number and extent of these series of natural forms, as well as the character of the primitive forms themselves, then the enemies of the Christian cosmogony will no longer be able to taunt us with having to accept the permanence of the systematic species as an article of faith.*[10] What has it to do with theistic cosmogony whether a hare and a rabbit, a horse and an ass are related or not? The recognition of a personal God, the Creator of all finite beings, is no more inseparably connected with the theory of permanence in zoology and botany than it was with the geocentric system in astronomy.

If the theory of descent holds its ground, and takes the place of the old theory of permanence, the theory of creation, and with it the Christian cosmogony, remains as firmly established as ever. Indeed the Creator's wisdom and power are revealed in a more brilliant light than ever, as this theory shows the organic world to have assumed its present form, not in consequence of God's constant interference with the natural order, but as a result of the action of those laws which He Himself has imposed upon nature.

We see therefore that, in this department also, true science leads us finally to a fuller recognition of God.[11] It is a mere delusion on the part of modern atheism, in its various forms and shades of opinion, to fancy that the theory of evolution has enabled the world to dispense with a Creator; for, the more manifold and the more independent is the evolution of the organic world according to the laws inherent in it, the greater must be the wisdom and power of the law-giver who created this world. The Darwinian, or rather Haeckelian, theory of chance, which derives all the conformity to law in nature from an original lawless chaos, by means simply of 'the survival of the fittest,' may at the present day be said to be discarded by science. But the monistic view of the universe, which professes to find the first cause of the orderly arrangement of the world

---

10 This italicised passage gives the reason for the bitter attacks made by monists upon the 'natural species.'
11 On this subject see K. Braun, *Über Kosmogonie vom Standpunkt christlicher Wissenschaft*, 1905, especially chapters 8 and 9. Also J. Reinke, 'Darf die Natur uns als Offenbarung Gottes gelten?' (*Türmer Jahrbuch*, pp. 139-167, especially pp. 162, &c.).

in the world itself, and not in a personal Creator substantially distinct from it, is no better than the materialistic theory of chance; for the so-called God of monism, whom it identifies with the world and everything therein, proves to be a true medley of irreconcilable and inexplicable contradictions, when considered in the light of sound reason. We are told that God is the most perfect being, having from all eternity the ground of His existence in Himself; but at the same time He is a God who must develop His own being in and through the world. Such a monistic God would be pitiably incomplete and dependent, for His very existence would depend upon the existence of every midge, and fly, and creature in which He develops Himself. To have invented such an idea of God and to seek to make it take the place of the theistic conception of Him, are achievements of modern lack of thought, not of modern science. But, on the contrary, the recognition of a personal God, who, in virtue of the fulness of His own being, created the world out of nothing, is still demanded by sound human understanding, and is therefore a true postulate of science.[12] Although God is present and acts in all His creatures, He is essentially distinct from the world and independent of it, and has shone forth from all eternity with the same unchanging purity and perfection. All the ephemeral deities of modern monism must give way to this only true God of Christianity.

At the present day men are fond of attacking the theistic cosmogony by saying it is an 'untenable dualism' to recognise a God as essentially distinct from the world. Nobody has yet proved this dualism to be untenable, though monism certainly is so. I am not one of those who 'prefer the most pitiable confusion to dualism' (C. Stumpf). There is in reality only one true kind of monism, and that is the unity of the first cause of all finite being—God in His infinity.'[13] People are fond of quoting Charles Darwin as an authority in support of the modern theory of evolution, but he did not feel that blind hatred of the Creator which characterises Haeckelism. Although we know from some of his later statements that he inclined to agnosticism, he never altered the closing words of his chief work, the 'Origin of Species.' Even in the sixth edition, published in 1888, after his death, this beautiful passage occurs: 'There is grandeur in this view of life, with its several powers, having been originally breathed by the Creator into a few forms or into one; and that, while this planet has gone cycling on according to the fixed law of gravity, from so simple a

---

12   The accounts of the theory of creation given in modern scientific works are most inadequate. See, for instance, Lotsy's *Vorlesungen über Deszendenztheorie*, I, 1906, pp. 5-8. Lotsy there rejects the atheistic and the pantheistic hypotheses regarding the origin of the world, but professes himself unable to accept the theistic view, which he seems to prefer, because 'the idea of self-existence is absolutely unintelligible.' This is true only of those who have never opened a book on Christian theodicy.

13   Cf. the third edition of my work on *Instinkt und Intelligenz im Tierreich*, 1905, p. 276.

beginning endless forms most beautiful and most wonderful have been, and are being evolved.'

Very similar is the opinion expressed by Lyell, the great geologist, in writing to Charles Darwin, on March 11, 1863. He maintains that the acceptance of a phylogeny of the organic species by no means enables us to dispense with the idea of creation. 'I think,' he says, 'the old "creation" is almost as much required as ever, but of course it takes a new form, if Lamarck's views, improved by yours, are adopted.'[14]

---

14   See Francis Darwin, *Life and Letters of Charles Darwin*, II, London, 1888, p. 193.

9. Harold C. Morton

(ca. 1925)

Morton, H.C. 1925. *The Bankruptcy of Evolution*. Marshall Brothers Limited, London. Our extract is from Chapter X: "Evolution" within rigid limits: the one, strictly limited, proven sphere of "evolution", pp. 164-184.

Thus Darwinism, as the *method* of the Descent of Species, is rejected by the Men of Science of to-day: and the Doctrine of Descent, by some unknown method or methods deriving the forms of organic life from one, or from some few, original forms, lacks all substantiation and has not established the very slightest claim upon the credence of mankind. Is there then nothing at all that remains? nothing, that is, except the knowledge of our ignorance of origins? Or if there is something yet remaining, is it of importance enough to warrant attention? The answer is that something certainly does still remain to us: a process to which we often apply the name "Evolution" is a fact, although a fact of *very limited* scope: and inasmuch as it *is* a fact, it is on that account alone worthy of the closest attention. It was the vastness of the claim of Evolution which beyond all doubt lent it its fascination, and it is that also which has caused its slowly recognized failure. A very limited Evolution may fascinate no more, but as [a–sic] matter of fact there is a very limited sphere in which Evolution is established and in which the Darwinian theory of Natural Selection may hold a place. "Natural Selection is a *vera causa* as far as it goes" is a claim which may be true: but in that case *its proven sphere is confined within the bounds of the distinct type or Species*. It is thoroughly worthy of establishment both that there is such a movement as is indicated, that possibly it proceeds by the method of Natural Selection as one of its methods, and that its sphere of activity is severely limited. If the modern outburst of research and thought has brought to an end at length the vast unwarrantable evolutionary dream, it has abundantly justified itself.

The "Evolution" I refer to is evolution on a very small scale, acting only within the "Species": and if I might coin a word by combining Latin *parva*, "small" with the other Latin word "*Evolutio*," I would gladly distinguish this from the old ambitious and discredited Evolution by naming it Parvolution, or by a combination of the word "Varieties" with "Evolution" denominate it "Varvolution."

The title of Darwin's great work was, when strictly interpreted, a somewhat modest one—"The Origin of *Species*": and it seems clear that Darwin himself, though he allowed his scientific imagination wide range, hesitated to go so far as many of his followers have gone. The Evolutionist has claimed vastly too much. The exuberance of his claims has been almost infinite, and it is this exuberance which has aroused the intense antagonism between Religion and Science which was thus inevitable and has wrought such harm. Darwin did not assert that the widely different types of life have come from a common ancestor. Even when he hesitates in the "Origin" as to whether certain Varieties are to be called Species, deciding upon the latter name, and then allows himself to refer to genera also: and when he goes on in his "Variation of Animals and Plants" to include Orders and Classes in his evolutionary scheme—even then, all he claims is that "all the members of the same Order or Class are descended from a common ancestor." He never declared, for instance, that Vertebrates, Mollusca, and Arthropoda are descended from a common ancestor. Far as he went, he left it to others to stretch a tenuous theory as far and even farther than this. Darwin himself inclined to the belief that life appeared upon the Earth in several different forms, and that their descendants remain distinct to-day. He did not trace everything alike back to some life-form which arose amid what Martineau so aptly termed "the fucous slime of waste sea-shores." It is well that Bateson should chastise this exuberance of the Evolutionists and say that the suggestion of the spontaneous formation of formaldehyde as the first step in the origin of life reminded him of Harry Lauder, in the character of a Glasgow schoolboy, pulling his treasures out of his pocket and saying: "That's a washer—for making motor-cars!" The thoroughly theoretical character which still adheres to evolutionary propositions is well illustrated in the language of Evolutionists. Prof. Macbride, for instance ("Zoology," pp. 88 and 89, 1922), only says what a Species *"will* do," and how all the vast complexity of Classes, Orders, Tribes, Genera, Species, within the limits of the Phylum *"will* come about." What a Species *has* done is not indicated. Indeed, the extraordinary licence, not to call it looseness, which some exponents of Darwinism allow themselves, is shown by such a statement as that of Prof. Macbride, that "the sole question at issue" between the Darwinian and those who reject his theory is whether "the tremendous slaughter among wild animals" "subserves the welfare of the Species or not"! Yet in the same chapter he goes on himself to say that Darwin's assumption of the heritability of differences between members of the same litter or family is unsupported by fact and hence that continued selection of individuals showing slight differences from their brethren is not true. Moreover, he says that Lamarck's theory, "though not popular with the majority of naturalists at the present time," seems to offer by far the most hopeful solution of the origin of Variation. Most assuredly these also are differences between Darwinians and those who reject his theory. Or again, Prof. Macbride in this same "People's Book" on Zoology says that the only instance of a natural species giving rise to a new "elementary species," i.e. a Mutational Variety, breeding true, which De Vries has been able to discover is "the case of an evening primrose." A very slight acquaintance with De Vries' volumes will show this statement to be quite incorrect. How vastly different from this carelessness of statement and from these exuberant claims are the words of A. R. Wallace, who speaks with such great prestige. His contention in comparison with others shows the greatest restraint. "Every fresh discovery in Nature," he said, "fortifies that original hypothesis. But this is the sane and honest Evolution, which does not concern itself at all with beginnings, *and merely follows a few links in a fairly obvious chain.* As to the chain itself, Evolution has nothing to say. For my own part I am convinced that at one period in the Earth's history there was a definite act of Creation, that from that moment Evolution has been at work, and guidance has been exercised" ("New Thoughts on Evolution," pp. 13 and 14). Prof. Hoffding's words are most true, that Darwin's followers sometimes grew dizzy, and in so far as Darwin also soared to some heights which were purely speculative, we can hardly deny that there was a trace of that dizziness in the Master himself.

The real proven sphere of Evolution is simply *within the type.* If that type be called a "Species," then Evolution rightly says that Variations occur in great numbers within the Species, and that some are perpetuated, being selected in some manner or manners, one method of selection being quite possibly what Darwin called Natural Selection.

It cannot be admitted that Darwin's derivation of all present forms from a few original and unexplained typal forms has any evidence to substantiate it. From each of those original forms Darwin would derive many Orders, Genera and Species which are perfectly distinct to-day. There is no proof whatever of such derivation of present-day Species. No single instance is known where one form has been transmuted into another by Natural Selection or by any other means. The words of Prof. Bateson, in his Presidential Address when President of the British Association, are very conclusive on this matter:—

> "Formerly single origins were generally presumed, but at the present time numbers of the chief products of domestication—dogs, horses, cattle, sheep, poultry, wheat, rice, oats, plums, cherries—have in turn been accepted as 'polyphyletic,' or in other words derived from several distinct forms. The reason that has led to these judgments is that the distinctions between the chief Varieties can be traced as far back as the evidence reaches, and that these distinctions are

so great, so far transcending what we actually know Variation capable of effecting, that it seems pleasanter to postpone the difficulty, relegating the critical differentiation to some misty antiquity into which we shall not be asked to penetrate. For it need hardly be said that this is mere procrastination. If the origin of a form under domestication is hard to imagine, it becomes no easier to conceive of such enormous deviation from type coming to pass in a wild state. Examine any two thoroughly distinct Species which meet each other in their distribution, as, for example, Lychnis Diurna and Vespertina do. In areas of overlap are many intermediate forms. These used to be taken as transitional steps, and the Specific distinctness of Diurna and Vespertina was on that account questioned. Once it is known that these supposed intergrades are merely mongrels between the two Species, the transition from one to the other is practically beyond the power of our imagination to conceive. . . . I take this to show how entirely the facts were formerly misrepresented" (p. 14).

Thus, it being quite impossible not indeed to prove, but even merely to conceive, how even Varieties became distinct the one from the other, the effort to conceive the process is abandoned, and the process relegated to some misty antiquity to which we shall not be asked to penetrate! It is much more certain that no change from one *type* to another has ever been known, or can even be conceived. Therefore it is the Evolutionist appears before the public like an Homeric God, enveloped in a mist—of antiquity.

Evolution within the type is all that can be legitimately posited, and that Evolution amounts to no more than the stabilizing of certain Variations. *That there has not only been Variation within the type, but that there has been a great deal of it, there can be no question—nor is the most convinced Creationist concerned to deny it.* Such a statement as Mr. Philip Mauro's—that apart from the human race, the organic world is static—is far removed from the facts. A more accurate classification will probably assign many so-called Species to the category of Varieties within the Type. "Evolution within the type," says Prof. W. B. Scott, in his "Theory of Evolution," "might be admitted without conceding the possibility of deriving one type from another." So Prof. Hoffding says: "It has also been shown by the experimental method, which in recent biological work has succeeded Darwin's more historical method, that types once constituted possess great permanence, the fluctuation being restricted within clearly defined boundaries" ("Darwin and Modern Science," pp. 447 and 448). Mendelism, which some Evolutionists are quoting as though it supported the variability of types and the Doctrine of Descent, in reality reveals not the variability but the rigidity of specific types. The word "Species" to-day must have a strict and concrete meaning, in distinction from the word "Variety": and while Species remain fixed, Varieties appear in great number and a large proportion of them by crossing. De Vries declares:—

> "The constancy of Species is a demonstrated fact: their transmutability is still a matter of theory." Then he goes on at once (p. 205, "The Mutation Theory"): "This is the old objection against the theory of descent. Lamarck, Darwin and Wallace met this difficulty by assuming that the immutability was only apparent and was due to the fact that the changes are so slow that in the short time during which we are able to observe them they cannot be detected. This, however, is a mere assumption, as I have already shown."

Certainly it is only Varieties whose evolution has been proved; though it must be borne in mind that it is quite conceivable that a true classification will reveal a very limited number of original untransmutable typal forms, call them what we may, within which typal forms many varieties have arisen. Evolution within the type, or Parvolution as I have ventured to call it, may thus be a very considerable thing.

That many striking Varieties have arisen it is simply foolish to question; and perhaps the real character and achievement of that "flux of things," which Evolution seeks to interpret, is nowhere better illustrated than by the Human Species, from a consideration of which Species modern evolutionary theory took its rise. It is worthy of a great deal of emphasis that it was from the study of social theory that the conception of Natural Selection had its beginning. Malthus' Essay on Population gave to Darwin, and also to Wallace, and also "came within an ace" of giving to Spencer, the vision how everywhere, in the struggle for existence which the scarcity of sustenance everywhere involves, those who possess any superiority win and live while the inferior lose and die. Darwin read Malthus in 1838 and gained from it the idea which for twenty years he resolutely developed until in 1859 he published his "Origin." In 1858, while ill with fever at Ternate, Alfred Russel Wallace found himself recapitulating in his thought the argument of Malthus' book, which he had read twelve years before. As soon as fever permitted he rose and wrote hastily a Paper embodying the same idea of Natural Selection at which Darwin had been working for twenty years. Thus it was a process which Malthus adumbrated, and Darwin and Wallace clearly perceived and seized, *a process proceeding in the realm of human affairs*, which revealed the secret of Natural Selection.

But not only so. There seems little doubt that the *faith* in Evolution was fostered, not perhaps consciously but none the less deeply and truly, through the social transformations of the age. The eye sees only what it brings with it, the power of seeing: and the reason why Darwin, Wallace and Spencer saw in Nature Struggle and nothing but Struggle, the ruthless Gladiatorial Show with all its tale of death, just where later observers see co-operation even more plainly marked than struggle, love in an Eden rather than fierce fight in a gladiatorial arena, is that the horrors of the French Revolution, and the ghastly bondage of the early English Industrial Revolution, made the eye quick to see struggle but slow to mark co-operation. Similarly, the conception of life which shows itself in the adage "practice makes perfect," rather than in the alternative adage "genius is born not made," is the conception that determined the line of Lamarckian thinking and found the explanation of differences in the effects of use and disuse. So Geddes and Thomson[1] lay the greatest emphasis upon the social origin of evolution theories. "That the idea of Evolution has originally been projected from the social plane into that of the other sciences," says "Chambers' Encyclopædia," "is a proposition which can only be doubted by the specialist who has not inquired into the history of his ideas. Evolution in social affairs has not only suggested our ideas of Evolution in the other Sciences, but has deeply coloured them in accordance with the particular phase of Evolution current at the time."

Let human affairs, then, from consideration of which the great Darwinian movement sprang, be our illustration of what the process of Evolution, by Natural Selection or by some other as yet unperceived method of conserving germinal variations, is able to accomplish. Although the single or multiple origin of the human race is still under discussion and is in scientific thought an open question, it is probably true that science leans rather toward the monophyletic or single origin: while believers in the Bible maintain, of course, the single origin also. The believers in the Bible should be the last to deny the actuality of a rigidly limited Evolution (Parvolution), and should most clearly perceive the scope of the evolutionary process as illustrated in the life of Man. For starting, as we hold, with one original pair, the evolutionary process has produced all the endless varieties within the Human Race which we see throughout the world to-day. There is no proof whatever, nor vestige of it, that any earlier distinct type has evolved into the type called Man (Homo Sapiens), any more than that from that type itself any other new type has ever been formed. All evolutionary change has been within the type: but how great have those changes been, in every realm, possibly in improvement and certainly in deterioration! Take Man (Homo Sapiens), both in his physical, his mental and his social characteristics. From the

---

1   See "Evolution," pp. 247 and 248.

first parents of the Human Race have come, in matter of physique, races white, red, brown, yellow, black: races tall, medium, and dwarf: races with the hair of the head fine in texture and gently curling or waving, and races with hair thickly curling and approaching the character of wool: races with brachy-cephalic, and races with dolicho-cephalic skull: races with thick lips and flattened features, and races with thin lips and features aquiline—and so on in long succession the physical differences run. In mental characteristics what large differences have come to be. Place a Greek of the great time when the whole Athenian democracy could be counted on to appreciate at a first hearing a play of Æschylus, side by side with an Australian Aborigine: place a Hebrew, with his conception of the One God of Justice, Holiness and Love side by side with a Hindu burdened by his multitude of mainly horrific deities: place a Greek of the Golden Age just mentioned with his brilliant secular intellect side by side with a Hebrew of the Golden Age of the Prophets, with his penetrating insight and thrilling statement of the Mind and Will of Jehovah! What vast contrasts! And these have come to pass by the process called Evolution within the limits of the type called Man. Or take social organization— and contrast Despotism with Democracy, or contrast Democracy with its equal respect for all classes and personalities with Bolshevism of the rigid limitations and the frantic hates, or contrast Monarchy with Oligarchy as two realized orders of Society—and while it is clear that Evolution does not of necessity mean progress, it may and often does mean most striking differentiation. It all takes place within the type: but within the type the Human Race shows, especially to those who believe in the single origin of the Human Species, how vast is the scope of change.

What happens within that fixed type of existence classed as Homo Sapiens takes place also within every other type. *How* it takes place is a question as yet very far from being authoritatively answered. Darwin's theories are, as we have seen, for the most part abandoned: and all that the leaders of scientific research will say is that Natural Selection is a *vera causa* as far as it goes! The very remark is almost scornful in its easy-going acquiescence. The facts from which Darwin turned away as being closely akin to Creation, if, that is, they did indeed constitute the origin of new Varieties, have been carefully studied by De Vries and formulated into a theory which need not arouse the antagonism of the Creationist, and may prove to embody the main evolutionary process. Prof. Hugo de Vries, Professor of Botany in the University of Amsterdam, seized upon those big Variations ("sports," "single Variations," "discontinuous Variations") from which Darwin had turned away, and contended that in them we may find the secret of evolutionary changes. He terms them "Mutations" or "Elementary Species." They are the large Variations which leap, unheralded and fully made, into existence, or at the least into notice. They remain fixed and breed true from the beginning. De Vries does not question that many Species have undergone vast changes during the course of centuries, and no one knows (presumably because they have not been under observation) whether they have taken place gradually or by leaps and bounds. But he is deeply impressed by the constancy of Species. "The constancy of Species," he says, "is a demonstrated fact; their transmutability is still a matter of theory." And in reply to the Darwinian plea that the immutability or constancy is only apparent and is due to the shortness of the time of our observation and the slowness of the changes, with the true scientific insistence on fact he replies, "This is a mere assumption."

Within Species, taking the word in its broad typal sense, De Vries submits that new Varieties arise by Mutation. Some of his illustrations of the emergence of these new Varieties are full of interest. For instance:—

> "About the year 1590 Sprenger, an apothecary in Heidelberg, found in the garden where he grew plants for his business (amongst which was Chel. majus) a new form of Chelidonium which differed from C. majus in the possession of deeply-cut leaves and petals. He called it Chelidonia Major foliis et floribus incisis, and sent some examples to Jean Bauhin, Gaspard Bauhin, Clusius, Plater, and other well-known botanists of his time. All of them declared that the plant was unknown to them and new. It had never been found wild before nor has it ever been found since: although from time to time it has escaped from gardens. It comes absolutely true from seed, has maintained itself till the present day, and is very generally known in Botanical Gardens. Miller, Roze, and many others have tested its constancy by cultures extending over many years and have observed no reversion to C. majus. I have repeated the experiments with the same result.
>
> "We may conclude therefore that C. laciniatum arose about the year 1590. Unfortunately Sprenger does not say whence the seeds came which gave rise to it, whether from seed saved by himself from C. majus, or from some other source. The former is the more probable, since otherwise he would have known from whence he had obtained it." ("The Mutation Theory," pp. 189 and 190.)

Again:—

> "Strawberries without runners belong to the species Fragaria Alpina, and are known under the name of Gaillon-Strawberries. Forms are known both with red and with white fruits. The history of their origin is recorded by P. P. A. de

Vilmorin in the Bon Jardinier. He found a single individual bearing this character in a crop of the ordinary Fragaria Alpina. The seeds of this individual gave rise solely to plants without runners: the new sort was absolutely constant from the beginning (p. 192).

"The Cauliflower and Kohl-Rabi were raised from isolated monstrosities of Brassica Oleracea. The Chou de Milan des Vertus likewise arose spontaneously from another sort of cabbage and soon became one of the most popular vegetables in the Paris market." (p. 192.)

Special space is given by De Vries to the Mutations or Elementary Species of the Evening Primrose, Œnathera Lamarckiana: from which he grew 50,000 plants, among which, in the course of a few years, no less than seven Elementary Species appeared.

The sudden appearance in the same manner of the Shirley Variety of Poppy will probably impress the general mind even more, inasmuch as it is now so general a favourite. The Rev. William Wilks, who for thirty years was Vicar of Shirley, found, one June morning in 1880, in the corner of a cornfield just outside the Vicarage garden, a wild red poppy with all four petals narrowly edged with white. "I marked the flower and saved the seed-head," he says. "Next year out of 200 plants three or four had white-edged petals. Then, after years of selection, I got flowers of pure white, pale pink and other colours, with golden instead of black centres. These flowers are now to be found growing all over the world, and are known as the Shirley Poppies."

Prof. Bateson and Prof. de Vries are the two leading investigators in the realm of Variation, and in the mystery of Variation the secret of Evolution lies hidden. Prof. Bateson's view of the meaning of Variation is of the highest interest and importance. The progress of his thought from the year 1894, when he published his "Materials for the Study of Variation," on to his Presidential Address before the British Association (Melbourne) in 1914, and then to his definite condemnation of Darwinian Evolution in an address at Toronto, 1922, is full of interest. His tremendous onslaught upon the whole old theory of Variation in the Presidential Address deserves to be read and closely noted. He declares that he holds to Evolution: but we do not know how it came about and it is doubtful if it is continuing to-day. In our present ignorance, he says, our speculations about origins have no more value than the speculations of the old Alchemists about the origin of the Elements. He believes that scientists began far too soon to form theories, long before the facts had been ascertained. We are as yet too abysmally ignorant to speculate at all: but as facts begin to be ascertained, Variation begins to present itself as "unpacking." Evolution in that case proceeds by the dropping not by the adding of characteristics: its procedure is in such case not from the simple to the complex but from the complex to the simple: and hard as it is, he says, to conceive of the first form of living matter (which he still conceives of as "protoplasm") containing in itself complexity enough to produce all the endless forms of life, yet we "must open our minds to the possibility" that Evolution is from the complex to the simple, and not vice versa as has been heretofore supposed. For example, Sutton's Crimson King Primula gave off a few years ago the Coral King Primula, a salmon-pink variety, by dropping one colour element, and has always bred true. There is no doubt that Variations thus occur, viz. by the dropping of a factor either in whole or in part: but, apart from this Variation by Subtraction, the only other Variation is, he believes, with Lotsy, Variation through crossing. New factors only occur in this latter way. And then he goes on, on pages 20 and 21 of the Address, to enunciate the possibility, which is steadily asserting itself as the view of sound and careful thinkers, viz. that such Evolution as we to-day can trace has taken place *only within the type*:—

> "Distinct types once arisen, no doubt a profusion of the forms called 'species' have been derived from them by simple crossing and subsequent recombination. New species may now be in course of creation by this means, but the limits of the process are obviously narrow. On the other hand, we see no changes in progress around us in the contemporary world which we can imagine likely to culminate in the evolution of forms *distinct in the larger sense*. By intercrossing dogs, jackals and wolves new forms of these types may be found, some of which may be species; but I see no reason to think that from such material a fox could be bred in indefinite time or that dogs could be bred from foxes."

Thus it is admitted that *we do not know* how distinct forms in the larger sense which I have called distinct types, originated; and Bateson, a really eminent investigator as distinct from an exponent of other men's conclusions (even Huxley, for example, called himself "Darwin's bulldog"), declares our ignorance to be too great to admit so much as an evolutionary *theory* of such origins. His own profession that he still holds to the theory of Evolution and still traces all forms of life back to "protoplasm" merely shows the bias of his mind toward the Doctrine of Descent, and is exactly to be described, with apologies for the entirely improper adjective, as a "pious opinion." No mere expression of pious opinion can weigh with us as against the reasons which have led us to discard the Doctrine of Descent as unproven. But *within the type* changes manifold are taking place. Bateson and De Vries both admit that the known changes are taking place there and there only; and De Vries propounds the Mutation Theory, with which, in the sense that factors are sometimes in whole or in part mysteriously and suddenly dropped, Bateson agrees. The position resolves itself into this: that to-day Evolution can only be traced within the type, the occasioning cause being either crossing, or else Mutations which we are not able to explain, but may perhaps describe as the dropping of a factor from the constitution of the parent.[2]

It is a vastly different conclusion from that which had been reached, say, in the eighties of last century. Then it was concluded that the mystery of the Universe had been fathomed and the chief secret of Life laid bare. Science heard herself chanting a mighty Epic, at once History and Poesy, covering all the course of Time. To-day she can only hear herself move haltingly through the pages of one brief chapter of that History. The Mighty Orchestra which filled all space has fallen into silence, and now only the homely shepherd plays for us a melody upon his flute. "The centuries follow one another, perfecting a small wild flower." But this is true music; and the Mighty Orchestra was both pretentious and barbaric in its theme. Or to vary the figure yet again, let us say that fifty years ago a strange glamour fell upon the Scientist, who turned Poet and saw the Universe as in an enchanted dream. To-day, the glamour past and gone, he sees some limited spaces of the Earth with eyes grown clear—and begins to marvel at the dream.

The fact is that, beside Creation, there is not even a theory of Origins to hold the field to-day. There is nothing to even contest the affirmation of a Creation whose typal forms still remain, and are the basis of the multitudinous Varieties existing at the present time. Creationism does not postulate a static world. There is constant movement within Species. Perhaps, as the Theory of Mutation suggests, and the so-called "Neo-Darwinians" are inclined to believe, at a given moment, after periods of quiescence, the entire Species is moved by a force that makes for Variation. Or perhaps there is no such periodicity. It is not a matter of any great moment. Periodic or not, we have no knowledge of any Variations that change the type; and Variation within the type is in no sense contrary to the Creationist position. "My Father worketh even until now, and I work," was the declaration of Jesus Christ. To the Rev. Dr. Erich Wasmann belongs the credit of having perceived years ago the real conclusion to which the mighty outburst of research initiated by Charles Darwin is actually leading. He affirmed that a distinction must

---

2   "The appearance of contemporaneous Variation (Prof. Bateson means thereby the supposed abounding mass of chance fluctuating Variation) proves to be an illusion. Variation from step to step in a series must occur either by the addition or the loss of a factor. Now, of the origination of new forms by loss there seems to me to be fairly clear evidence, but of the *contemporary acquisition* of any new factor I see no satisfactory proof, though I admit there are examples which may be so interpreted." (Bateson, Presidential Address, Brit. Assoc.)

be made between what he called "Systematic Species," i.e. the Species of the ordinary classifications, which are very numerous, and "Natural Species," each of which includes many of the "Systematic Species" within itself: and he maintained that while the Systematic Species have arisen by descent from within the Natural, we are shut up to the theory of the direct Creation of the Natural Species, of which there is at the close of the long investigation no other conceivable origin. When we carefully distinguish the pious opinions of the great leaders of scientific investigation from their definite and very moderate affirmations, we realize that all need to fear the destructive influence of that rigidly limited Evolution, which alone is proven, upon Christian Biblical Theology has passed away. This does not, of course, apply to the contentions of the "camp-followers," such as the writers of schoolbooks and the theologians—who still imagine Darwinism to be the dominant biological theory, and the Doctrine of Descent to be accepted by all intelligent men. These are living in a past generation of scientific thinking, and that makes them dangerous.

But the true leaders realize that the mightiest assault which Research ever made upon the strongholds of ignorance and the greatest outburst of Thought which human history records have reached their halting-place. Admittedly they can proceed no further until an accumulation of Facts offers material for theory and paves the way for understanding. Meantime the outstanding result has been to place upon a strong philosophic basis the Record of Creation—as an ancient account of Origins, capable of furnishing a reasonable explanation, closely akin to that Mutation Theory of the origin of Varieties within the Species which grows in strength today, and holding the field securely because there is no contestant.

10. Byron C. Nelson

(1893–1972)

Nelson, B.C. 1929. More about the origin of species. *The Bible Champion* 35(10):539-540.

We do not want the BIBLE CHAMPION to become a place of argument for those who are of the household of faith, nor a journal for biological discussion; yet a different opinion regarding the origin of new species from that held by Mr. Whitney may be of interest to readers of the CHAMPION.

Mr. Whitney's view is that certain forms may have descended from a common ancestral pair which were in the ark, even though those forms are now unable to cross and produce fertile offspring. He mentions the American coyote, the European wolf and the African jackal as being cousins; by which he means that they have descended from a common pair. On the basis of breeding experiments, this may well be so, for it is known from these experiments that those three forms, together with our domestic wolf-like police and shepherd dogs, are perfectly inter-fertile, and do, when they mate, produce offspring of unimpaired fertility. It is easy to believe that inter-fertile forms have a common ancestry.

We believe that all men the world over, however much they differ, being all perfectly inter-fertile, are descended from a common pair. The same thing holds good in the animal and plant kingdoms.

The fox, however, evidently did not descend from the same ancestors as the dog, but seems to belong to another natural species group; for there are a number of fox varieties existent throughout the world which are fertile toward one another and produce fertile offspring, though they are all totally sterile toward all the members of the dog-wolf-coyote-jackal group.

Mr. Whitney mentions the leopard, lion and tiger as being cousins, and therefore likely to have descended from the same common pair. I am inclined to believe this, adding to the group also the puma, jaguar, ocelot, lynx, and even our own domestic cat. But here we are talking without any breeding data to guide us, for experiments have not been carried on between these cat forms to show us whether they are inter-fertile and produce fertile offspring. Between some of these cats first generation progeny have been born, and among some of the smaller varieties it is known that the first generation of offspring are perfectly fertile. But as to the fertility of hybrids between lions and tigers and tigers and leopards, nothing is known. So, though we may talk about cats as having descended from a common pair, and though we may be of that opinion, based on what evidence there is at present, we really have no such good grounds for thinking so as we have regarding the wolf-dog-jackal group.

In my opinion the bison and the ox, mentioned by Mr. Whitney as having a common ancestry, have not descended from a single pair, but each was represented in the ark separately. Whoever may be interested in the breeding relations of these two species, may consult the *Journal of Heredity*, Vol. V. pp. 189-198; W. F. Hornaday's *The American Natural History*, and the *Report* of the animal Husbandry Division of the Dominon of Canada, Department of Agriculture, for 1894-1897.

From these accounts of breeding experiments carried on for many years between cattle and bison, it is apparent that there is a severe barrier of sterility separating them. Hybrids have been produced, some of which (males) have been fertile. But a combination of the two species has not, and evidently cannot, be secured and maintained. Whatever hybrids have been produced by costly experiments, have reverted back either to the cattle or the bison type in a few generations. This phenomenon of reversion is the usual result when truly distinct species, and not mere varieties, are crossed.

My point is this: We ought to concede to development what is necessary, but not more than is necessary, or is justified on the basis of present scientific evidence. New species—meaning by a species a "group of organisms of marked characteristics in common and freely interbreeding" (Bateson)—are not being formed today. The evolutionists themselves admit that they cannot find it to be so. For example, Professor Louis T. More says: "With all our contriving we have never been able to produce a new species." Bateson says: "New species may be now in the course of creation by this means (i.e., by interbreeding), but the limits are obviously narrow. On the other hand, we see no changes in progress around us in the contemporary world which we can imagine likely to culminate in the evolution of forms distinct in the larger sense. By intercrossing dogs, jackals and wolves new forms of these types are being made, some of which may be called new species. But I see no reason to think that from such material a fox could be bred in indefinite time, or that dogs could be bred from foxes."

In his notable address at Toronto in 1922 Dr. Bateson said that the event for which evolutionists were waiting was to find that a new form of plant or animal has arisen from perfectly fertile parents which was not able to cross back with the parent forms, but showed the same sort of sterility that exists between bison and cattle, or between foxes and dogs, or between horses and asses. He added: "From time to time a record of such an observation is published, but none has yet survived criticism."

I have made it a point to investigate every report published on what Bateson said the evolutionists were waiting for. They are very few. Bateson wrote about an important one in plants about 1914, but in 1922 he found that it could not "survive criticism." Another was reported by Professor Plough, of Amherst, in 1924. It is mentioned by Morgan in his book, *Evolution and Genetics*. I was interested in this case (it concerned fruit-flies), which Professor Plough said he was further investigating. In reply to a letter of mine in which I had asked him what his further investigation had disclosed, he said that what has happened "quite destroys its value for evolutionary theory."

One professor of genetics in an eastern university admitted to me that there were no established cases today of a new species having arisen. New varieties are arising by the hundreds. Most notably has this been discerned in the fruit-fly. But none are new species, because none of them are sterile toward their parent forms. Another biologist and evolutionist, head of a biology department in an eastern university, expressed himself to me very hopelessly regarding men's abiilty ever to find an authentic case of the origin of new species.

If we admit, for example, that domestic cattle (of which there are fifty or sixty distinct known varieties, all inter-fertile) and the bisons have a common ancestry, though they are now sterile toward each other, where are we going to stop admitting things? If the ox and the bison came from a common pair, maybe the musk-ox did too, though that animal is sterile toward both cattle and bisons. The musk-ox is classed by zoologists between sheep and cattle. They hardly know which it resembles most. So, if the musk-ox gets into the group, why not the sheep? Then why not the goats? There are members of the deer genus that are considerably like sheep. Why not let them in also on the common ancestry with the cattle and bisons? Then why not go further and let in the deer and the antelopes, and then the elands, and so on? Where are we to stop admitting a common ancestry for God's creatures, and on what basis are we going to stop where we say we are going to stop?

It may be charged that, if we do not broaden the variety of forms that came from common pairs in the ark of the Noachian deluge, the ark would have been too small to contain all of them. But such a fear arises merely from not really considering the great size of the ark.

For those who are interested in this particular phase of the creation-evolution problem, I may say that some time this coming winter a third edition of my book, *After its Kind*, will be published, and will contain two large appendices on "mutations" and "natural species," which will deal very fully with the matters I have here been discussing. The publication will be announced in the CHAMPION, so that those who are interested in these important problems may read what is said in those appendices.

11. Dudley Joseph Whitney

(1883–1964)

Whitney, D.J. 1929. The origin of species. *The Bible Champion* 35(9): 475-479.

Darwin's great bid for fame was his theory about the origin of species. First he demonstrated that there had been splitting up of species: that Galapagos turtles, for example, were a different species from turtles elsewhere, though they evidently had the same ultimate ancestors. Then he advanced his theory of how the changes in species came about. He believed, and most of the world of science has long believed, that Darwin explained how it was that many species of owls came from one owl species; how many species of clovers came from one species of clover; how many species of monkeys came from one original monkey species. The leading principles of his theory were set forth in the preceding article.

Now, Darwin was wrong in his explanation. Almost the whole world of science is agreed about that; but they are hopelessly at sea in deciding how species changed. They agree that species have changed (and they wrongly call that evolution), but they do not know and cannot think *how* they changed.

As a creationist, taking the Bible simply and directly for what it says, I am now going to present a theory for the origin of species which will stand the test of science better, I assert, than any other theory that can be presented. If the biologists are really anxious to have a theory for the origin of species which will stand analysis, I ask them to consider what follows.

In explaining my own theory, it will help us if we are able to see why Darwin's theory fails. His theory, as has been explained, is that small variations are continually occurring with plants and animals, and those variations which help the plants and animals to survive more effectively will endure and become permanent, so that, for example, some general rabbit species became the ancestor of both jack rabbits and cottontails.

If a person will read *Evolution, the Way of Man*, by Vernon Kellogg, he will see several reasons why Darwin's theory does not work. Changes enough to make new species never came little by little, as Darwin's theory assumes; if they came *naturally*, they came suddenly by mutations. This is simply to say that, if long-legged, lanky jack rabbits descended from ordinary rabbits, the descent was sudden, perhaps, in one generation, just as if the seed of a wild field daisy should grow into a giant Shasta daisy all at once. The thing that I want to discuss is the possibility of these sudden changes, and the possibility of these changes making new species. If my audience is not an audience of scientists, yet I hope that they can follow the line of thought by the use of ordinary common sense and simple observations of nature.

Mutations, or notable changes from parent to offspring, are not at all uncommon. As a student of botany at college, I ran across several myself in one term with wild plants, and I have seen them frequently since. A flower with six petals, for example, may produce a seed from which a plant will grow whose flowers will have ten, or twelve, or twenty, petals. A rabbit in a litter might possibly have ears like a squirrel, or black fur instead of grey, or something of the sort. It is not at all uncommon for calves to be born with no more horn in their heredity than there is in a colt.

Our problem is to figure how new species could develop through such mutations. Readers must understand the very important fact that mutations nowadays do not make new species. Did they ever do so? I say that they did, and in due time will explain how I think this came about.

We will go back to the rabbits again to illustrate the possible origin of species. As I said, Darwin thought that the change from ordinary rabbit to jack rabbit occurred little by little, generation after generation, and the change to short-legged, compact-bodied cottontails came the same way. Let us see how it would be if, perchance, in a litter of baby rabbits (the parents being built like common domestic rabbits), there should be a baby which should be a mutant and grow up to be a typical jack rabbit. The question is: would a thing like that cause jack rabbits to originate? This is supposing that the only rabbits on earth up to that time were just common, average rabbits. No! The prospects for the origin of a new rabbit species, a jack rabbit species, through an event like that would be exceedingly remote, and there are reasons why.

In the first place, in a state of nature the struggle for existence is extreme. The average wild animal which reaches maturity leaves only two offspring to survive and to reach maturity, and each of those has only half his blood. The ordinary plant produces only one seed which produces a mature plant. This is, speaking about averages. A rabbit may, it is true, be the parent of half a hundred rabbits before it perishes, few of which will live to maturity, and a plant may produce from a thousand to several million seeds, yet *as an average thing* plants and animals leave only two offspring, each with half its blood, to survive and produce progeny in their turn. If the average were more than this, one can see very readily that such plant and animal species would soon overrun the earth.

Now, our imaginary jack rabbit might survive all right, particularly if his longer legs and greater speed helped him to outrun his enemies, but there would be two almost insurmountable obstacles to prevent his descendants from surviving so as to develop a jack rabbit species.

The first would be the difficulty in having the right kind of a mate. It would be a marvel if he found a lady jack rabbit to mate with, since all the rabbits on earth up to his time were just average rabbits. It would be rather remarkable if he happened to mate with that individual if she were in existence, since so many other rabbits of the ordinary kind were being produced. Almost inevitably he would mate with an ordinary rabbit, and his progeny therefore would be mostly ordinary rabbits too. If, in spite of everything, several second generation jack rabbits survived, they also would in the ordinary course of events mate with average rabbits and their progeny therefore would almost inevitably be just ordinary rabbits.

Note this point particularly, therefore, for it has much bearing on what comes later: If, in a state of nature, an individual appears much different from its parents, one which under favorable circumstances, could be the ancestor of a new species, the mating of that individual will almost inevitably be with ordinary individuals so that its differences from the parent type will be overcome, and very few of his offspring would be likely to survive.

There is just one chance, practically speaking, for its descendants to keep distinct from the ancestral type, and that is, that other individuals of its type are produced from the same parent and that it mates with one of those individuals. That, however, is in-breeding, which is usually weakening, so it cannot help much.

And then, of course, as was pointed out earlier, the struggle for existence is so severe that in nature very few individuals survive, in comparison with the animals born or seeds produced. The fact of the matter is that, although the occurrence of these mutations is universally admitted by biologists, they agree that they do not provide a cause for the origin of new species any better than the cause which Darwin suggested.

And yet, after all is said and done, *species have changed.* At least, I believe so, and I believe that some extremely great changes have occurred. The American coyote is certainly a cousin to the European wolf and the African jackal; the bison is certainly a cousin to the ox; the American panther is certainly a cousin of the leopard, and the leopard is a cousin of both the lion and the tiger. Unless I am badly mistaken the American turkey is nothing more or less than the equivalent of the Asiatic peacock, as little as they seem alike at first glance. How did the changes take place? The evolutionists say they occurred. I agree that they occurred; yet the evolutionists have no explanation as to how such things took place that will even begin to suit them.

This is my theory. I outlined it several years ago in the BIBLE CHAMPION in connection with the origin of human races without attempting to point out its bearing upon the origin of distinct species. Species split up and divided and subdivided when there were very few individuals of any kind living. Instead of a struggle for existence when few animals survived, numbers multiplied perhaps rapidly, perhaps slowly. Instead of their being a multitude of mates to chose from, brother and sister matings of necessity occurred, and there was in-and-in breeding for generation after generation, or until numbers were abundant once more.

Suppose, now, for example, that in all the earth there was but one rabbit pair, and the rabbits multiplied and spread out, and separated as they did so. In the second generation there would be brother and sister matings, and as the animals migrated and became separate from other pairs, brother and sister matings would occur in the third generation, and in the fourth generation and so on until rabbits were numerous all over and a great choice of mates was possible. Suppose also that environment, or food and climate was very much different from what the ancestors of the rabbits had been accustomed to. That would have a tendency to cause variation and the less fit animals would not thrive, while the more fit ones would. Such a thing would naturally cause a decided difference in rabbits in different parts of the world, or in foxes, or deer, or bears, or owls, or ducks.

The situation, in brief, is this: there has been much change of species which we are trying to account for. Darwin tried and failed. No one else has tried and succeeded very well, yet there has been change of species. Variation between parent and offspring is the starting point. How do we get that in the first place?

The experience of plant and animal breeders helps us there. It is what gave me my clue. Few things will cause variation (or mutations) as much as the mating of individuals which are closely related, and that will frequently do it.

Secondly, nothing in the world will cause such mutations to become *intensified and made permanent* but continued mating with related individuals which also have like nature. However, *in nature as it is now* there is not very much mating of closely related individuals, and if there is, it is not continued into the second and third generation. It is done in plant and animal breeding, and new and permanent varieties develop from it, but it does not occur in nature.

Suppose now–and see how well this fits in with Genesis–that all rabbits were wiped out of existence but one pair and that their descendants were to replenish the earth with rabbits. There would be in-breeding and in-breeding, something to stimulate variation, something to intensify it after it had occurred and to make it permanent.

Once, however, rabbits again became abundant, mating would no longer be with near relatives; and, anyway, there would be a big choice of mates, and variation in one direction would tend to offset variation in another: present-day conditions would be developed.

Yet we hear this argument for fixity of species presented *with the idea that it is defending Genesis*: "New species do not originate now; therefore we ought not to believe that they ever did."

No, they do not originate now ([1]perhaps they do even at that), but look at the difference in conditions now and once before: once (after the Deluge) there was a totally different kind of an earth from what there was before the Deluge and only a few animals to replenish it. There was in-and-in-and-in-breeding for generations then, which would give a chance to originate new species; but nothing like that exists now, save in the hands of the plant or animal breeder.

In an article on the "Origin of Human Races" several years ago in the BIBLE CHAMPION I went into the method of developing permanent variation in far more detail than I have given here, and if any person cannot follow the line of reasoning now and can get that article I hope he will do so.

Let me emphasize the fact that this theory for the origin of species is not a wild fancy nor some unscientific speculation by a man who knows no science. I venture to say that practically all biologists of standing will agree that there is much of value in it, even if they will not agree that it is a *sufficient* theory, and I will say a word or so about that later.

It was submitted to one of the best known educators and scientists in America. His reply (as Doctor Keyser has said in his letter) was:

"Your hypothesis with regard to isolation is, I think, quite sound. In fact, I have lately published an article showing that isolation is a primary factor in the origin of species. [Exactly what I am saying.–D. J. W.] Species

---

[1] I am strongly of the opinion that what are in effect new species originate now naturally among injurious insects. Every few years some insect which had before been harmless, living upon wild vegetation, takes to some cultivated crop, usually of a kind related to the wild host plant, and becomes a serious pest. For the most part the insect and cultivated plant had been in proximity for years; then suddenly, or, rather, within the span of three or four years, the insect becomes a serious pest. It seems evident that this is not because the normal wild insects all change, but because one or two insects vary somewhat, and go over to the cultivated plant, their descendants in-breed and become still more adapted to the cultivated plant and soon are at home on it. In fumigation for scale insects in California, notably with the red scale, there are strains of scales which are very gas resistant. Certainly those are descended from closely related individuals. In fact, resistance to fumigation has developed greatly in scale insects. The place to find how species have changed in the past, as demonstrated particularly by the geographical distribution of species, is not with the large, well known animals, like wolves and deer or rabbits, but with the lower orders of animals, like insects and snails. Fresh water fishes also provide a fine lot of examples.

originate in some degree of separation, and there is no species that does not have geography in its history somewhere."

Readers can therefore see that this is good science which I have been presenting. I might add that my Fundamentalism and absence from high position with some university or other public institution seem to have kept editors of scientific papers from publishing this theory when I presented it to them.

Now, there is something immensely amusing about all this. The biologists (or we can say, the evolutionists) have been frantic with eagerness to discover some way to account for the origin of species. This accounts for it. Dr.— says it is good. He is one of the best known and most highly respected scientists in America, and one of the oldest. He has published a paper to that effect himself.

Do the evolutionists now throw their hats in the air and shout, "Eureka, we have found the *modus operandi* of evolution at last"? No; you can be very sure that they don't. If they accept this theory of the origin of species, it will be with a very glum face. *That theory of the origin of species means the ruin of their theory of earth history, and a vindication of Genesis.* Bible defenders are the ones to shout aloud! The origin of species which works is the origin of species of Genesis! Three cheers and a tiger.

I ask again, therefore, Shall we, as Fundamentalists, fight the idea of species change? Shall we insist upon the fixity of species? No! a thousand times, No! We will proclaim the fact that species *have* changed, and have changed in a way that fits Genesis admirably, and fits evolutionary geology not at all.

See here how the situation rests. The evolutionists assert that the earth is millions upon millions of years old and that plants and animals have existed for long ages.

At all times therefore, practically speaking, the earth would be well supplied with every kind of plant and animal that there was room and food for. In fact, it is one of the fundamentals of Darwin's reasoning, and of all evolutionary reasoning, that reproduction is far greater than the survival; that *the individuals of any species are so numerous that comparatively few can survive.* Since this is so, how then, according to evolutionary geology, would there be in-breeding, and so the development of new species? It would not happen.

Oh! it might happen if the enemies were so numerous that few animals of a kind could survive, but that surely would be an unsatisfactory position for the development of a new and successful species.

Some disease might come and destroy all individuals but two or three; but animals so susceptible that all but a few would be destroyed by disease would seem to be poor material for a new species either.

Some great deluge or other earth-wrecking catastrophe might come along and destroy all but a very few. Ah, yes! But will the evolutionists enjoy that solution? Will they feel overjoyed that they have found something to replace Darwin's origin of species? The lack of enthusiasm which has greeted this theory, which not I alone, but one of the great scientists of America, has given to the public, is a sufficient answer.

And now I have covered a very great theme with a very few words, and left unsaid pages upon pages of details that might prove instructive to biologists. It is to be hoped that the course of reasoning is clear to those readers who are particularly interested in the whole problem of the history of creation.

It is always good in a matter like this to give a summary, to show what the discussion all amounts to. In this case the significance ought to be clear: There has been much species change. The idea of species change has been fought on the supposition that it was anti-Genesis; yet as science advances, it is pro-Genesis and anti-evolution.

There is just one way to account for the origin of species: at the time of the origin of those species there must have been very few individuals of the parent stock, so that there was much in-breeding. Probably there was a radical change of environment also. These things would not occur, for all we can see, in a long drawn out series of geologic ages; they could occur in the kind of earth history described in Genesis. Genesis wins again; Genesis wins every time against evolution when the evidence is examined fairly and well.

I have discussed this matter of species change on a naturalistic basis, as I would discuss it before a gathering of scientists. Actually I cannot believe that the changes occurred by chance alone, merely as the normal result of in-breeding and change of environment after the Deluge. As I have said before in these columns, since God guides the flight of the sparrow, He must have guided the course of heredity of plants and animals from the beginning of creation to the present. Still, if the problem is discussed from a naturalistic standpoint, this theory of the origin of species seems to be the only one that will stand any kind of inspection.

I have found both in biology and geology many hard, hard problems that seem to be in opposition to the Genesis account, but for every one of those that I have found I have found six equally hard problems in opposition to anti-Genesis or evolution. Time and time again, in this place and that place, in features which were supposedly opposed to Genesis, I have found that the evidence actually pointed in just the other direction and sustained Genesis.

I will cite just one of these in closing. Readers may remember the rather common argument of certain noted evolutionists that the Fundamentalists have the problem of accounting for lots of species change quickly and so need more evolution than the evolutionists. For instance, men changed from one parent stock to black and yellow and brown and ruddy (white) in only a few hundred years, while the evolutionists have tens of thousands of years to make the change. This is one of H. H. Newman's favorite arguments.

All right, Sir, with the greatest joy we will join issue with you on that basis. You try to get the changes to black and yellow and brown and white and red in tens of thousands of years by Darwinism (which does not work) or in any other way that does not work. You will fail. Come now, see if you won't fail. Tell how it is done.

Then turn to the method of isolation: where there are very few individuals to work with, one man and his three sons and their wives. Have those families separate, and the families of the second generation and the third generation separate. In brief, have the change in color occur by the marriage of very close relatives for several generations. Then you will have a way to account for the origin of human races which will have some standing in biology, and it will occur *quickly*. In other words, Genesis does it–it accounts for the change. When the evolutionists pointed to the Fundamentalist's belief in a quick change in heredity with a sneer, the sneer ought to have been directed to old-line theories of evolution. The triumph is that of Genesis.

I stand ready to face the problem of evolution on every point that the evolutionists will bring up. I hereby assert that they cannot bring forward one single argument for real evolution but I will point out a serious fallacy in it that every honest, clear-thinking scientist ought to see by a little careful inspection. The farther along true science goes, the better Genesis and the rest of the Bible are sustained.

12. Douglas Dewar

(1875–1957)

Dewar, D. 1931. *Difficulties of the Evolution Theory.* Edward Arnold and Company, London. Our extract is from Chapter II: The Changes in Organisms Effected by Breeders, pp. 8-13.

Breeders, by taking advantage of the phenomena of variation and heredity, have produced the various races of domesticated animals and cultivated plants.

Darwin made the results of breeding operations one of the mainstays of his theory. He pointed out that some of our domestic breeds differ from the wild form to such an extent that, if met with in a state of nature, they would be considered new species, or, in a few cases, new genera. Of pigeons he wrote (*Origin of Species,* 6th ed., p. 17): "I do not believe that any ornithologist would place the English carrier, the short-faced tumbler, the runt, the barb, the pouter and the fantail in the same genus." Had Darwin been content to apply his theory of evolution to the origin of new species and genera, the operations of breeders would have afforded strong experimental evidence of its correctness.

These operations, however, seem to tell against the evolution theory, because breeders, although they have been at work for hundreds of years, have not yet been able to produce a new breed which can possibly be deemed to belong to a new family.

All the breeds derived from a common stock, no matter how much they differ from one another in appearance, are fertile when bred *inter se,* and all clearly bear the stamp of their ancestral form; all the breeds of pigeons are clearly pigeons, all those of horses plainly horses, all those of dogs undeniably dogs. The animals themselves appreciate this; a puppy of any breed at once recognizes an individual of any other breed of dog as one of his own kind.

That breeders have not been able to produce a breed which does not present every one of the features that characterize the zoological family to which it belongs, seems to indicate that the extent to which any organism can be changed by degrees is strictly limited.

The question naturally arises: As all the efforts of breeders have resulted only in minor changes in animals and plants, is it likely that natural selection or any other natural force can effect greater changes?

To this question three answers have been given by evolutionists. The first is: "Yes. The breeder has been at work for only a few centuries, while the forces that bring about evolution have been operating for many millions of years. It stands to reason that the breeder in so short a time cannot accomplish that which has been effected by natural causes since living matter originated."

This would be an effective reply, but for the fact that *the breeder*, no matter on what animal or plant he experiments, *after he has effected a number of minor changes in any given direction, is suddenly brought to a standstill*; in a comparatively short time he reaches a stage at which he cannot accomplish more, no matter how much he try.

It may safely be asserted that none of the existing breeds of animals or plants will ever undergo extensive developments in the directions in which they have already been changed; any changes made in them will be in other directions.

The fact that breeders are invariably brought to a standstill, no matter on what animal or plant they operate, or in what direction, is fatal to the evolution theory as enunciated by Darwin and developed by his successors, unless it can be explained away.

The second and third of the answers to the question asked above are ingenious attempts at this.

The second answer—that of de Vries and the other mutationists—is: the breeder has been unable to achieve the same results as nature, because evolution—the gradual transformation of organisms—is the result of the accumulation, not of minute variations, but of mutations or saltations that occur only periodically. During the comparatively short time at which breeders have been at work no big mutation has arisen in any of the organisms on which they have been operating. In support of this view is the fact that "sports" or mutations do occasionally crop up in animals and plants; when these occur breeders sometimes make use of them. The turnspit dog, the ancon sheep, blue and yellow budgerigars and the Shirley poppy are all breeds that were produced suddenly as the result of a sport or mutation.

This answer is no more satisfactory than the first, because, although some "sports" differ considerably from the normal type, no sport is known that differs fundamentally in any feature from the normal type. A shortening of the limbs, or a change in colour of the plumage, even though considerable, is but a superficial change, one of degree, not of kind.

Thus, the obvious rejoinder to this explanation is: "Until a sport appears differing fundamentally from the type, the theory that evolution is the result of the accumulation of mutations is pure hypothesis. Moreover, a sport differing fundamentally from its type would appear to be a special creation."

The third answer to the question is more subtle than either of the others, although it is at least as old as Epicurus. It is that the breeder has failed where nature has succeeded, because he has been operating on unsuitable material, namely on species the evolutionary tendencies or powers of which are nearly exhausted.

The evolution of those who give this answer is very different from the evolution of Darwin, Haeckel and other biologists of the last century. The evolution of the former is change by fits and starts, evolutionary outbursts after long periods of stagnation; that of the latter is slow, stately, ceaseless change.

This modern view of evolution is thus set forth by L. Cuénot [*L'Adaptation* (1925), p. 374]:

> "We are then led to believe that the evolutionary outburst (*élan evolutif*) has been the appanage of a series of rare forms, of small range, which have disappeared without leaving relics, after having exhausted their potentiality of variation in giving rise to the ancestors of the great natural groups; the ramification of the mammalian tree, to continue the simile, seems to have been complete by the middle of the Tertiary, the axis and petioles have dried up irrevocably; only a certain number of leaves are still green and fully alive, many others have dried up for ever. The green leaves are still capable of evolution and producing secondary leaflets, but no new group can appear, the evolutionary sap no longer circulates. The best proof of this is that new families have not been formed for millions of years (the estimate of the duration of the Tertiary period as three millions is too low); all existing mammals belong to specialized groups, from which it is inconceivable that they should emerge. The same applies to many other orders of the animal kingdom: incontestably the evolution of reptiles, birds, amphibians, fishes, echinoderms, molluscs, crustaceans, sponges has completely finished; they may still produce species and new genera, but they have not within them undifferentiated material capable of evolving into unexpected forms and new mechanisms; they exhausted their evolutionary creative potentialities during the Secondary and Tertiary periods.
>
> I do not mean by this that evolution has definitely ended on the earth, and that we know all the possible formulæ of life... I readily believe that there is still a reserve capable of giving rise to new beings quite unlike any that existed formerly, or exist to-day. I look for these in microscopic families of uncertain affinity, disregarded by almost all zoological treatises, marine or freshwater organisms such as the Echiuroidea, Tardigrades,

Dinoflagellates, Archiannelids, Rhodope, terrestrial forms such as the Myrientomata."

The above passage is a masterpiece. Darwin himself could not have done better. Its full significance may perhaps not be fully appreciated by some readers until after they have perused this book.

The hypothesis of Cuénot is designed to meet most of the serious objections to the evolution doctrine: the meagre results obtained by breeders, the absence of nascent organs and structures in animals, the lack of fossils testifying to the gradual origin of peculiar types, and the fact that the animals on oceanic islands all belong to families that occur on the mainland and the plants to mainland natural orders.

There is, however, not an iota of positive evidence in support of this hypothesis and Cuénot makes no attempt to point to any natural forces capable of bringing about this strange kind of evolution.

A theory of this nature cannot be disproved, but there is evidence which casts strong suspicion on it.

According to the hypothesis, the older the group, i.e. the longer it has lived on the earth, the more complete should be the drying up of its evolutionary sap. Now, the fishes appear on the Earth in the Silurian, while mammals first occur in the Trias, in other words, fishes have existed on the earth fully twice as long as mammals. As, according to Cuénot, the evolutionary sap has dried up in the mammals to such an extent that the breeder cannot produce a new genus of mammals, he ought not to be able to effect any appreciable change in the far more ancient fish. As a matter of fact, fish appear to be quite as plastic as mammals and birds. The only species of fish on which the breeder has operated extensively is the Crucian Carp of Asia; as the result of these operations all the breeds of goldfish have been produced. These differ from one another and from the ancestral form quite as markedly as do the breeds of dogs and pigeons. The retriever, spaniel, greyhound, St. Bernard, foxhound, dachshund, toy terrier and Dalmatian do not differ one from the other more than do the following breeds of goldfish: telescope, nymph, fantail, celestial, fringe-tail, lion-head, veil-tail, oranda and comet.

If Professor Cuénot wishes to establish his hypothesis he should breed a new family from one of the organisms in which he supposes the evolutionary sap still to flow. Similarly, the mutationists should breed a new family by selecting suitable mutations.

Until one or the other effects this, the proper course is, provisionally at any rate, to put a simple rather than a far-fetched interpretation on the results of breeding operations. Breeders and fanciers should be regarded as witnesses hostile to evolution.

13. George McCready Price

(1870–1963)

Price, G.M. 1938. Nature's two hundred families. *Signs of the Times* 65(37):11, 14-15.

In previous studies of this series, we have considered some very important facts and principles which must serve as the foundation for the answer to this question. Only a very brief summary of these facts can be given here by way of introduction.

We have found that life must have been created. One of the most firmly established of all scientific facts is that living things cannot now be produced from the nonliving. Neither in nature nor by any hocus-pocus or clever manipulation in the laboratory can a living plant or animal be produced. This great truth is known as the law of biogenesis. And it becomes the absolutely secure foundation on which we may reason regarding the way in which living things must have come into existence. The opposite idea, known as spontaneous generation, is regarded by all men with scientific training as utterly impossible.

Yet there is no entity called life; that is, we know nothing of life in the abstract. We know only living things. Hence, it is in order for us to ask ourselves what kinds of living things must have been made in the beginning?

In our previous studies we have found that there is no evidence of transformism (commonly called evolution), or the change of one kind of life over into another. Not only do the plants and animals around us breed true to type, but we have found that the bacteria and protozoa also breed true for astonishingly long periods of time. If these microscopic forms of life did not thus breed true, there could be no such thing as a "pure culture," and no science of bacteriology.

But again we ask, What kinds of life must have been created in the beginning?

Scientists have divided the animals into certain large groups which they call the *phyla*. The number of these groups is variously given as from eight or ten up to twenty, Dr. Austin H. Clark of the Smithsonian Institution favoring the latter number. Each phylum is divided into a certain number of *classes*; the phylum Chordata, which includes the fishes and the mammals and all the vertebrates, being divided into the Amphibia, Reptilia, Mammalia, and various others. Each of these classes is again divided into one or more *orders*; the Mammalia including the Carnivora, Rodentia, the Proboscidea, the Primates, and many others. The orders are still further subdivided into *families*, the families into *genera*, and the genera into *species*. Thus the term "species" is applied to the smallest unit or group of animals to which definite characteristics can be assigned.

The Families' Exclusiveness

Now it is evident that all these groups–the phyla, the classes, and all the rest of them, even the genera and the species–*are not entities*, they are mere idealized collections or abstractions. They have no existence whatever except as we try to imagine a number of individual organisms to be separated from all others and grouped together. The only things that have objective reality are the *individual organisms*. It is evident that in any system of clear thinking we must suppose that it would be some of these individual organisms which were created in the beginning, and that from these primal specimens their descendants have been produced by what we call the natural processes of reproduction.

Now the dozen or more *phyla* have been named as they are by scientists because they represent creatures so absolutely different or distinct from one another that not even the evolutionists can imagine how one phylum could have grown or become transformed into another. Not even the wildest imaginings of anyone can make it reasonable that one of these phyla could be changed into another.

But this very same principle is true also with regard to the *classes*, and even the *orders*. For example, we have no scientific knowledge of how the vertebrates could have originated from any of the nonvertebrates. Some evolutionists have declared that the class Aves (birds) may somehow have originated from the reptiles. But this is quite incredible and without any scientific evidence in its support. As proof of this statement we have the disagreements among evolutionists regarding the details; for no two of them can agree as to how or from what type of reptiles the birds were evolved.

Similarly, it is safe to say that there is no scientific evidence to show that the placental mammals have sprung from the marsupials or the monotremes. Dr. Austin H. Clark, the eminent zoologist, goes much further than this. He takes into consideration the entire record of the fossils, as well as the facts known regarding the modern living types; and he says that the whales and the seals have always been distinct, and we do not know of any possible way by which one of these groups could have developed into the other. He says: "Just as whales were always whales, seals were always seals. No intergrades between the seals and other mammals are known."

The fact that no intermediate types are known, either in the living or in the fossil form, is the foundation for these statements by Dr. Clark. But he goes on to make a similar statement about some of the ordinary mammals, as follows:

"Among the more familiar mammals, the cat and the dog lines are always separate. No forms intermediate between cats and their relatives and dogs and their relatives are known, even though both cats and dogs are collateral members, together with the seals, of the Carnivora."–"*The New Evolution,*" page 181; 1930.

We thus arrive at the very crux of the whole problem of evolution. We have the great *families*, which have been divided into *genera* and *species*. The concept of species is a very confusing one; and it was largely on this confusion that Charles Darwin seemed to make out a plausible case for his theory of transformism. Within our modern knowledge, either from wild nature or from breeding experiments, we may rightly conclude that new kinds which we might properly call *new species* have arisen within what may be termed scientific observation. A few instances are known where what are called distinct *genera* have been crossed with other distinct genera. Thus it is not safe to say that "new species" have not arisen under scientific observation in modern times. Here is where evolutionists have confused the issue. But we may admit that many new types have arisen within such a group as a *genus*, or may even admit that the genera themselves prove to be cross-fertile with one another, without any danger of extending this process further. We may admit that many changes have come about *within the family*, that families have split up and have produced many various forms, without being obliged to admit that this process of splitting or differentiation has gone any further than this.

For there is absolutely no shred of scientific evidence to indicate that one of the great *families* of animals has been produced from any other family. As Clark remarks above, the cats (Felidae) and the dogs (Canidae) have always been distinct, and there are no intermediates or intergrades between them. The cats include such well-known animals as the lion, the tiger, the leopard, etc., there being several dozen of these cats scattered over the world. Similarly, the dogs include not only our domestic types, but also the wolves and the jackals, the foxes, and some extinct forms. Now while we may readily admit that all the cats have sprung from one original stock, and perhaps all the dogs are similarly related by descent, yet it is only a matter of common sense and strict science to say that there is absolutely no proof whatever that the dogs and the cats have had a common origin.

It seems to me that a great simplicity is thus introduced into our study of nature, for the *families* become the units of living things; and while we may admit any reasonable evidence of change *within the family*, yet we are on solid scientific ground if we say that these families have remained constant down through all the centuries and have never changed or become transformed into different families. In passing it may be remarked that there are only about 113 living families of mammals in the world today, with about 129 that are regarded as extinct, according to one of the latest systems of classification. Thus we have a comparatively small number of absolute units with which we would have to deal, when we consider the problem of the kinds which were originally created. Similar principles would prevail throughout the animal kingdom; and by taking the family as the unit of stability, and its subdivisions as having come about by splitting or differentiation, we can arrive at an understanding of nature that is in full harmony with what is revealed in the Bible.

Also by regarding the family as the immutable unit from which the genera and species have been produced by splitting or subdivision, we greatly simplify the problem of how Noah could have preserved samples of all the animals in the ark. Instead of many thousands of kinds, he would have been obliged to care for only one or two hundred kinds; and the same principle would apply to all the other animals that he was called upon to provide for, as the record is given in Genesis.

Clark also gives the weight of his scientific authority to the statement that man cannot be proved to be related in any way to the apes. He declares:

"Man is not an ape, and in spite of the similarity between them there is not the slightest evidence that man is descended from an ape."– Page 224.

Similarly he declares:

"In the light of all the evidence available at the present time, there is no justification in assuming that such a thing as a 'missing link' ever existed, or indeed could ever have existed."–Pages 226, 227.

It is only fair to state in this connection that Clark holds to something that he calls a theory of evolution, in spite of the admissions just made. He does this because he accepts at face value the common teachings of the geologists; but in the light of what has been said in previous numbers of this series of articles, as well as in my published books on geology, it is impossible for me to have any confidence in these geological theories. If we accept the Flood as the cause of the geological changes, we shall have no trouble in believing the record in Genesis that a great variety of plants and animals was originally created and that from these primal kinds the types with which we are acquainted have sprung by what we term natural processes of reproduction.

The believers in the record of a literal creation ought to take new courage. They have too long been cowed and browbeaten by the noisy claims of the evolutionists. The latter have long claimed to have scientific facts on their side. But in the light of what we now know, it is exactly the other way around. The doctrine of an original creation is now seen to be supported by an abundance of well-attested facts, all of which as we now know them support this idea of a literal creation in the beginning. And great numbers of scientific facts are positively against the theory of transformism, or what is usually termed evolution.

Here we may rest the case for the present. There is an abundance of evidence that the record in the Bible is true. This evidence is now available for all those who desire to inform themselves; and in the light of the situation in the world today, it would seem important for all believers in the Bible to make themselves familiar with these scientific facts.

The publishers of the SIGNS OF THE TIMES will be glad to supply literature dealing with this subject to any who desire it.

14. Harold W. Clark

(1891–1986)

Clark, H.W. 1940. *Genes and Genesis*. Pacific Press Publishing Association, Mountain View, California. Our extract is from Chapter Four: Confused Species, pp. 85-106.

Hybridization, or crossbreeding, is a prolific source of new kinds of plants and animals. Breeders use this method in order to bring about new combinations of hereditary qualities that have not been known before. In spite of the common prevalence of the custom, the exact degree to which crossing may occur is still a matter of controversy. Recent studies have thrown light on the question, and a host of interesting facts are now available for consideration. The evidence which is accumulating seems to connect the problem directly with that of genes and chromosome numbers.

One of the earliest known examples of the influence of chromosome numbers on hereditary characters was that of Oenothera, the common evening primrose. This plant normally has fourteen chromosomes—seven pairs. In the reduction to the haploid number, the division may be uneven, one daughter cell receiving six and the other eight. A plant developing its pollen or ovule with six chromosomes would, if crossed with the normal seven, produce a plant with thirteen chromosomes. The latter case has actually been observed, and it differs markedly from the normal plant in form of leaf, habit of growth, and other characters. Another variant has been observed with twenty-eight chromosomes, evidently produced by the failure of the chromosomes to divide properly, thus doubling the number at the time of fertilization. Many structural features of this variant are exaggerated, such as size, height, and leaf thickness.

One of the most interesting examples of the origin of new groups with varying chromosome number is that of *Biscutella laevigata*, a member of the mustard family distributed over central Europe. Some races have thirty-six chromosomes, while others have eighteen. The races with eighteen chromosomes are confined to the valleys of the Rhine, Elbe, Oder, Danube, and some of their tributaries. The races with thirty-six chromosomes are widely and continuously distributed over the mountains, including the Alps, Carpathians, the mountains of Italy, and the northern part of the Balkans. The mountain race of *Biscutella* must be considered as having been produced from the original valley form by the doubling of the chromosome number. Subsequently this new race spread over the whole mountain region of central Europe.

Datura, or Jimson weed, has been observed to throw variants with unusual chromosome numbers in the same way as the evening primrose. Numbers ranging from sixteen to thirty chromosomes have been found. Wheat is known to fall into three classes, einkorn, hard, and soft wheat, with fourteen, twenty-eight, and forty-two chromosomes respectively. These go back to prehistoric times, and it is highly probable that they have been produced by variations on the original number fourteen.

Many species of roses, which are reckoned as true species in the strict Linnaean sense, have chromosomes in multiples of seven. The same is true of Rubus, or blackberries, and Crataegus, or hawthorn.

In chrysanthemums, Rumex (sorrel), and roses, species are found to have $2n$, $4n$, $6n$, and $8n$, which could come from multiplying the chromosome number evenly, and some have $3n$ and $5n$ chromosomes. Here a $2n$ would have to unite with an n, or normal haploid, to produce the $3n$. The $5n$ would likely be produced by the union of the triploid $3n$ with the diploid $2n$. Chrysanthemum chromosomes are multiples of nine, and forty species of Senecio are known whose chromosomes are in multiples of ten.

In New England over twenty hybrid species of Rubus are recognized, and it is generally supposed that most Rubus species are of hybrid origin. These vary from nearly complete interfertility to nearly complete intersterility. Roses, Crataegus, Datura, Oenothera, fruit flies, and potato beetles seem to be in the same situation. Bananas, pineapples, oats, and dahlias have been found to have varying chromosome numbers which might indicate similar conditions in these species.

In modern genetics the status of a hybrid is established by the presence of different genes rather than by the classification of the parents. Every individual produces germ cells with many different hereditary characters carried in the genes. Similar combinations of these in the offspring will produce like characters. If therefore the genes in the offspring were different from both parents, a hybrid condition would be recognized. The degree of difference varies widely in different cases. It may involve a few or many genes. If few were involved, the offspring would not appear noticeably different from the common stock. If many were involved, the hybrid conditions would be easily recognized among them.

This situation has a definite bearing on the question of fertility. The chromosomes in many interspecific and even in some intergeneric hybrids may combine readily if they have groups of similar genes. In such cases fertility would not be impaired in any appreciable degree. As a rule, the difficulty of obtaining a fertile hybrid increases with the numerical and qualitative differences in the chromosomes. For example, common corn with ten chromosome pairs crosses easily with Mexican corn, which has the same number. Two moths, A and B, both with a chromosome number of twenty-nine, cross readily and produce fertile offspring. Some cases are known, however, where this does not hold true. Two peas, *Pisum humile* and *P. sativum*, both with seven chromosomes, produce a high degree of sterility in the offspring.

Peculiar effects are produced when the chromosome numbers are different. *Viola arrensis* with seventeen chromosomes may be crossed with *V. tricolor*, having thirteen. In the first generation irregular forms are produced, some of which are sterile. In the second generation a number of new forms are produced, which are constant and fertile. Drosera (sundew) with ten and twenty chromosomes have been crossed, producing a hybrid with thirty. A twenty-four chromosome crepis (cress) has been produced by crossing *Crepis setosa*, having four chromosomes, with *C. biennis*, having twenty. In poppies forty-two chromosomes were obtained by crossing a seven chromosome species with one of thirty-five. This bred true continually. In *Primula floribunda*, having nine chromosomes, a cross with *P. verticillata*, also with nine, produced a sterile hybrid with nine. A bud from this latter had a chromosome number of eighteen, and was fertile.

Whenever germ cells with altered chromosome numbers are combined, diversity naturally follows in succeeding generations. Many combinations do not result in viable forms. In succeeding crosses, many aberrant chromosomes are eliminated, while others find partners. New assortments may be produced, with complete setup of chromosome pairs; thus new plants are produced, with different characteristics from any before known.

In wheat seventeen different types of chromosomes are found. That is, a certain chromosome will contain certain genes in one kind of wheat but different genes in another kind. Some types appear in only one of the species, some in two, three, or four. This suggests hybridization as a means of producing the different kinds. These facts are vitally significant in the problem of species formation.

Many more examples might be given to show the peculiar behavior of plants in regard to chromosome numbers. As a general rule hybrids resemble their parents to the degree in which the parental chromosomes are represented. Moss hybrids show many sets of chromosomes, and whole series of moss plants can be arranged, graded in order to correspond to the degree to which either parent has contributed to the chromosome combination.

One of the most remarkable studies along this line is that conducted on Galeopsis hybrids. Four species were studied, having the following haploid chromosome numbers: *pubescens*, eight; *speciosa*, eight; *tetrahit*, sixteen; and *bifida*, sixteen. Crosses between *pubescens* and *speciosa* produced a twenty-four chromosome sterile offspring. This must have come from the union of the haploid number of eight from *pubescens* with the unreduced number, sixteen, from *speciosa*. The plants thus produced were again crossed with *pubescens*, with the result that a thirty-two chromosome number was produced. The new plant would not unite with *pubescens* or *speciosa*, but did cross readily with either *tetrahit* or *bifida*, whose haploid numbers were like its own, sixteen. It was therefore called an "artificial *tetrahit*," and was described by the investigators as the "first case where a Linnaean species has been synthesized by means of species hybridization and chromosome summation."

II

Lotsy, in the early part of the twentieth century, put forth the idea that hybridization was the principal means of producing new species. At that time it was believed that crosses could occur only between numbers of the same species. Therefore the problem remained unsolved, for a great volume of genetic material was accumulated which could not be explained as long as this belief prevailed.

Radical changes in viewpoint have been brought about recently as the result of genetic studies. In 1925, R. Ruggles Gates, of King's College, London, said: "The old view that forms which produced fertile hybrids must belong to the same species has completely broken down, as has the converse conception that in plants sterile pollen is a proof of hybridity."— *American Naturalist*, May-June, 1925, page 198. Similar ideas are now appearing in standard textbooks.

In 1938 a new text, *A Survey of Biological Science* (Harpers), declared that modern genetics had entirely destroyed the idea that species could not combine with other species. Not only are modern textbooks admitting hybridization as a common means of producing new species, but some are suggesting that it is possibly the *only* way new species are ever formed.

Part of this change in attitude toward hybridization has been due to the accumulation of data entirely unknown at the beginning of the century, part to a clearer definition of species, and part to the knowledge that chromosomes may be subject to change. One must be fully conversant with the latest information on all these phases of the subject in order to properly appreciate the role of hybridization in the problem of the origin of species.

To what extent may hybridization occur? How distantly may two individuals be related, and yet find it possible to hybridize successfully? These questions have received various answers, but most of them are the result of prejudice or opinion rather than investigation.

Most of the experimental work on hybridization has been done on plants, because of the ease with which it may be performed. Experiments which have been done on animals lead us to believe that the principles are the same. It must be recognized, of course, that the more complicated generative mechanism in animals makes the incident of possible hybridization necessarily considerably less than in plants.

The chance of a possible cross between two forms is apparently governed to a certain degree by the chromosome number. It is not to be implied that two forms with different chromosome numbers could not cross, although apparently too great a discrepancy would be likely to make crosses unlikely or impossible. Illustrations have already been given.

The critical point in reproduction is the synapsis, or union of the chromosomes, at the time of the meiotic, or reduction division. The two chromosomes of each pair, one from each parent, come together just before they are distributed to the separate cells being formed. If they are so diverse one from the other that the genes in one do not match those of the other with a fairly close approximation, proper reduction appears impossible. In such failure, reproduction could not take place, for new germ cells would not be produced. The individual would therefore be sterile. The case would be all the more obvious if whole chromosomes were present without any partner to match them at the time of meiosis.

A plain example of the above is seen in crossing a tetraploid ($4n$) with a diploid ($2n$) partner. During the production of the germ cells the tetraploid has its chromosome number reduced to $2n$ (half of the tetraploid number), and the diploid to n. The union of $2n$ and n gives a triploid. This form may easily be viable, and may grow to perfect maturity. Yet when it attempts to reproduce, it may be sterile, because the odd chromosome has no partner, and meiosis may be impossible. There is one possibility of reproduction taking place. If all three chromosomes were to go into one germ cell instead of separating, and this cell should unite with another formed in a similar manner, a hexaploid ($6n$) individual would be formed. Since its chromosomes could now unite in three pairs, it might be perfectly fertile. Because of its different chromosome number it would possess new qualities, and would become a new species. Whenever, therefore, hybridization may bring about new constant-number chromosome combinations, new species would appear. Such cases have been known, and doubtless have occurred not infrequently in the past. The situation in roses, chrysanthemums, and other plants, given in preceding pages, readily illustrates this principle.

The origin of *Spartina townsendi*, previously mentioned, seems to be an illustration of the same principle. The diploid chromosome number of one of its parents, *S. stricta*, has been found to be fifty-six. That of the other parent, *S. alterniflora*, is seventy. If *S. townsendi* came from the crossing of diploid gametes, it would possess one hundred twenty-six chromosomes. This number it actually does have.

A similar case is found in the wild iris of America. *Iris setosa* has a diploid number of thirty-eight; *I. virginica* has seventy; *I. versicolor* has one hundred eight, exactly the sum of the other two.

Many other examples of like nature are known. It will be noted that the new species possess the sum of the diploid number of both parents. If the regular reduction occurred, the haploid, or single chromosomes, could not match in synapsis. With diploid numbers present in the gametes, however, synapsis is possible, and the new combination would be fertile.

To attempt to review the recent discoveries along these lines would unduly burden the pages of this volume. The literature is voluminous. Hundreds of cases have been investigated. Dobzhansky says:

"The experimental allopolyploids represent an impressive array of novel types created artificially by combining various previously existing species. Some of these synthetic types can be properly regarded as new species. Indeed, they possess complexes of morphological and physiological traits not present in any known species, and, in addition, are fertile and true breeding forms similar in this respect to any 'good species' found in the natural state. Last but not least [they] are...isolated from their progenitors by the barriers of incompatibility and of steriltiy of the hybrids."—*Genetics and the Origin of Species*, page 207.

He then proceeds to marshal evidence to show that nature has used this method "on a grand scale for the production of new species."

In addition to the chromosome factor in hybridization, the problem of similarity of structure must be recognized. Plainly two species, in order to cross and to produce viable offspring, must be closely alike in general morphology. No one would dare suggest that plants as different as a rose and an oak could have any possibility whatever of crossbreeding. Likewise two animals as unlike as fish and a mammal could not be expected to hybridize. The embryonic processes that cause the growth of organs and structures from the fertilized egg could not possibly produce an intermediate between two forms whose anatomical features were radically unlike with respect to embryonic origin or ultimate morphology.

While one must be guarded in respect to this point, it might not be wise to assert dogmatically that hybrids between somewhat distantly related species would be a certainty. Crosses are known between species, genera, families, or even orders. Just how far the idea could be carried, or has been carried in the past, no one can say with certainty.

A third factor, that of the structure of the generative organs, must be taken into account. Certainly these must be of such a nature as to make interbreeding possible. In this respect, taxonomic relation is no indication of the possibilities, for some closely related species are separated by barriers of physical incompatibility, whereas many related species are physically capable of interbreeding.

The factors thus far enumerated apply to both plants and animals. In animals, a fourth factor must be considered, the mental or nervous reaction that would give two different kinds the inclination to mate together. It has been commonly assumed that the mating urge is absent unless the animals are within the same species. This assumption is unwarranted, because observations indicate that relationship or even possibility of interbreeding does not appear to be the controlling factor. Animals of different species are not so adverse to mating together as is generally supposed. There seems to be no rule governing the inclination of two animals to mate. Some species are closely restricted to their own kind, while others seem to be stimulated by almost any other animal as well as their own kind. This applies to both male and female. In birds, mating instincts may be stimulated by decoys and dummies. As a general rule, judging from experimental data, sex complaisance rather than repugnance seems to be the more common.

Hybrid forms are commonly known between different species of plants, insects, birds, and some of the larger animals. The old idea that the mule is invariably sterile is not necessarily correct. As to the horse group, the horse, ass, zebra, and quagga all interbreed freely, but fertility of the offspring has not been fully investigated. The University of Texas had a fertile mare mule at the agricultural college for several years. Part of her offspring were sterile, and others proved to be fertile. When bred to a jack she had a sterile female foal like a mule. When bred to a stallion she had a fertile horselike colt which bred with mares in normal manner. Darwin, in *Animals and Plants,* reported a cross between a male ass and a female zebra. The hybrid offspring was crossed with a mare, and produced a second hybrid.

An interesting case comes from experimental work done at the University of Chicago. Fishes have been crossed with others in different suborders, and were fertile for several generations. Two species in the same genus proved to be more vigorous than their parents.

In Montana the forest service men have reported a hybrid between a moose and an elk. This was known for several years. Some time ago a cross between a stag and a mare was reported from an estate in England. A personal letter from "Believe It or Not" Ripley describes the animal and tells the village in England where it was seen. It had the head and forequarters of a deer and the hindquarters of a horse, and was nine months old when reported.

Zebu, yak, and cattle have been crossed, with many fertile offspring, both male and female. In the cross between the gayal and zebu or gayal and cattle, the males are usually sterile, but the females fertile. The generally higher percentage of fertile females is usually attributed to the fact that the sex chromosome is diploid in females, and more likely to undergo normal meiosis.

In studies on hybrids, care must be taken to guard against the danger of judging conditions in nature by the results seen in experimental work. Failures to produce successful crosses in experiments should not be taken as proof that such crosses are impossible or that they do not occur in nature, since animals are subjected to differing conditions under experimental work, and may not respond as they would in nature. In his book, *The Species Problem*, G. C. Robson, of the British Museum, declares that a consideration of the number of successful crosses that have been made under experimental conditions, and the large array of observations recorded in menageries and gardens, gives the impression that hybridization is of frequent occurrence.

A summary of the possible results of crossing gives the following:

1. Parents may be so diverse that no cross is possible.
2. Hybrids may be so weak that they cannot reach maturity.
3. Hybrids may be vigorous but sterile.
4. Hybrids may be fertile and vigorous.
5. When parents are alike, offspring will show no change from parental conditions.

These results are probably due to many laws rather than one law, and only by a large amount of investigation will the complete truth be known. It is apparent, however, that crossbreeding is, and in the past has been, a fruitful cause of new species of both plants and animals.

III

To those interested in Biblical records, it will be worthy of notice that the writer of Genesis plainly refers to hybridization as a means by which many changes were made from the original kinds which God had created. This reference has been strangely overlooked alike by both advocates and opponents of the literal creationism of the Genesis record.

When God created animal life, He said, "Let the earth bring forth the living creature after his kind." Genesis 1:24. This was a command for creation, not for propagation, as many creationists have assumed. Naturally it should be taken for granted that God intended all kinds to propagate as He had created them, but there is no fiat forbidding, biologically, a perversion of His plan. On the other hand, both the biological and the geological evidence supports the contention that a perversion of the original plan did take place to a surprisingly large extent. In fact, the acceptance of the Biblical story of the fall of man and the subsequent degradation would demand a recognition of a very pronounced corruption of other features of the creation as well as of man.

In the story of the Flood are the most significant words, "God looked upon the earth, and, behold, it was corrupt; for all flesh had corrupted his way upon the earth." Genesis 6:12. An analysis of this statement reveals two important facts—first, that *all flesh* was involved in the general corruption, and second, that all flesh had *corrupted his way upon the earth*.

It is commonly taught by those who accept the Biblical record of the Flood that the destruction of the earth came only as a means of clearing it of wicked men. This is a very restricted concept, and fails to recognize the full significance of the event. The Scripture clearly states that *all flesh* was included. Genesis 6:17; 7:21. The testimony of the Scripture, according to its own definitions, is that both animal and human life was involved. Wilhelm Gesenius, noted for his Hebrew scholarship, supports this view in his comments on these verses.

As to the statement, "had corrupted his way," it is obvious that whatever is meant, the condition must have been serious to call down the dire vengeance of God. A synonym for *corrupt* is *adulterate*, which means to mix with other kinds than what is supposed to be present. Other definitions are *tainted*, which has the same implication, *contaminated*, or invaded by foreign substance, *polluted*, or to be impure from a mixture with matter from without, also *debased*, *depraved*, and *defiled*. In man, since he is a moral creature, corruption could come in a moral way by a departure from the principles of right. In other creatures no such spiritual corruption could be possible. Some other means of corruption must be sought in order to satisfy the full meaning of the text. To say that nature was corrupted simply because of man's sin is not sufficient. The presence of degeneration in the form of thorns and thistles, which are generally considered the curse laid on the earth because of the result of man's departure from the right, would not be a cause for destruction of the earth by a Flood. Furthermore, the conditions produced by the Flood have favored the development of such degenerative changes a thousandfold as compared to what we find to have been the case previously. Something else must have been involved.

Gesenius tells us that the expression "his way" refers to the manner of life, the plan, scheme, or habitual mode of life. This plainly indicates that living creatures so changed or perverted their modes of action or conduct as to have departed from the original plan of God, until all were corrupt, or confused, contaminated, defiled, debased, and perverted. In no other way could animals, having no moral responsibility, have fulfilled the statements of the author of Genesis.

The fact that part of the corruption in animal life was due to intermingling of the original kinds is indicated by the command given for the preservation of the animals in the ark. In Genesis 1:21, 24, and 25 we read that the animals were created each "after his kind." The same is true of plants, shown in verses 11 and 12. In chapter 6, verse 20, Noah was commanded to bring the creatures "after their kind" into the ark. In chapter 7, verse 14, the beasts are referred to "after their kind" as they went into the ark. Again in chapter 8, verse 19, it is said that every creature came forth "after their kinds." Thus we see that they were created after their kinds, they came into the ark after their kinds, and they went forth after their kinds. On the other hand, they were not commanded to multiply after their kinds, but were found to have corrupted their way upon the earth, and for this reason to have been destroyed with sinful man. The original "kinds" which God had created were preserved in the ark, but the confused species that had come about as the result of corruption were destroyed. Today their bones are dug up, and testify to the scientific accuracy of these plain statements in Genesis.

IV

It would seem that all the factors are now at hand for a complete answer to the problem of species. Recent studies in cytology have revealed many facts regarding the behavior of chromosomes and genes which were entirely unknown to early students of genetics. A review of the latest experimental evidence indicates that species may change their characteristics because of (1) new combinations of genes, (2) changes in chromosomes due to irregularities in division and distribution, and (3) hybridization or combination of chromosomes from different species. The material upon which natural selection and isolation may work for the production of new species is furnished by the mutant genes. The limits to which mutations may go are determined by the pattern of the genes of that particular species. Changes which modify the chromosomes beyond the pattern make development impossible or produce sterile offspring. Many new kinds are produced by hybridization, but here the limitations for successful propagation are very closely circumscribed.

The bearing of these studies on the problem of evolution is of major significance. Those who know these principles the best are the ones who most frankly admit that, while there is abundant and quite satisfactory evidence for the existence of those mutations which result in new species, there is no satisfactory way in which these facts can be made to explain the origin of the larger groups. In other words, *there now exists*, thanks to the very latest genetic evidence, *a clear insight into how new species are produced, but no explanation for the general theory of evolution.*

V

The rarity of what could be considered true intermediates between the larger groups, such as families, orders, and classes, or even between genera and species in most cases, serves to emphasize the rule of persistence of types. If evolution had taken place, intermediate types should reveal a gradual transition from one type to another. Cases which have generally been regarded as intermediate evolutionary stages reveal the presence of distinct characters which, upon critical examination, indicate hybridization instead of evolutionary progress, for it must be noted that hybrids do not usually show blending of characters. Thus in a hybrid form certain structural features will show their derivation from one ancestor and certain from another. Seldom do many of the structural features show intermediate characteristics between those of the two lines of ancestry. Goldschmidt's work on insects shows this fact clearly. For hundreds of generations he bred certain races of gypsy moths in an attempt to produce new types, but they persistently bred back toward the ancestral features and manifested the original characters distinctly. Austin H. Clark brings out the same fact in regard to other insects. The principle appears to hold true wherever observation has been made on hybrid forms.

The fossil records indicate that the intermediate forms may have been much more common in the past than now. Many series of animals such as elephants, camels, horses, which are generally supposed to represent evolutionary sequences, may have been merely taxonomic series. Some specimens have been found which would appear to be hybrids between well-established species in such series. There is no way to tell positively whether a skeleton represents a real race of living animals which produced offspring in a normal manner, or whether it was an aberration, unless sufficient numbers are found to prove that it multiplied freely.

Birds are surprisingly similar to reptiles in general anatomical features. At least thirteen structural features are common to the two groups which are not common in other groups. Many fossil birds possess reptilian features which are unknown among living species. The most famous of these is *Archaeopteryx* (ancient bird), which has been found in the rocks near Solenhofen, Germany. This creature had no horny beak, but possessed jaws with a row of small teeth. The wings were like those of a modern bird, but had the same number of joints as the forelimbs of a lizard. The plumage was birdlike, but there were no contour feathers on the head, neck, and much of the body. The tail was long, with separate vertebrae, like those of a reptile. On each joint of the tail were two quill feathers. In more technical features we find four definite skeletal likenesses. One writer describes *Archaeopteryx* as a "true bird" with "many features of...reptilian ancestry."

Archaeopteryx is usually considered as proof of the evolution of birds from reptiles. The foregoing facts suggest that it could be reasonably explained as a hybrid. While a cross between a bird and a reptile is not known to occur today, such an occurrence is not entirely beyond the range of possibility.

The lower mammals give what might possibly be considered evidence of the crossing of mammal stock with the reptiles. In the monotremes we find *Ornithorhynchus*, or platypus (duckbill), and *Echidna*, or the spiny anteater. To understand the position of the monotremes it is necessary to study the marsupials, to which the kangaroos and the opossums belong.

The marsupials are known as pouched animals, from their peculiar habit of carrying the partially developed young in the pouch, where they are nourished by milk until they complete their development. The scheme is unique, nothing like it being found in other groups. Marsupials show distinct mammalian characters such as the presence of true teeth, a reduced coracoid bone, and a pectoral arch of mammalian type. In some features they are different from all other mammals, for example, in the presence of the "marsupial bone" on the underside of the abdomen to support the pouch. This bone is attached to the hipbones.

The marsupials are classified as lower mammals, with the monotremes at the bottom of the mammal line. The monotremes, however, show distinctly intermediate features between the reptiles and the mammals. They possess a cloaca, as in the reptiles, a common canal into which the digestive, reproductive, and urinary systems empty. Skeletal features are generally reptilian. The coracoid bone is reptilian, or avian, rather than mammalian, as is also the pectoral arch. There are no teeth—the mouth is more like that of a bird or turtle. Perhaps the most striking feature is the partial development of the marsupial bone in the region of the marsupium —a useless structure, since the monotreme lays eggs. In addition to this, there are poorly developed mammary glands. The body is covered with hair like that of a mammal.

The origin of this unique creature might be explained on the basis of crossing between some reptilian and mammalian forms. It cannot be an evolutionary stage, for two reasons. First, the reptilian and mammalian characters are mixed, not blended. Secondly, the marsupial bone is not found in forms below or above these two groups.

Among common living animals and plants a student occasionally finds one that could easily be explained as having come by hybridization. In California the oracle oak looks like the black oak in every way except that the leaves are evergreen, and somewhat like the coast live oak which grows in the same region. Hybrid willows are very common. The tanbark oak partakes of characteristics of both oak and chestnut, yet it is neither an oak nor a chestnut in typical form. Certain birds possess a combination of features of two families, as, for example, the Townsend solitaire, which is sometimes called the flycatcher thrush, inasmuch as it shows characteristics of both flycatchers and thrushes. The hyena has several features of both dogs and cats, as can be readily seen by anyone who studies its appearance. The wildebeest of Africa has both horse and cattle characteristics.

The question may be raised, "Why call these hybrids? May they not be as valid creations as any others?" It must be admitted that dogmatic assertions cannot safely be made; nevertheless it should be pointed out that according to the creation record, plants and animals were made each "after his kind." The original types must have been so distinct that there would be no difficulty in deciding in which category a plant or animal should be classified. The confused species dug up from the rocks and in some cases living today are a plain suggestion of crossing of original types.

Most of Dobzhansky's reticence and Bateson's and Goldschmidt's pessimism regarding the application of genetics to the problem of "evolution" would be removed if they, and all who are trying to solve the problem, would recognize the Bible account of creation, the subsequent corruption of types, and the Flood. Significantly, Dobzhansky points out the effect of the new discoveries regarding hybridization on the "phylogenetic tree." The question at issue would be simplified if the "evolutionary pattern" were to be regarded as a series of lines, or cables, instead of a tree. These, according to the creationist viewpoint, would run parallel to one another, but might occasionally branch or come to an end. The races and species would become composite groups which are to a certain degree independent of one another. Whenever species formation through crossbreeding occurred, the parallel lines of branching cables would fuse together, and form a network of smaller branches. A recognition of these principles would eliminate much of the difficulty that arises when these confused species are explained in the story of evolutionary advance.

To the creationist the present situation regarding genetic problems is highly gratifying. Accepting the Genesis record of the direct creation of plants and animals each "after his kind," he is able to explain the origin of the present species of living things from the original type forms by the various processes of "descent by modification." The Bible stands scientifically vindicated, with no necessity whatsoever for a recourse to evolution.

15. Frank L. Marsh

(1899–1992)

Marsh, F.L. 1947. *Evolution Creation and Science*. Second edition. Review and Herald Publishing Association, Washington, D.C. Our extract is from Chapter 10: The Genesis Kind, pp. 235-258.

Owing to the statements of Genesis to the effect that plants and animals were created in distinct kinds, creationists naturally have much to say about Genesis kinds. But it is a characteristic of creationists to become extremely vague when asked to point out these kinds in nature today. Not a little criticism comes from evolutionists over this indefiniteness. They argue upon very reasonable grounds that if plants and animals were created in the beginning in clear-cut basic forms, and if there has been no evolution of new basic forms since, then why should the creationist not be able to point out these basic groups today? In plain language, the evolutionist says that the creationist should either point out these units today, or keep still about them.

Even though we are very much aware that the evolutionist has much to say about the "fact" of evolution of new kinds although he is *completely incapable* of explaining their origin in a scientific manner, still I believe he is justified in demanding that the creationist delimit the Genesis kinds. I am happy to say that the creationist can do this in a concrete and scientific manner. When the creationist, at the request of the evolutionist, has demarcated the Genesis kind, then it would be no more than fair play for the creationist to demand of the evolutionist that he in turn present similar concrete and scientific reasons for believing that evolution of new kinds has occurred, or keep still about such a fantastic, i.e., unscientific, affair.

II

The first chapter of Genesis states very clearly that the Creator formed all the kinds of plants and animals during the first six days of Creation Week. The record does not say that simple forms were created first and that these were then evolved into present-day complex forms through natural processes. Genesis 1:11,12, states that seed-bearing plants, that is, the "highest" forms of plants, appeared in the same twenty-four-hour period in which all other plants appeared. The same is true with animals. Cattle and other "higher" forms, including man, appeared on the same day. There is not the slightest hint in the story that these days were longer than our present solar day. Each one during creation week was made up of an evening and a morning, just as are our solar days now. At the close of the six-day period the earth was entirely outfitted with all the basic kinds of plant and animal life. The creation was not merely begun at that time. The record is that it was *finished,* and the seventh day was set apart as a special day to commemorate the *completion* of the creation of all organic forms.[1]

III

In speaking of the formation of plants and animals, the Genesis record emphasizes one fact which was apparently of great importance. Ten times during the short recital of events it is stated that plants and animals were made "after their kinds." This indicates that the discontinuity between kinds was just as great at their first appearance as it is today. Under the power of the Creator the earth "brought forth grass, and herb yielding seed after his kind, and the fruit tree yielding fruit,...after his kind." God created "great whales, and every living creature that moveth...after their kind, and every winged fowl after his kind." "And God made the beast of the earth after his kind, and cattle after their kind, and every thing that creepeth upon the earth after his kind." These words portray a world of organisms just as complete in its basic taxonomic groups as is our world today.

What is the significance of this expression, "after his kind"? The statement manifestly means that God formed these organisms after some orderly plan which He had previously drawn up. Witness of the orderly nature of this plan is found in the present possibility of a logical classification of the plants and animals of the world. It would seem that the kinds of Genesis should constitute the true basic units of any system of classification. These units likewise appear capable of being grouped today into larger categories such as the great divisions of taxonomic botany and the large phyla of systematic zoology.

Linnaeus, the founder of modern taxonomy, a creationist, endeavored to assign species names to what he thought were Genesis kinds. However, in building the categories of his system he employed a method that was entirely artificial, that is, his system was built upon *external* appearances. However, the modern biologist knows that the true test of blood relationship is not morphological entirely, but rather, is largely physiological.

The truth of this statement becomes obvious when we study the morphological differences between the two sexes of the same "species" in such forms as the marine worm *Bonellia,* certain angler fishes, and butterflies, moths, and other insects which manifest polymorphism.

---

1   Genesis 2:1-3.

The principal evidence of blood relationship in these cases is the fact that these diversely formed members of a pair will mate. A system of classification based upon such evidence is described as a *natural* system. It is interesting to observe here that the fertility test, a natural test, now being applied by certain taxonomically inclined evolutionists as Dobzhansky and Ernst Mayr, in the determination of where one "species" ends and another begins, obviously frequently comes nearer to discovering the boundaries of the Genesis kinds than did the artificial system of the creationist Linnaeus. Linnaeus had the right idea as a basis of his classification, but he employed the wrong method in discovering the kinds. A purely artificial system could never discover the true basic units among organisms, because these units were primarily based upon *physiological* characters.

IV

How can the creationistic scientist be sure that physiological characteristics formed the real differences between Genesis kinds? First, from a philosophical point of view, this would be a logical assumption. Genesis states that the Creator created organisms in what would appear from the context to be the same complexity of kinds that we have today—there were grass, herbs, and trees, whales, birds, cattle, man, and all the rest. If these forms were different only in their morphologies, then crossing could occur wherever mechanically possible—and this situation would exist in innumerable cases. This would mean that extreme confusion of kinds would occur in case possible instincts against crossing were broken down through some natural degenerative process. Cohabitation across kinds occurs not infrequently today, most commonly with a human being as one of the partners. By such extreme hybridization God's original plan of discreteness of kinds would be completely frustrated. In other words, it is illogical to assume that the Creator would make organisms physiologically identical, and thus capable of crossing in innumerable cases, and thereby defeat His own plan of discontinuity among kinds.

V

Second, from a scientific point of view the opinion that Genesis kinds are physiologically discontinuous is completely in harmony with all scientific records of breeding behavior. In the last chapter we have observed that in every authentic case of hybridization of animals the partners were always so nearly alike morphologically as to be without question members of the same basic kind. In plants hybridization has occurred across what might at first glance appear to be distinct kinds, as, for example, the radish and the cabbage. But closer inspection in such cases shows that the differences lie entirely in the vegetative structures. The reproductive structures, for instance, in the radish and cabbage are identical. In fact, taxonomists place these plants in genera situated in juxtaposition in our classified lists. The cabbage genus and radish genus contain extremely variable individuals, and the constituent varieties grade quite continuously one into the other.

Everywhere we look today we see physiologically isolated groups of organisms reproducing after their kinds. Sunflowers, beans, corn, ducks, horses, and dogs stand as clear-cut kinds. There is really little difficulty morphologically to differentiate these basic units in nature. And where the morphological boundaries of a kind lie there likewise commonly lie the physiological boundaries. Scientific records reveal that different kinds of organisms are not capable of hybridization, even to the formation of a true zygote, or fertilized egg. There is no evidence that natural laws have changed since the world began. One of the most obvious of these laws is that neither man and apes, cats and rabbits, sunflowers and goldenrods, nor any other kinds can cross. Therefore, from the scientific standpoint it appears that Genesis kinds, from creation to our day, have existed as physiologically isolated units.

VI

A third reason for assuming that physiological characteristics demarked the original kinds is found in the fossil record. The creationistic philosophy holds that perhaps about forty-three centuries ago the entire earth was overwhelmed by a flood of waters. The animals and plants which were living on it, along with any of their remains which were lying on the earth's surface at that time, were buried by this Deluge, known as the Noachian Flood. These organisms and remains which were buried either by the waters of that Flood or by the wind which followed it[2] constitutes most of the fossils which are dug up today. If the original kinds had been physiologically identical and thereby capable of crossing, and if they crossed, we would have a situation wherein the original kinds would have lost their identity, and the world of animals and of plants would commonly have presented a picture of continuous succession of forms which would bridge all morphological gaps between kinds. This would produce a world that would appear exactly as evolutionists would have us think it would appear if an accelerated movie could be seen showing all changes which are assumed to have occurred through the millions of years as the simple changed to the complex.

But the real proof that such hybridization was not possible (and that evolution did not occur—but more of that in a later chapter) is found in these fossil remains of the antediluvian fauna and flora. We were told very recently by the evolutionistic paleontologist, G. G. Simpson, of the American Museum of Natural History, that the most conspicuous thing

---

2   Genesis 8:1.

about the fossil record is not that of *continuity* of forms but rather of *discontinuity*. He says:

> "The facts are that many species and genera, indeed the majority, do appear suddenly in the [fossil] record, differing sharply and in many ways from any earlier group, and that this appearance of discontinuity becomes more common the higher the level, until it is virtually universal as regards orders and all higher steps in the taxonomic hierarchy."[3]

A. H. Clark, of the U. S. National Museum, also an evolutionist, likewise stresses this very manifest discontinuity in the fossil record.[4] The creationist recalls that the Noachian Flood occurred in the seventeenth century after Creation. Surely, if crossing of Genesis kinds had been possible in those early centuries the fossil record would be rich in hybrid forms showing the characteristics of their parents, and the parents would likewise occur in the record. But, as we have just observed, the record shows no bridging of morphological gaps. No forms which are obviously hybrids between kinds occur. The same kinds of plants and animals occur just as clearly demarcated in the fossils as they do in the living forms, oaks, walnuts, ferns, horses, eagles, elephants, and all. If there is any evidence of confusion it is not between kinds but rather among the varieties of a kind.

VII

A fourth reason for assuming that physiological characters were the basis of demarcation of original kinds, and perhaps this should have been placed first, is the fact that the physiological qualities of an organism, ignoring environmental effects for the moment, determine what its morphology shall be. A giraffe, and not a hog, develops from the zygote of the giraffe because of the functional effect of the giraffe genes in giraffe chromosomes upon giraffe protoplasm. If all animals had the same chemical substances in their genes, their fertile eggs would develop into organisms having the same morphological structures. Therefore, the stated fact that God created organisms in their great diversity of form, "each after his kind," is merely another way of saying that the original kinds, because they were diverse in their morphology, were likewise diverse in their physiological, i.e., chemical, qualities, and for that reason were incapable of crossing, even to the extent of forming a fertilized egg.

---

[3] George Gaylord Simpson, *Tempo and Mode in Evolution*, p. 99. (See also pp. 105, 106.)
[4] Austin H. Clark, *The New Evolution*, pp. 100, 101.

VIII

Thus, in the light of these reasons, logical and scientific, we find that we have a very concrete way of discovering membership in a kind. Two organisms are members of a kind if their germ cells will join in true fertilization. We actually recognize several degrees of cross-fertility. To illustrate: between some "species" of salamanders the fertilized egg will go no further in its development than the gastrula stage; in rat × mouse hybrids and in goat × sheep hybrids the fetus dies just before birth; in the chicken × guinea cross the hybrid is vigorous but apparently always sterile; in the horse × ass cross the hybrid is a vigorous individual which is occasionally fertile; in the cow × bison cross the hybrid males are sterile, but the hybrid females are fertile; the dog × wolf hybrid is fully fertile in both sexes. But the point I would make here is that in *all* cases where cross-fertility is possible, even in those where fertilization goes no further than to produce an embryo that dies at some early developmental stage, the participants are always so nearly identical morphologically as easily to be considered members of the same Genesis kind.

IX

In the light of this consideration the question presents itself, Is it possible to distinguish Genesis kinds by their morphology alone? My answer would be No. When morphology alone is depended upon, there is always extreme uncertainty where to fix the boundaries of a kind. Forgetting everything else but morphological characters, we would certainly place the Pekingese in a different kind from the one to which the Russian wolfhound belongs. But because we know the history of domesticated dogs we place all such in a single "species." Dependence upon mere morphology might cause us to place foxes, jackals, hyenas, and even wolves in separate kinds, but breeding data reveal that they are all cross-fertile and thus obviously quite similar in their physiological make-up. Because of their cross-fertility they bring forth after their single kind. All tame dogs and wild dogs make up a well-knit unit, or kind, today when their physiological characters are considered.

Appearance alone might cause us to place the pigmy man into one kind and the Nordic man into another, but cross-fertility shows them identical as to kind. We might even puzzle over the morphological similarity between man and the chimpanzee. Every bone, muscle, and nerve of the man is found in the chimpanzee. They both have the same chromosome number, twenty-four pairs. Are they members of the same kind? Here recourse to the test of fertility, i.e., to their physiological make-up, shows them to be members of two different kinds. This is true, because no man has ever hybridized with any member of the group of higher apes.

X

This brings us to another angle of the problem of determination of original kinds. If the members of any two groups of individuals are cross-sterile, do the two groups constitute, or at least belong to, two different kinds? Dobzhansky and Epling have considered the fact of cross-sterility between what used to be races A and B of the vinegar fly, *Drosophila pseudoobscura*, to be sufficient ground upon which to assign a new species name to race B. The latter, because of their act, is now known as *D. persimilis*.[5] For the same reasons Dobzhansky has erected the new species, *D. equinoxialis*, which is reproductively isolated from *D. willistoni*, although there is a "virtual lack of morphological differences."[6] The vinegar fly, with its many "species" and varieties, in the light of its similar morphology within the group and the not infrequent hybridizations which occur across members of the group, is obviously a single unit in nature. Any infertility which occurs between members of the group or kind, has been built up by various natural processes of variation. Dobzhansky and Tan have shown how this has occurred between the smaller groups now known as *D. pseudoobscura* and *D. miranda*.[7]

Thus it is obvious that the fertility test alone cannot determine the boundaries of all kinds. To illustrate, it would be extremely absurd to argue that *D. equinoxialis* and *D. willistoni*, in which there is a "virtual lack of morphological differences," are members of two different kinds merely because they are reproductively isolated. In such instances our sense of sight tells us that they are members of the same basic group. There are doubtless many such cases in nature. However, this situation does not cloud the picture of the edges of the Genesis kinds, because the similar morphology of vinegar flies, for example, and the fact that hybridization among some members of the group does occur leaves no doubt that they are a single basic unit. Members of their group never cross with cheese-maggot flies, stem-eyed flies, frit [sic–fruit] flies, or any other "related" groups. The fact of fertilization between some members of these morphological groups makes clear that there is a basic physiological unity in the group in much the same way that we use the mathematical axiom which states that two things equal to the same thing are equal to each other. It is thus found that the creationistic taxonomist has, in the fertilization test, a very real and concrete way of determining, by a natural method, the edges of the original units as they exist today. The artificial method, that of comparing morphological traits, is needed only here and there to clear up cases where natural processes of change have disrupted

---

5   Theodosius Dobzhansky and Carl Epling, *Contributions to the Genetics, Taxonomy, and Ecology of Drosophila pseudoobscura and Its Relatives*, p. 6.
6   Theodosius Dobzhansky, "Complete Reproductive Isolation Between Two Morphologically Similar Species of *Drosophila*." *Ecology*, July, 1946, vol. 27 pp. 205-211.
7   Theodosius Dobzhansky, *Genetics and the Origin of Species*, pp. 144-147.

the gene order so seriously as possibly to change the physiological characters sufficiently to build up a chemical incompatibility between the germ cells.

XI

Progressive evolutionistic taxonomists of today are giving more and more recognition to what they term the polytypic species. The polytypic species, called *Formenkreis* by Kleinschmidt, consists of two or more geographically isolated groups which are cross-fertile when brought together. An illustration is found in the wild goats (*Capra*) of Eurasia and Northern Africa. On the various mountain ranges of this area, seven "species" are recognized, situated on the Pyrenees, the Alps, the Caucasus (two "species"), the Himalayas, the Sinaitic, and the highland of Abyssinia, respectively. These "species" of goats are all cross-fertile when brought together, and therefore, constitute a single polytypic species. If they were being named today by such enlightened taxonomists as Ernst Mayr, a single species name would be assigned to them. Such taxonomists are unconsciously recognizing the basic units in nature, the Genesis kinds. Thus the fertility test is already recognized and is in good repute today. Of course, in using it to discover the borders of the kind, it is necessary to use it in its larger aspects only. This use will uncover the widest borders of the basic units. Used in its smallest aspect, as employed by Dobzhansky and Epling in assigning a new "species" name to race B of *Drosophila pseudoobscura*, it merely demarks physiological races which have developed and are developing within the kind.

In the light of Genesis and pertinent scientific data, it appears that if the taxonomist wishes to erect his categories upon a truly natural system, he must recognize the Genesis kind (polytypic species, *Formenkreis*) as the basic unit among living things. The fertility test supplemented by similarity of morphological characters will make the discovery of these units possible. In an earlier book[8] I have suggested the name barä'min (plural *baramins*), built upon the Hebrew words *bara*, "created," and *min*, "kind," for these units. I suggest this word because it gets entirely away from the idea of *species*—a word which has come to mean something different for each person who employs it. I have no objection to the use of the word *species* for any of the varieties or races of a baramin, but we must bear clearly in mind that the modern "species" and the Genesis kind are often entirely different groups.

Huxley is of the opinion that the fertilization test when applied alone is not tenable in the discovery of basic units, because forms that cross "are often markedly distinct morphologically and do maintain themselves as discontinuous groups in nature."[9] However, Huxley is

---

8   Frank L. Marsh, *Fundamental Biology*, p. 100.
9   Julian Huxley, *Evolution: The Modern Synthesis*, pp. 162, 163.

looking for *superficial differences* while I am looking for *basic similarities*. Morphology springs from physiology and is, therefore, subordinate to it. If two forms are markedly distinct morphologically and are still chemically similar enough to be compatible at the union of their germ cells, then they obviously belong to a single basic physiological group. These are the groups that the creationistic taxonomist is looking for, and the groups any taxonomist is looking for who wishes to discover the real natural taxonomic units among organisms.

XII

The usual evolutionistic conception of origin of modern kinds of organisms is commonly represented by a "phylogenetic tree." That is, from a common trunk the limbs arise and divide and subdivide into the kinds of today much as twigs are related to the main trunk of the tree. Where the trunk takes its origin is significantly omitted by evolutionists. This type of diagram indicates the evolutionistic assumption of the blood relationships of all living things. One tree serves to represent the history of all modern forms. There are other evolutionists, illustrated by A. H. Clark,[10] of the U. S. National Museum, who assume a separate tree for each phylum. This is called the polyphyletic theory of origins. These theorists likewise ignore the important point of where their various trees take their origin.

The creationistic scientist, in diagraming the history of the modern forms of life, must needs employ a forest of trees, each separate tree representing a Genesis kind. This is necessary because if a Creator formed each kind of animal by a separate and distinct act of creation, *none* of the kinds will be blood related. They may show a number of characters in common, such as a notochord in early development, a dorsal vertebral column in the adult form, and even may all have hair as adults and still not be blood related one with another.

XIII

That these Genesis kinds were created as more or less complex units seems reasonable and, in fact, necessary to assume in the face of fossil evidence. The fossils are obviously the remains of antediluvian animals and plants which, according to Genesis, were buried in the Noachian Flood. These fossils show considerable wealth, in many cases, in the matter of ecological races. This is illustrated by the horse group. Because all the "horses" except our modern *Equus* have become extinct, we cannot discover whether the various fossil horses were members of a single baramin or not, but from their similar morphology it seems possible that they may have been. The *Eohippus*, with its four toes in front and three toes behind, apparently was equipped both in feet and dentition

---

10   Austin H. Clark, *The New Evolution*.

to frequent the forest aisles and lowland borders where the ground was soft and the tender-tipped bushes furnished abundant browsing material. *Miohippus* and *Merychippus*, each with three toes on each foot but with the central toe quite well developed, and with teeth adapted to eating grass, were apparently fitted to graze over rougher, drier ground at forest edges. *Equus*, with its single toe and with teeth suited to grazing, was fitted to live on the hard, dry, grassy plains in full sunshine.[11] Fossil evidence fails to show that these "horses" lived at different times, but it does show that they were morphologically adapted to fit into different ecological niches.

This same variability is shown in the fossil remains of other Genesis kinds. This leads us to deduce on very sure ground that about seventeen centuries before their burial[12] their respective ancestors had been created in all this wealth of ecological adaptation. From this wealth of ecological varieties it becomes clear that the antediluvian world was rich in its variety of ecological niches.

XIV

In the light of this fossil evidence it is logical to assume that the Genesis kinds were created in two or more varieties in all cases except man. Man was the steward-king of the earth and capable of adapting himself to many different environments as he explored his dominion and viewed his subjects, the lower animals.

The plants and animals, on the other hand, were fairly fixed in their niches, being adapted to specific environments. In the hare-rabbit kind, for example, there very possibly was a variety suited for life near the cold tops of high mountains, quite like our arctic hare and varying hare of today. Another variety possibly was suited to life on open, sun-flooded plains, as is our jack rabbit today. Another variety was possibly suited to life in less open country as our present-day cottontail rabbit. Still another may have been adapted to life along water courses and bodies of water as is our modern swamp rabbit. Being members of the same kind, these varieties would be capable of hybridizing should they meet just as are our modern "species" of hares and rabbits.[13]

In order to clarify my conception of the Genesis kind, or baramin, I represent in the diagram on this page [*page 177*] three simplified ancestral trees of three kinds. The Genesis record makes it clear that but one variety of the man kind was created. In the cases of other kinds we are forced to build our conception of the original picture from modern and fossil forms. I place the asslike variety and the horselike variety in the same kind because these animals will cross today. The result, the mule, is by

---

11   Alfred Sherwood Romer, *Man and the Vertebrates*, pp. 143, 144.
12   Genesis 1-8.
13   M. F. Guyer, *Animal Biology* (3d ed.), p. 505.

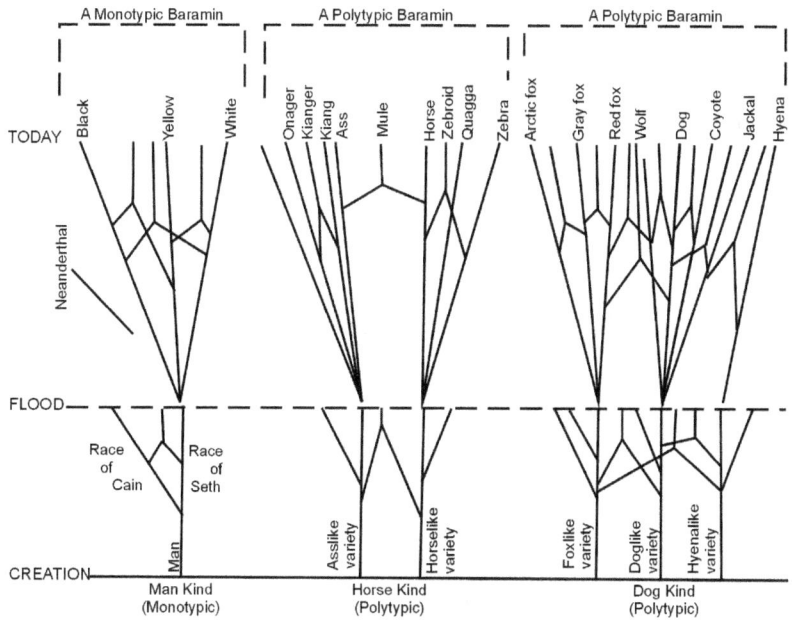

Diagram of Three Genesis Kinds

The ancestral trees of the horse kind and of the dog kind are simplified and are intended merely to suggest the effects of natural processes of variation within each kind since creation. The Neanderthal line of the man kind has not been attached to any racial line because no data are available at present to indicate to which it belonged or whether this man was a hybrid within his kind or a mutant.

no means always sterile.[14] It appears inaccurate to assume that horse and ass have descended from the same ancestor because of the discrepancy in chromosome count. It is impossible to see how, through any natural process, the horse with its nineteen pairs of chromosomes and the ass with its thirty-three pairs, could have developed from the same ancestor. Therefore I assume, as the diagram indicates, that their ancestors were originally created varieties of the horse kind.

In the case of the dog baramin every continent today has its wild dogs and foxes. These seem to fall quite naturally into dogs, foxes, and hyenas when morphological characters are considered, but all are cross-fertile. Therefore, as shown in the diagram, I assume that there may have been at least three original varieties of the dog kind. It appears appropriate to designate those baramins which were made up of two or more original varieties as *polytypic*, and those, like man, which consisted of a single race, or variety, as *monotypic*.

---

14   *Yearbook of Agriculture*, 1936, pp. 184, 185.

Because of natural processes of change and because of the thousands of races and even kinds which have become extinct since the Flood, it is difficult now to get a complete picture of the baramins as they were created. But through the very real laboratory test of fertility it is possible clearly to mark off the boundaries of all the kinds today. A great deal of work is yet to be done to accumulate data sufficient to give us anything like a comprehensive mapping of the kinds.

XV

In discussing the subject of "species," Ernst Mayr, of the American Museum of Natural History, makes the following comment:

> "As the new polytypic species concept began to assert itself, a certain pessimism seemed to be associated with it. It seemed as if each of the polytypic species (*Rassenkreise*) was as clearcut and as separated from other species by bridgeless gaps as if it had come into being by a separate act of creation. And this is exactly the conclusion drawn by men like Kleinschmidt and Goldschmidt. They claim that all the evidence for intergradation between species which was quoted in the past was actually based on cases of infraspecific variation, and, in all honesty, it must be admitted that this claim is largely justified. But there is one serious flaw in the arguments of Kleinschmidt and Goldschmidt: they fail to define what *they* consider a species."[15]

I believe that Mayr makes a very valid criticism here. In this chapter I trust that I escape that criticism by calling attention to the fertilization test as furnishing a definition of the Genesis kind, or baramin. Any organisms, however diverse in their morphological details, which are capable of accomplishing true fertilization, even though the ensuing development cease at an early stage, are members of the same baramin. This test, purely natural in character, will reveal the truly basic relationships among plants and animals.

---

15 Ernst Mayr, *Systematics and the Origin of Species*, p. 114.

CORE Issues in Creation

Established in 2005, the CORE Issues monograph series presents high quality scholarly work from or related to a young-age creation perspective. This monograph series is not for the publication of scholarly critiques of alternative positions (other venues exist for that kind of publication). Rather, CORE Issues has been created to publish any monograph in any discipline (philosophy, theology, physics, geology, biology, archaeology, linguistics, etc., etc.) which substantially contributes to the systematic development of a positive, young-age creation model. Original monographs will thoroughly review the conventional and creationist literature on the subject, offer a constructive interpretation of the subject's data, integrate well with other disciplines as the model is constructed, and advance creation model development. Other monographs offer reprints, compendia, or translations of significant historical works that are currently unavailable. CORE Issues is peer-reviewed and will strive for the very highest scholarship standards. CORE Issues is a joint publication of the Center for Origins Research at Bryan College and Wipf & Stock Publishers.

CORE Issues does not publish works written only by Bryan College faculty but encourages outside submissions. Researchers may submit monograph proposals (full manuscripts are not accepted) to CORE either electronically at info@bryancore.org or by regular mail:

CORE Issues editor
Bryan College 7802
721 Bryan Drive
Dayton, TN 37321

Previous Volumes in the **CORE Issues** Series

1. A Creationist Review and Preliminary Analysis of the History, Geology, Climate, and Biology of the Galápagos Islands, by Wood (2005)
2. Johannes Buteo's The Shape and Capacity of Noah's Ark, trans. by Griffith & Monette (2008)
3. Animal and Plant Baramins, by Wood (2008)

www.ingramcontent.com/pod-product-compliance
Lightning Source LLC
Chambersburg PA
CBHW071453150426
43191CB00008B/1329